PRAISE FOR *SCHOOL OF GRIT*

What an honor for me to be one of the first to read *School of Grit*. It's a remarkable and honest book, written by a remarkable and honest man. Adversity is a building block for individual character. I met Brad during our freshman year of high school during baseball conditioning. He would always ask me to run more steps with him, challenging me with his honest smile and annoying endurance. Almost 30 years later, he hasn't changed a bit. This is a special book that will help people. Something that Brad has always been about.

COMMAND SERGEANT MAJOR JOSHUA BROWN
United States Army

Many people desire to be more mentally tough, more emotionally resilient, and even grittier, but very few are willing to do the work. As you read *School of Grit*, be aware of where your grit begins to build. This book is a game changer.

LARRY HAGNER
President/Host, *The Dad Edge Podcast*

Your account of Kokoro was riveting. I found myself continually saying silently in my head, "Are you friggin kidding me?! How in the hell could he do that?" The onslaught. I really loved how you intertwined both the Applications and the Challenges. It moved the writing out of the realm of pure memoir to in service of others. Really well done.

BRETT MAGPIONG
Executive, Performance Coach and Speaker

My buddy Brad Ritter inspired me with his book *School of Grit*. He taught me to think about how little I've truly evolved all these years. I ended up complaining about the same things and not feeling fulfilled or a word he uses, purposeful. It is time for me to create a more purposeful version of myself and I have to say goodbye to my old self.

TUAN NGUYEN
Dad Techpreneur, Chief Marketing Officer at Efani

This book should be required reading for anyone who has punched their ticket to a crucible experience.

BERT PACAL
Ski Patrol Director, Park City, Utah

Talk about a tough weekend. Brad's experience at Kokoro Camp may have only been 50 hours long but it contained a lifetime of lessons he shares here in the *School of Grit*. Lessons that anyone can take action on now and change their life forever. If you are ready to see what you're made of, this book is a must read.

COLE BERSHBACK,
Author of *Total Potential* and Founder of Total Potential Mom

I finished the book this afternoon and I loved it. This is what I wanted to read as soon as I learned you completed kokoro camp years ago. The evolutions you went through were rough and educational all at the same time. Reading the story was amazing. The lessons learned at the end of each chapter pointed out things to take away and immediate action that could be taken on things. I'm going to go through all of those again.

JOHN W. FORSBERG
President, PQ Software LLC

GET READY TO GET FIRED UP! Brad takes you along on his journey to test and find himself at the SEALFIT Kokoro Camp, the toughest training camp on the planet. He was up for over 50 straight hours and you will be amazed at the mental and physical toughness required to get through this. The book reads like an adventure novel. I couldn't put it down. I was right there along with the author (vicariously only, thank God.) The best part of the book is that each chapter ends with lessons learned that you can apply to your everyday life to become a better person—lessons that you can put to use right away. If you want to get fired up, grow, and recharge your vigor for life, grab this book immediately. It is fantastic! One of the best I have read.

BARRY KARCH
Owner of The Real Estate Power Houses, podcaster at The Real Estate UnSalesperson

SCHOOL OF

BRAD RITTER

SCHOOL OF

UNLOCK YOUR POTENTIAL THROUGH PURPOSEFUL ADVERSITY

Published and distributed by Merack Publishing.

Library of Congress Control Number: 2022900729

School of Grit: Unlock Your Potential Through Purposeful Adversity

ISBN Paperback 978-1-957048-09-3 Hardcover 978-1-957048-11-6

DEDICATION

To my wife Leslie who allows me to
do crazy stuff and train as much as I want.

To my daughter Hallie and my son Brody, never be afraid of being
judged. Have the courage to suck at something new.

CONTENTS

FOREWORD

The last time you got knocked on your butt by an unforeseen crisis, I bet you wished you had been more prepared, physically, mentally and skill-wise. Am I right? It makes sense. But I wonder if that realization caused you to take positive action to prepare for the next crisis? On that point, I am willing to bet the answer is no.

Preparation for the unknown is uncommon behavior. Most just don't do it for a variety of reasons.

There are two big mistakes most people make in this regard: The first is to hope that "it" won't happen to them—that they are somehow immune to the accident, cancer, tornado, earthquake, plane hitting the building, etc. The second is that if "it" does happen, then they will be able to dig deep to find the reserve power and courage to get through it. The problem with number one is that bad shit happens to everyone. Crisis does not discriminate. But the bigger problem is with number two. Failure to develop the mindset to overcome adversity, in advance of a major crisis, can be a fatal mistake.

The 2020 Covid 19 pandemic, economic lock-downs, lost jobs and businesses were the latest smackdown. You may doubt that it is even possible to prepare for unknowns like these. This game of life is designed to throw curveballs at us. Are we supposed to just let the balls smack us in the head, then stumble a bit before reflecting to see how much we learned from the suffering we endured?

I don't think so. There is another way to learn to play. That is what a School of Grit is for.

In this Volatile, Uncertain, Complex and Ambiguous (VUCA) world, the most important skills to possess are awareness, mental toughness and resilience… in a word, grit. To learn these requires that we subject ourselves to rigorous and extensive training. We must not take for granted the limitations we have been taught is our natural state. Training requires that we challenge what we believe is possible. We must learn that we are capable of so much more than we can imagine.

The resilience and courage to deal with radical change and extreme challenge doesn't require special physical skills. Rather, grit comes from a specific and trainable mindset, what I call a "sheepdog strong" mindset. The sheepdog adapted a specific mindset which makes them capable of protecting sheep from the preying wolves. You can adapt and develop this same mindset to protect yourself, and others you love, from society's wolves. And that same mindset will allow you to skillfully navigate natural (or unnatural) disasters which may come your way.

In the SEAL Teams, when I got sucker punched by an enemy or suffered some screw-up, I learned to say: "Good. Embrace the suck and grow from this." I did not get hung up on shame or blame, but developed the resilient mindset to move forward fast through the obstacles. I learned to expect things to suck, to be messed up and out of my control. That expectation set myself and my team up for success—and vastly motivated us to train even harder for the unknowns. What we trained was our mind, our emotions and how to respond positively to the challenges. That is what a good School of Grit teaches... to be prepared physically, mentally and emotionally for whatever, whenever.

My experience was that we can only develop grit by overcoming resistance to adversity. Adversity builds character quickly, while comfort and prosperity erode it slowly. We live in the most prosperous and comfortable time in known history (at least in the developed world). Therefore, one must seek out adversity to build a sheepdog mindset. My intention when I created SEALFIT was to offer the most severe of training academies—one where individuals could forge deep awareness and mental toughness, and gain the resourcefulness to deal with any challenge, the larger the better. Hundreds of Navy SEALs and thousands of hardy civilians have endured SEALFIT training, and gone forth to thrive in VUCA environments. Brad Ritter is a sterling example of one of these graduates. You can learn some of what he learned through this excellent book... but to really know what he knows, you will need to attend a School of Grit.

You may design your own School of Grit, or find one like SEALFIT. There are many options available that can be surfaced with a little bit of research. Don't be like the majority who avoid hard training because they are conditioned to be like the sheep— too busy, too distracted and too adverse to the discomfort. They are at risk of getting eaten by wolves.

I say to you dear reader—strive to bring the challenges to you before the crisis is dropped on you unwelcomed. Put yourself into situations of extreme discomfort to desensitize from that discomfort. Let the temporary pain of weakness leaving your mind bring you permanent peace. Embrace the suck and do the uncommon. Get gritty... and everything else in your life will become easier and better.

Do this and you will know what Brad Ritter knows. You will also find that the path of grit is fun and infinitely rewarding.

Hooyah!

Mark Divine

Navy SEAL Commander (ret)

Founder of SEALFIT, Inc., Unbeatable, LLC, and the Courage Foundation (501c-3)

Best selling author and host of the Unbeatable Mind podcast www.markdivine.com.

PREFACE

If you're tired of the same old routine, stuck in a rut, or struggling to find your purpose; if you feel trapped in the corporate rat race; or if you have your life's laundry cycle set to lather, rinse and repeat, then this book is for you.

How much did they pay you to give up on your dreams? As for me, I settled for a measly $25K a year in salary and full benefits, which was my first "real" job after graduating college. I thought if I could just make $30K a year as a bachelor, I would be rolling in the dough. Then, like so many do, I got married, settled down, went into further debt, and had kids, all while chasing that next 2–3% increase in salary from year to year instead of chasing down the truth.

The truth is, it's important to know who you really are deep down inside and what you were meant to do or become during your relatively short existence on this planet.

But why? Why would I settle like a lot of you who might be reading this right now? Because it provided me with a false sense of security.

In reality, no job is really "secure." And the more time I put into work, the more I alienated my family due to long hours and travel. I had been accustomed to chasing money and in the process, I'd drifted away from myself. I didn't even know who I was anymore. Truth be told, I'm not sure if I ever did. It was time to break those golden handcuffs. I'd gotten too comfortable.

Have we gotten soft as a society? I would argue yes, in most cases. It boils down to this. We have built a society and culture of comfort. We don't challenge ourselves and are okay with settling and being mediocre. People tend to shy away from hard work. They look for the path of least resistance and are attracted to the easy way. You see it everywhere, from advertising promoting losing 10 pounds in just 10 days to the plethora of get-rich-quick schemes out there. People want the magic pill that will cure their troubles. They have lost the joy of hard work. Guess what . . . no one is coming to save you. If you don't like your current situation, it's on you to get yourself out. And there is a way out, but it's uncommon.

You have to do the daily work and create the discipline to change. Take time to better yourself and those around you. Focus on others' needs instead of your own. I see it all too often (and was guilty of it myself). People expect things to be handed to them and want instant gratification. They don't realize the struggle and the daily grind it takes to get to where you want to be. It's not about how many times you've succeeded. Ask yourself how many times you've failed. You learn. You keep going.

That's what makes this country so amazing. You can truly do or be whatever it is you put your heart, mind, body, and soul into. It sounds cliché, I know. I almost edited that part out. But it's true, all of it. All you have to do is make the choice to be uncommon.

But that's just it, and that's where I see the breakdown. There are many books written about how to get rid of stress in your life. Get rid of stress? Seriously? Unless you plan on becoming a monk and living at the Shaolin Temple to reach enlightenment, it's probably not going to happen. That's like trying to change the direction of the wind by pissing into it. What you need to do instead is change your relationship with stress. More on that later. Stress usually comes from some sort of adversity. People fear adversity. An idea will pop into your head that sounds amazing, but at the first sign of adversity, what do most people do? They tuck tail and run and move on by going around the situation or abandoning their thought processes altogether. They succumb to *fear*. To me, that's the ultimate F-word . . . not the F-word that Ralphie got soap in his mouth for saying (cue the movie, *A Christmas Story*). Think about it. Fear affects everything you do. It affects where you work and live; whom you talk to, ask to the dance, or marry; how you talk to your boss; what sports you try out for; what you ask your customers; and whether you follow your dreams or let them die. All of it is tied to a certain level of fear.

Word to the wise: Embrace adversity. Run toward it and not away from it. Go looking for adversity, or what I call "purposeful pain," and let it mold you like a sword being forged in fire. That is your School of Grit. Think of it as your own personal boot camp; allow it to mold you into the person you were born to become.

This book is about my own personal journey and how I took a giant leap of faith and signed up for what's been called the "world's toughest civilian training on the planet." It is the type of thing that truly pushes a person out of their comfort zone and attacks them on every level—physically, mentally, emotionally, intuitively, and spiritually. This book is about a man who was struggling to find his place in the world. He took a chance and bet on himself when others didn't understand and even doubted his sanity and whether he could make it. It's about a dad who rejoiced in adversity and looked fear in the face and told it to give up.

If I could offer only one piece of advice to use for the rest of your life, it would be this: try new things, do stuff that scares you, and master your inner dialogue. You learn a lot about yourself when you step out of your comfort zone and push your own perceived limits—that's where the real growth happens. Nike got it right with their tagline, "Just do it." I like to take that and put my own spin on it. "Do hard stuff and grow your grit."

I never intended to sit down and write a book and it's proven to be one of the hardest things I've ever done. After Class 38 graduated from Kokoro Camp in July 2015, I sat down with my family and went into great detail about that weekend and my experiences. I've been reliving my stories to my family, friends, and coworkers ever since. I finally sat down to write this book back in January 2017, after much encouragement from those very same friends, family, and coworkers. It started out as a passion project to my wife and kids in case something were to happen to me, that way they'd always have this to remember me by, as part of my legacy exercise someone told me to do (and I encourage you to do the same sort of exercise). But then I realized that my story might help others who were just like me. Do you ever feel like you were meant for more? Are you tired of playing small ball? Do you want more authentic relationships with your spouse, girlfriend/boyfriend, kids? Perhaps you're struggling with work/life balance? Do you ever ask yourself, "What's my legacy? What will people remember me for?" If you answered yes to any of these, then please keep reading.

This is a firsthand account of my experience being trained by Navy SEALs, arguably some of the toughest men on the planet. We'll dig into my background and why I would ever choose to get beaten down by Navy SEALs for over 50 hours straight in the first place—without any sleep. The events of my life and the training that took place in California have been recounted to the best of my ability. As you can imagine, cramming 50 plus hours of the weekend at Kokoro Camp into a readable book means that I had to condense my story a good bit. I have not included all of the activities of the weekend. Certain names I will not divulge to protect the identity of those coaches who may still be involved in highly classified missions around the world.

I'll teach you the lessons the SEALs taught me and at the end of each chapter I'll present you with an Application to Life, in a section called Pack Your Rucksack. This application is a real-world example from my own life of how I use those lessons as a father, husband, employee, etc. One more thing, each chapter has its own challenge. These challenges have been designed to push you past your comfort zone so you can begin growing your grit today. What are you waiting for? Let's get to work!

INTRODUCTION

Don't pray for an easy life. Pray for the strength to endure a difficult one.

—BRUCE LEE

Have you ever seen a TED talk? I'm betting most of you have. But have you ever seen a TED talk that changed your life? Well, in 2014, my life changed forever after watching one on YouTube. I was standing in my master bathroom, looking at myself in the mirror, getting ready to go to work, just as I normally do. I was home alone. My wife, who is a schoolteacher, had already left for work and she had dropped our kids off at daycare. The morning began just like any other. But this was no ordinary morning. Something was speaking inside of me. Only this time, I finally listened. Maybe it was God. Maybe not. All I can tell you is that it's been there my entire life, slowly growing, like a small spark that had turned into a fire. Up until that point, I did what most do, and I didn't really listen to that voice. I'd brush it off as nonsense and move on to my next activity, never stopping to understand it. Year after year after year, that voice had finally sparked a fire inside of me, and the voice grew louder and more frequent. As I looked at myself in the mirror on that day, I asked myself three simple questions.

"Who am I?"

"What am I here to do?"

and

"What's my purpose?"

And you know what? I couldn't answer a single one. Not even close. It scared me. To think at 35 years old, I had no idea what I wanted to be when I grew up. So that day, I decided to call in sick to work; I wasn't going to go. Something was telling me at that particular moment in my life, work just wasn't a priority. It was time to make myself a priority for once. So, I stayed home. And I did what many people do. No, I didn't start watching TV, even though I was behind on *Game of Thrones* Season 4. I got on the internet instead and did a Google search on passion and purpose. And as you can imagine, several results popped up, about 257 million to be exact. And after about an hour of sifting through all the different links and stories and blogs, you know what? I was nowhere closer to finding any answers. In fact, I was even more confused. I had analysis paralysis.

Then I went to YouTube thinking maybe a video would help, and I typed in the same thing, "passion and purpose." This resulted in another several million hits. But this time, one particular video stuck out to me on the first page of results.

It was a six-minute TED Talk video on something called *grit*, delivered by a psychologist named Angela Duckworth. You may or may not have seen this TED Talk conference, but I'll sum up her message. She claims that grit is the number-one indicator and predictor of success in life. And you know what? Scientists still know very little about how to build it and grow it.

Angela's definition of grit is the power of passion and perseverance toward reaching a long-term goal. Grit also means courage, resolve, and strength of character. As Angela points out, grit can be grown from the inside out and also from the outside in. That got me wondering, how many goals and dreams have I given up on in my life? A lot more than I care to admit.

Angela also provides a free grit test you can take to get your own score. I thought I was tough and figured, why not, I'll take this test that will prove to me what I already know... that I'm a boss. At least, that's the lie I told myself. You can find her grit scale here: AngelaDuckworth.com/grit-scale/

It's only 10 questions, and I encourage you to take it, just like I did. On a scale of 0 to 5, with 0 having no grit and 5 being the grittiest toughie on the planet, I scored a whopping 2.2. Good enough to score higher than 20% of Americans, according to the results. I guess you could say I just wasn't that gritty, and that did not sit well with me at all. I started to question everything. Had I become too comfortable with life? Answer: Hell yes, I had. I wasn't really living; I was just going through the motions.

I watched her video again and again and again. And I started internalizing her message. I knew I was onto something. I had bought into her message, hook, line, and sinker and even purchased her book from Amazon shortly after watching her video for the 10th time.

The message that resonated with me was that I needed to grow my grit and resilience... but how? You see, up until that point, I had never really tested myself in life, and I didn't know what I was truly capable of or how gritty or resilient I could be. Have you ever pushed yourself beyond every measure, passed what you thought was possible, over the brink? Sadly, I hadn't, and I was 35 at the time. I wonder how many people go through their entire life without testing their limits and finding their true selves. I was playing small ball in life, and it was time to go big. I'm different from most of the people that you might hear speak at a conference, read about in a book, listen to on podcasts and other interviews, or watch in videos or on TV. You see, most of these people by all accounts have lived incredible lives. They have tons of life experience or experienced loads of adversity and trauma. Their life résumés read like a presentation speech for a lifetime achievement award. I'm just the average Joe. Life had come pretty easily to me up to that point.

I'm a white middle-class male. My parents are still happily married. I had a wonderful upbringing. I'm the oldest of four siblings, and my family remains very close to this day. School also came pretty easy to me. I wasn't a straight-A student, but it wasn't very hard for me to get B's, so I never really had to apply or push myself.

It was fairly easy for me to make friends. I followed the rules. I went to college. I played sports. I went on to marry the love of my life, and we have two wonderful kids, both completely healthy. We have a big house in a very sought-after neighborhood. No, it doesn't have a white picket fence. But you know what? I don't want one. I had bought into the American dream. Work hard, go to school, work for a company for 30–40 years, and vacation down in the Gulf of Mexico.

After hours of examining my life, I came up with the following explanation for how I got to where I was. My life had been a little too easy. Do you think that's possible? That life can be too easy? I know it's possible because I lived it. I've never really had to experience true adversity—the kind that can be life-altering. Now, I'm not saying I grew up in a bubble and was never picked on or had daily struggles. I'm human just like anyone else.

I'm talking about real adversity. It could be growing up as the only ethnic minority in your school or small town and dealing with racial issues. It could be battling obesity at a young age and being called *fat* all your life. It could be dealing with a learning disability and being called *stupid.* It could be growing up dirt poor and everyone knowing about it. It could be losing a close friend or family member at a young age or other traumatic events a child shouldn't have to go through. It could be living with the fact that your parents are divorced and you think it's all because of you. It could also be dealing with a life-threatening illness such as cancer. Adversity, in my opinion, is the key ingredient to growing grit and resiliency. My new mission in life was to bring adversity to myself rather than wait for it to happen. I call this *purposeful pain.* Purposeful pain can be defined as intentional discomfort. Volunteering to be in an uncomfortable situation can bring purposeful pain. This can result in feelings of anxiety, fear, nervousness, or just downright physical trauma. It can be anything from signing up for your first 5K to going after your MBA or PhD, from learning to play a musical instrument to public speaking.

The point is, the more you expose yourself to these types of scenarios, the more chances you have at failing, which allows the opportunity to grow your grit and develop mental toughness and emotional resiliency.

You can grow your grit every single day of your life. Imagine that for a second. Every day, you have the opportunity to do something that makes you uncomfortable so that you can really grow. Now, think about how your mind and body would respond if you made this a practice. I'm not saying life would be easy. What I am saying is that life would be *easier.* It's not a matter of whether or not life will throw curveballs your way, it's a matter of when. I promise, if you commit to a daily practice and push yourself, you'll be ready for the biggest battle there is: the battle of life.

PACK YOUR RUCKSACK

Check your ego at the door.

News flash: The world doesn't owe you a thing.

In my mind, it was all coming together, or at least I assumed it was. I thought companies would come knocking down my door, and I'd have job offers left and right. Large salaries with all the benefits—a 401(k), a company car, and expense accounts— filled my brain with daydreams. The problem was, no one came knocking. It was all a pipe dream. It was 2002, and I had just graduated from college. I worked full-time while going to school and was able to graduate with a four-year degree (which took me five years to achieve, by the way, but who's counting).

Unfortunately, the economy wasn't doing so hot. Our country was at war, and many folks were out of jobs. In addition to that, I was competing for entry-level gigs against people who had master's degrees and several years of "real-world experience." Everywhere I interviewed, it was the same old song and dance: "Come back when you have experience." How do you get real- life work experience when no one wants to take a shot on a recent college graduate?

After several months of interviewing and getting nowhere, I elected to work two jobs. My day job would give me the necessary "experience," and my night job would provide me insurance. I needed insurance because I was about to turn 23 and could no longer be on my parents' policy.

By day, I was working a paid internship at an inside sales and marketing research firm that paid $10/hour. By night, I was working the graveyard shift at a local shipping giant at the Indianapolis airport. My schedule consisted of the following: wake up at 6:00 am and get ready for work to be out the door by 7:00. Then a 45-minute commute to sit behind a desk and solicit sales leads from 8–5. I'd leave the office and hit rush hour so the 45-minute drive easily became an hour or more to get home. Once home at 6:00 or so, I'd eat dinner and try to get some sort of exercise done without any real purpose or a program and then be in bed by 9:00. I'd sleep from 9–11 then roll out of bed to report to the graveyard shift, where I'd spend the next four hours loading planes with cargo. Typically, I'd get home around 3:00 am and then go to bed until 6:00 am. Lather, rinse, repeat.

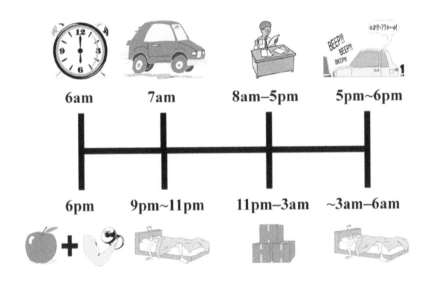

The same cycle of working two jobs meant getting a combined five hours of sleep at the most each day. Lack of sleep and a pitiful "woe is me" attitude started taking a toll on me and my family. My physical training started to decline, which resulted in a loss of muscle mass and weight. This had a major effect on my attitude, and I'm sure I was a total jerk to be around (just ask my wife and coworkers). Was this the American dream? Where's the white picket fence and the big house with a yard that I had been promised?

My life was at an all-time low. It took everything I had to not fall asleep behind the computer at my internship. That job was boring, and there wasn't a real career path for me there. While at my night job, I couldn't help but think, *What am I even doing here?* I felt entitled, and that I was above certain people there. *I have a college degree and I can't get a good full-time day job?* I felt like the world owed me something.

That was my first truly humbling experience of eating a giant piece of the adversity pie in my life. You see, everything I had up to that point in life had come relatively easily. I had taken life for granted and hadn't faced any major setbacks yet. I didn't realize it at the time, but my life had been too comfortable.

I've always admired kids who know exactly what they want to be when they grew up, but that wasn't the case for me, and I believe it's not the case for most people. So, if you don't know, just take a breath. It's okay, but promise me one thing. Promise you won't go chasing the money right away. Income is somewhat important, but it will come later. More important than money is finding out what your passions and purpose are in your life. Spend your early years experiencing. Work can wait a little while. There's a trend in America that adults reach a certain age and have a midlife crisis. Do you ever wonder why that is? I think it's directly linked to folks who go after the money and career first instead of trying to figure out what they love or really like to do. In our society, it's commonplace that you start your career around age 20 and work for the next 30–40 years of your life hoping that you've saved enough to retire.

Thirty to forty years is a long time to work at a place you don't like, for a boss you don't like, doing the same stuff you don't like day in and day out. In other countries, young adults are encouraged to travel the world, try new things early on, and figure out what they are into. This leads to a higher job satisfaction rate and far fewer people suffering from a "midlife crisis." Take the time to do the deep work to really figure out who you are and what you like doing, not what you think you are or what someone else thinks you should do. Whatever you end up doing, though, just remember to check your ego at the door anytime you walk through one.

CHALLENGE

Do the Deep Work.

My first challenge for you is to do something that isn't taught at school (at least not while I was in a classroom). It's to do the deep work. What I mean by "deep" here is looking inward at yourself and spending quality time contemplating why you're here on earth. I had the benefit of finding a mentor in my early thirties, Mark Divine (more on him later), who helped me discover my passion, purpose, and principles (or the 3 P's). But don't wait as long as I did—or worse, never take action. With his Unbeatable Mind program, I was able to change my life's trajectory.

We all need a mission in life, something to drive us, something that will wake us up in the middle of the night because we can't stop thinking about it. You need something you can't help but talk about when your friends and family ask you what you've been up to. As Mark says, if our purpose is our only reason for being here on this planet, why wouldn't you have faith and an intense desire to fulfill it?

Throughout this book, I'm going to touch on lessons and challenges just like I have in the Introduction. The ideas are pretty straightforward, but as with anything new, they can be challenging to implement. Implementation is where most people (including yours truly) can and often do fall short. If you find yourself wanting to make a change or try one of these challenges and find yourself struggling, don't worry, that's the point. In the struggle is where real growth happens. Just don't quit.

Instead, I encourage you to seek out a coach who can help. A coach? That's right, someone to help guide you through your transformation. Think about it. You've had coaches most of your life. Ideally, your parents were your coaches early on, but if that wasn't in the cards for you, someone or something stepped into that void. If you played sports, guess what, you had coaches. Your teachers are coaches, and those teachers likely learned from a coach or mentor of their own. You can hire financial coaches to help grow your nest egg, entrepreneurial coaches to help run your business, personal trainers to help setup programming and nutrition. Why would or should this be any different?

Finding your 3P's is the foundation for your journey in all other aspects and domains of your life. One last plug here. It just so happens that I'm a certified Unbeatable Mind coach and operate my own coaching experience called, "*The School of Grit*." If you're finding it increasingly difficult and want help to become the person that, deep down inside, you know you want to be, turn to the back of my book for my contact info. Alright, enough of the sales pitch. Let's do this!

THE CRUCIBLE

Whether you think you can or you think you can't, you're right.

—HENRY FORD

You might be wondering which School of Grit I chose. Remember that grit test I took, in which I scored a 2.2? After doing some soul searching, I figured that the best way I could grow my own grit was to shock my system. I wanted to use the technique of growing my own grit from the outside in. There are several ways to grow your grit from the inside out, and I'll go into one of those at the end of the book, but it involves a lot of self-reflection and personal development. It's a total game changer, too, but I wanted instant gratification (remember when I talked about that earlier? I'm eating my own dog food now).

How was I going to grow my grit? *Maybe I'll sign up for a marathon*, I thought at first. Would that produce the sort of shock I was looking for? I didn't think so, although in its own right, running 26.2 miles is very hard to do. It just didn't have that lasting impression I was looking for. Plus, I knew lots of people who trained for a marathon, completed that goal, and then went right back to their old habits. I was on a quest to find something where I would truly be tested on all levels and that would be such a shock on my system it would have a lasting impact. A crucible experience should do the trick.

I turned to my old friend Google for the answer. I typed in the following phrase: toughest civilian training. Out of the hundreds of thousands of results, I zeroed in on the top hits on the first page. *Men's Journal, Huffington Post,* and *Outside Online* all had articles about something called SEALFIT Kokoro Camp. Even though I wanted something specific to civilians, several articles about who has the toughest military training popped up as well.

Every list I looked at listed the Navy SEALs as being the toughest training on the planet. (Sidenote: I think every branch of the military has tough training, and I'm the last person qualified to tell you which is most challenging). There must be something special about this Navy SEAL thing, else why would it be popping up everywhere? At the time, I didn't know much about them, so I did some YouTube searches to see what I could find. I found some videos from the Discovery channel about Class 234 who were going through what's known as BUDs. That stands for "basic underwater demolition" SEAL training. Since we're on the subject, SEAL stands for Sea, Air, And Land.

I was hooked. I couldn't stop watching these men and all the abuse they had to endure to earn the right to called themselves Navy SEALs. About four weeks into the program, there's a special week called Hell Week. This is when students train for five full days and nights without any sleep. It starts sundown on Sunday and ends sometime on Friday. What I witnessed that day blew my mind. How can someone function nonstop for five days straight without any sleep? It doesn't seem possible. How gritty do you have to be to endure something like that?

Armed with some mental imagery of what sort of training a SEAL candidate goes through, I turned to this SEALFIT Kokoro Camp that had been listed in most of the articles I was reading. I typed in that name and this popped up on their website:

THE CRUCIBLE

What if, over the course of 50 hours, you could tap into a limitless source of power you never knew existed? Imagine moving through life without fear, with total confidence in your ability to overcome obstacles and reach any mission or goal, no matter how big or challenging. That's what Kokoro Camp can do for you. It's a test that connects you to the very core of who you are, and what you're made of.

SEALFIT Kokoro Camp is, quite simply, the world's premier training camp for forging mental toughness, modeled after the US Navy SEAL Hell Week. Yes, it is brutal. No, it's not for everyone. You may not qualify or make it through the training. Yet, if you're ready for this challenge, you'll find it to be an experience that changes your life—FOREVER.

THE MISSION

Our mission is not merely to push you for its own sake, but rather, to help you develop mental toughness and insight 20x more than you ever thought possible. This 20x principle applies to all areas of your life— your health and fitness, career, income, relationships, and beyond. Once you see and "get" this fundamental truth, it becomes impossible to ever settle for less in your life.

As you cultivate the non-quitting warrior spirit over three days, you'll discover sources of discipline and focus while you sharpen your will and determination. Your ability to direct your attention on your goals and targets will be enhanced, and you'll learn to keep going until you reach them. No matter what.

Virtually every aspect of your mind, body, and spirit are trained and tested through 50 hours of intense physical and mental training. By pushing you to your perceived limits, and then far beyond those limits, your concept of who you are and what's possible will be revolutionized.

SEALFIT Kokoro Camp is the brainchild of Mark Divine. Mark is a retired Navy SEAL Commander who operates SEALFIT and Unbeatable Mind along with several other very successful ventures. He's also a *New York Times* bestseller and thought leader on human performance. The BUDs training has a failure rate of around 80%. The Navy hired Mark to create a program that would boost those retention numbers. Candidates who successfully completed his program had an 80% success rate of graduating BUDs training.

Kokoro Camp.

SEALFIT combines physical training with mental toughness training to help you get through virtually anything life throws your way. It was born out of the desire to help Navy SEAL candidates successfully complete Basic Underwater Demolition/SEAL (BUDs) training with a special emphasis on surviving Navy SEALs "Hell Week." They then discovered that civilians were interested in participating in Navy SEAL fitness training, and the program evolved to something much more. Beyond being a Navy SEAL fitness program, SEALFIT has become a way of life and state of mind for thousands of people around the world.

In the video above, Coach Divine says, "Rejoice in adversity . . . How do we grow as human beings? Through adversity. We grow by challenging ourselves beyond every measure. Warriors choose the severest of schools to forge their character—welcome to the severest school. Unless you're at Basic Underwater Demolition School (BUDS), you won't find any training that will compare to this weekend . . ."

Was this video made specifically for me? Could I do something like that? Hell, could I even survive something like that? Three days of nonstop beatdowns? That's crazy. And that's exactly the type of crazy I was looking for in my life.

That was it. That was my moment. I knew I had to do it. I was on a quest to find myself and test my character, and if three straight days of training without sleep couldn't provide it, I didn't think anything could. I knew I had to do it, and most people wouldn't understand why... but that didn't matter because *I* knew why I was going to do it. Now there was only one thing left to do: Sign up!

PACK YOUR RUCKSACK

What is your Why?

Why? This is arguably the least favorite question a parent can ever receive from their child. The typical parental response is "Because I said so," which is also my least favorite way to respond. Many books have been written about finding your "Why." My favorite is Simon Sinek's book, Start with Why. The book starts with a comparison of the two main ways to influence human behavior: manipulation and inspiration. Sinek argues that inspiration is the more powerful and sustainable of the two. I wholeheartedly agree. Why is it, then, that I find myself trying to manipulate my own kids' behavior instead of inspiring them? When they ask me something now, I try to get on their level and explain why doing what I ask is important to me, the effect it will have on them, and the end state I hope to create. But that wasn't always the case. I would sometimes get mad that they had the audacity to question my authority. Really? Like I'm some sort of Dad Emperor? Please.

That's the farthest thing from the truth. You'll find that if you can explain why to your kids, chances are they will follow through.

The same goes for work. Take any job in which you report to a boss or manager. If they try telling you what to do without explaining why they want you to do it, chances are your inner voice will resist. *What are they trying to change or implement now?*

As the manager, if you can simply divulge the inside information of why you're asking them to do anything, you'll increase the likelihood of your team carrying out your orders. Information is power, and employees love knowing what's really going on inside a company... not the cherry-flavored Kool-Aid that gets served at company conferences. You don't have to overthink it. That reason might be as simple as, "Hey, look, I don't agree with what the top management is asking for, but do me a favor and make this look good so we all look good." Be real. Be honest.

People can see through the smoke and mirrors. We're all humans, and we all want that sense of belonging and know the real reason behind the request.

CHALLENGE

Start with "Why."

Your "Why" is the reason you are doing anything at any given time. It's your fallback when things get tough. If you can't answer that question, you will likely fail. Similarly, if your "Why" is extrinsic versus intrinsic, and you find yourself in a truly adverse situation, your likelihood of making it to the other side is slim to none. You're going to need a bucket full of "Whys" throughout your life depending on the various situations you find yourself in.

So how do you start? Pretty simple actually. Did you know that asking yourself "why" three to five times can get you to the root of something? Try it. It works every time. Sometimes all you need is three while others may go seven or more, but eventually, the real reason is always revealed. I first learned this trick from my regional vice president when I was a "new guy" in the publishing industry (thanks, Tom). We used this tactic to get to the root cause of the issue our prospects were experiencing. Let me give you a quick example from my own life. Let's start with a problem or project first. Okay, I know just the one. Brad wants to write a book. Here's the internal dialogue.

1. Why do you want to write a book? *Because I want to.* Why do you want to? *So that I can teach others some lessons I learned.*

2. Why do you want to teach others lessons you've learned? *Ah, now we're getting somewhere... These lessons and the experiences I went through changed my life, and I want others to know that they are capable of more than they think they are. Specifically, I want my wife and kids to know they can do anything they put their minds to. Besides that, the book will be a part of the legacy I intend to leave for them. Cue mic drop.*

Simple, right? Now I want you to take any project, problem, or idea, and ask yourself three to five "Why" questions so you too can figure out the real root of the problem or the real truth behind the project or idea. Journal these insights so you can come back to them when the journey gets tough (because it will).

COMMITTING

Do, or do not. There is no try.

—YODA

I bet you're thinking that the very next thing I did after watching the video about Kokoro Camp and navigating their website was to sign up. After all, that's the meat and potatoes of this book anyway, right? Wrong. I had tons of self-doubt and really started to question myself. In fact, at first, I didn't think I could do it.

Remember the F-word? Fear was already infiltrating the decision-making part of my mind. But still, even with the fear wolf howling, there was something about this thing that I couldn't quite put my finger on. I just knew if I could make it, it would change me forever, sort of like a rebirth or reboot. I guess you could call it Ritter version 2.0. There would be the old me before the experience and the new one after. Weeks went by, but it was something that was constantly on my mind. I was starting to dream about being there.

I'd always kept Kokoro Camp at the back of my mind as the pinnacle of my journey toward self-mastery, and felt it was time to finally take the plunge. But (there's always a but), how was I going to afford the camp, plane ticket, and hotel? How could I invest the time in training to be ready, and when would I attend? When I discussed my plan with my wife Leslie, my family, and friends, most of them just shrugged it off or told me I was crazy. But I wasn't crazy. I was doing this for a reason. Perhaps the biggest reason of all was to find myself. Or maybe it just takes the right kind of crazy to get you there.

After months of self-doubt, I formulated a plan that I would attend Kokoro Camp if I finished the year at my employer as the #1 sales consultant. Overall, I figured the experience would cost around $3,000. That's a ton of money to me. My family could go on an awesome vacation for that amount of money, and I was having a hard time committing to something like that because it felt a little selfish. I deal with this mentality a lot. It's easy to feel selfish when you are spending time bettering yourself versus being with your family. But what good is being around if you're not at your best or bringing your A game? It's very important in life to make time for and work on bettering yourself in all areas— mental, physical, emotional, intuitional, and spiritual. Remember that lions eat first.

It's interesting what happens when you finally decide to do something and take massive action toward your goals. One day approximately three months after seeing that video, I told my boss that I was going to finish the year as the #1 sales consultant, which obviously brought a smile to her face.

The company I worked for at the time has a multiday national sales meeting once a year with almost the entire sales organization (about 500 people) to celebrate the prior year and kick off next year's strategy. There is an elegant awards dinner at which top performers are brought onto the stage and recognized. It's referred to as "prom" in our industry, mostly because everyone is dressed to the nines. Typically, the select few that do get their name announced walk across the stage, shake hands with top brass, and receive a gift. Most commonly, these gifts are physical things like watches, nice bottles of wine, clothing, etc.

I didn't want a material gift; I wanted an experience. And not just any experience—one that could change my life. I wanted Kokoro Camp. So that was my deal with my wife and my boss. I wouldn't go to Kokoro Camp unless I was a top performer. And if I finished #1 in the company, my gift would be a paid entry.

I was completely consumed that year, and I did everything I could to maximize revenue for the company and finish #1. I work out of my house, so I kept a picture of Kokoro Camp by my computer to remind me of my goal. When I'd be up early before anyone was up in the house, or working late when everyone was already in bed, I'd look at that picture and keep going, keep persevering, and never quit. I wasn't motivated; I was obsessed.

As you probably already guessed, I did finish that year #1 and was invited on stage to receive my award in front of 500 people. That was a pretty cool moment for me. Not only did I achieve my goal of being the best at my craft, but more importantly, I had finally punched my ticket for something I had been visualizing for well over a year.

Monday, January 12th, 2015, the very next day after I had flown home from the awards banquet, I took the plunge. There was an application to fill out along with a medical waiver, liability documents, etc., to sign up for Kokoro Camp. I had to include an essay on why I was doing it, along with the standards that I could perform. Not just anyone can do that camp. You have to qualify even to be considered to class up with your team, and the test would immediately disqualify most.

This was it! I paid the money and pressed submit. I felt like I was signing my life away, but finally, after a year of waiting and visualizing, I was locked in. There was no going back. Truth be told, I was really nervous while signing up. I had an accelerated heart rate, and my fingers were cold and clammy just typing the application letter. Putting words on paper, I had to write out my "Why."

Here is the email I sent Headquarters:

1. What do you hope to get out of the training?

    Ultimately, I want to be a better all-around human being. My why is for my family—to be a better husband and father. I'm the oldest of four and have always felt a duty to protect those around me, especially those who can't fend for themselves. I have a fire inside of me that has been burning ever since I can remember. I want to see that fire spread, and this is my chance to make it happen. I've visualized for a long time what I would do if I were to be in certain scenarios. It's time to put myself to the test. 100% true grit and never quit. I'm ready to meet myself for the first time and form friendships with my teammates that last forever.

2. How have you prepared your mind and body?

    Physically I've been training via the SEALFIT Operator daily WOD (workout of the day). (The workouts can be found here https:// sealfit.com/. More on this in the next chapter.) Most days I can get through 4 of the 5 elements. Baseline, strength, and stamina are my daily routine, while workload and durability are the two that I typically alternate between depending on time and resources. I enjoy trail running and obstacle course races as well. I visit a local CrossFit box every now and again for team competitions. Mentally, I've read *8 Weeks to SEALFIT, Unbeatable Mind,* and *The Way of the Seal* to help prepare.

3. Provide your stats for benchmarks of the program. Standards (these are to be performed in 2-minute intervals with a 2-minute rest in between). Also known as a PST or Physical Standards Test.

- Push-ups: 65 (50 minimum)

- Sit-ups: 69 (50 minimum)

- Air squats: 70 (50 minimum)

- Dead hang pull-ups: 15 (10 minimum)

- 1-mile run in 7:30 min (must be done in boots and utility pants on the road) (9:30 max)

- Murph in 45 min (1 hour 10 min max.) (Murph is a famous HERO WOD named after Lt. Michael P. Murphy, who was awarded the Medal of Honor. He was the first US Navy member to receive the honor since the Vietnam War. He called it body armor, and it consists of the following: a 1-mile run, 100 pull-ups, 200 push-ups, 300 air squats, and another 1-mile run—yeah, all while wearing a plate carrier that weighs at least 20 pounds.)

- Endurance standards to guide your preparation (not tested for performance, but completion):

  - 10-mile run in less than 1:20

  - 20-mile ruck hike with load in less than 6 hours

Two event failures (PST or Murph) will result in a drop from the course, and refusal to perform any event will be considered a nonverbal drop. Note that we highly recommend that you ramp up your endurance and stamina training. A standard CrossFit training regimen will not suffice.

You should run a marathon or half Iron Man and spend considerable time rucking with load.

Amazing what happens when you set an end goal with a deadline. I pressed the Send button and signed up for the camp in July 2015. It was time to take my training to a whole new level! I had roughly 28 weeks to turn myself into the hardest man I could become. Game on!

PACK YOUR RUCKSACK

Take massive action.

It's easy to sit in the comfort of your own home watching something on TV and tell yourself, "Yeah, I could do that." It's a big deal to actually put your skin in the game, sign up, and then go out and achieve it. I see it all the time, too. I'll have conversations with people who'll have goals, but when faced with adversity, most of them will put it off or come up with some sort of excuse. My dad once told me excuses are like buttholes: Everyone has them, and they all stink. So true. My excuse used to be that I didn't have enough time. Let me give you a few examples of what I'm talking about here.

What's your morning ritual like? I used to have one, and depending on the day, it consisted of sleeping in until about 6:30 or 7:00 and then immediately grabbing my phone to look for any work emails that might have come to my inbox while I was asleep. I'd then hop in the shower, and once that was over, I'd start making breakfast. Only, breakfast for me was cereal and a Pop-Tart (or a Toaster Strudel if I was treating myself). Once done with breakfast, I'd immediately sit in front of my computer and start answering work emails. Then I'd hit the road for work with an average commute of anywhere from thirty minutes to two hours depending on the day's plan... but not before giving my wife and kids a goodbye kiss. Sound familiar?

What's wrong with that description? Well, nothing if all you really care about is work and a sugary start to your day, not to mention zero physical movement. Your morning sets your tone for the day, and I was starting mine off playing defense. Try playing offense instead.

Years ago, I thankfully stumbled upon a book, *The Miracle Morning* by Hal Elrod. In that book, Elrod discusses how important a morning routine is and groups it into six parts—silence, affirmations, visualization, exercise, reading, and scribing—all of which can help improve our physical, emotional, mental, and spiritual self.

Does it sound like a lot? It certainly can be. That's why I suggest picking one and starting there.

Once you have silence down, then move on to exercise, or reading, or journaling. The point is to start making time for yourself. It can be anything from an extra 10–15 minutes in the morning to waking up at 4:30. Are you freaking crazy, Brad? Sounds early, I know. Why would I wake up at 4:30 or 5:00 if I didn't have to? My answer is so you can win the mind before setting foot on the battlefield of life. So I ask you now, "Why do you wake up in the morning"?

Jocko Willink is a retired SEAL commander, best-selling author, and podcast host. He coined the mantra, "Discipline equals freedom," and among his many books, he wrote a field manual with the same title.

Willink says, "Discipline is the root of all good qualities. The driver of daily execution. The core principle that overcomes laziness and lethargy and excuses. Discipline defeats the infinite excuses that say not today, not now, I need a rest, I will do it tomorrow. What's the hack? How do you become stronger, smarter, faster, healthier? How do you become better? How do you achieve true freedom? There is only one way. The Way of Discipline."

And what better way to start your new habit of discipline than winning the first battle in the morning? Do yourself a favor. Wake up early, and don't hit snooze. Listen, I know it's hard. I hate waking up early as much as I hate running. So why do it? Adopting a practice of doing things that suck every day will help build our grit.

You still don't want to wake up early, leave your warm cozy bed, and get a head start on the day? Well, then, I want you to write down a goal that you *would* like to accomplish. One month from now, pull out that same goal. Maybe you achieved it, which is great, and that's our mission here. Maybe you didn't achieve that goal, or worse, haven't even started doing the work to achieve it. If the excuse is that you don't have enough time, quit lying to yourself. Come to terms with the fact that you chose not to be disciplined, wake up early, and get it done.

My morning ritual now consists of waking up at 4:30–5:00. I gulp down a large glass of water and then spend 10 minutes meditating using a practice called box breathing. This breathing practice can serve multiple purposes. I can just focus on my breath, which makes it a concentration practice; I can use it to connect to my purpose, passion, and principle, and then visualize my day. I can also use it to let go of something. The point is, it gets my mind in the right thought patterns so I can play offense instead of playing defense all day. After my meditation session, I perform a 10-minute stretching/yoga routine that I have developed. That's 20 minutes of my time and energy that

I've spent 100% on myself and nothing else. My kids get up at 7:00 for school, so I'll spend the next 1.5 hours or so working on a mission. As of right now, that mission is getting this book complete, and it would have never come to fruition had I not formed the discipline to wake up early and write. Once 7:00 rolls around, I become a dad and a husband and focus my energy on my kids and my wife, and we alternate making breakfast. Yeah, I still eat Pop-Tarts from time to time. I freaking love those things, especially the brown sugar and cinnamon packs. But we always make eggs, bacon or sausage, cut fruit, etc. Then we're all out the door, ready to attack the day.

If you aren't happy with where you are right now, take massive action. Own your morning. Don't let it own you!

CHALLENGE

Create Your Morning Ritual.

You just heard what my morning ritual consists of. Now I want you to focus on your own. Remember, don't go from zero to a hundred overnight, unless that's your type of thing. Start off small. Master those new habits, and expand. Just try waking up 30 minutes earlier than you normally do, and spend that time on you—writing, stretching, working out, meditating, gratitude sessions, or learning a new skill. The list goes on.

Also, and this is a big one, pay attention to when you are sleeping and how much sleep you are getting. The prior night sets the tone for the morning. If you decide to stay up late, drink beer on your couch, and watch Netflix or football, you are setting yourself up to fail. Trust me, I know this one intimately. It's hard enough waking up to an alarm and not hitting snooze. Try being extra tired and a little hungover. Good luck with that. It all comes down to discipline.

Win the first battle of the day by skipping the snooze button. Commit to a new morning ritual. We all have time. You just need to carve it out for yourself. As the saying goes, lions eat first. Sidenote: On the rare occasion you already wake up early and can't squeeze any more time in, consider looking at what time you go to bed and your evening ritual of putting yourself to sleep.

TRAINING

Destiny favors the prepared in mind, body, and spirit.

—MARK DIVINE

After I signed up for Kokoro Camp, it got real. I suppose it's no different from signing up for a 5K race, half marathon, Spartan, Tough Mudder, or GoRuck event. There's something magical that happens when you commit and put a self-imposed deadline on yourself. The simple act of putting that date on the calendar locks it into your mind and gives you a real purpose for your training. I knew that no matter what, by July 24, which was less than 6 months away, I had to be at my best.

I had an agreement with myself, which I still incorporate to this day: Never *give up* on a workout once I've started. My theory on giving up is that once you do decide to throw in the towel, the option to repeat that behavior sits in the back of your mind. From then on, each time that thought enters your mind, you'll be more likely to succumb to the pressure. If you never learn how to give up, you don't know what that feels like, and you're more likely to push through since that's all you know.

Do you think that giving up is the same as quitting? They are not. I've quit lots of things I've started in life, and it's actually not a bad skill to master. Master quitting? Did I hear you right, Brad? Yes, you sure did.

Quitting something isn't necessarily bad depending on the circumstances. I've quit many jobs in order to expand my background and grow professionally, always being able to answer the question of "Why?" and "What will this set up for me long term?" I've quit lots of bad habits and friendships, too. It depends on the perspective and circumstances.

Giving up, on the other hand, that's a totally different deal. Giving up on something you care passionately about should never happen. These are the types of things that you hold so near and dear to your heart that there is no way you'd ever give up. Obviously, your wife and kids could fall into this. Your career might fit this, too, if it's aligned with your 3P's. A race or crucible might fill the bill here depending on why you are doing it and what it means to you.

Everything being equal, quitting is okay. Giving up . . . never! While preparing my body, I was completely consumed and immersed in the SEALFIT training program. I started to take my physical training very seriously and would meet with my army buddies a few days a week to train in a team environment, and then I'd perform a few solo sessions on my own. Training sessions were typically 2–3 hours. Yes, you read that correctly, 2–3 hours, a far cry from the hour of cardio and dumbbells I had been doing all my life. The SEALFIT OPWODs (Operator Workouts of the Day), basically programming designed for folks looking to get a special forces contract, consisted of the following:

- Baseline: Range of motion drills, active stretching, and a quick warm-up; typically 10–15 minutes

- Strength: One of six movements—either bench press, push press, back/front squats, deadlifts, or an Olympic lift. The average time spent was 20–30 minutes. No rush here.

- Stamina: A long version of HIIT (high-intensity interval training) to be performed at a constant chipper pace for around 20–40 min. Chipper means a speed that isn't your fastest or slowest but something you can maintain without stopping.

- Work Capacity: Most refer to this as a WOD in the CrossFit world, a short high-intensity workout where you go full speed for 10–20 min. Basically, if you aren't sucking gas, you aren't doing it right. Usually, you're doing a few different movements for as many rounds as possible (AMRAP) in a certain time limit.

- Endurance: usually running, rowing, or rucking for an extended amount of time.

In a typical week I would perform a SEALFIT OPWOD three times, usually Monday, Wednesday, and Friday. I would then incorporate bodyweight workouts from SEALGrinderPT.com on Tuesdays and Thursdays (thanks Coach Brad McLeod). Coach Brad has an excellent website for training athletes and is well known for having gone through BUDS not once, but twice. What I loved about his program is you can do most of it with your own body weight, no fancy equipment needed. Saturday was a long endurance session. I'd go for a 5–8-mile run, ruck for a couple of hours, or ride a bike. Sunday was typically a rest and recovery day, although I would usually walk, run, bike, or ruck for an active recovery session.

Sure, there would be weeks where obligations would get in the way, but I figured if tried to train every day, then I could consistently get in the necessary volume to deem myself ready for the crucible. The last thing I wanted was to show up to camp and have any doubts regarding whether I had trained hard enough. What I wanted in the end was to put in so much work, that my neighbors thought I was crazy. I actually had one ask me if I was training for the Olympics as I was carrying a 100lb sandbag on my back. Mission accomplished.

PREPARING THE MIND

It doesn't matter how physically fit you are, everyone has a breaking point. Whether it's 10 push-ups, 50, 100, 200... at some point, you will break. What separates people is what they do when they hit that breaking point. Do they push on and persevere? Or do they quit, tuck tail, and run? It became a necessity for me to train my mental toughness if I was going to be able to make it through that training. Whenever I set out for a physical training (PT) session or some other form of strenuous activity, there were four things I focused on: my breath, positive self-talk, visualization or mental imagery, and goal setting. These four assets are what Mark Divine refers to as the Big Four of mental toughness. They would prove to be my secret weapon whenever I was faced with a challenge or adversity and I still use them daily. I guarantee they'll work for you, too.

Don't believe me? Try doing 300 air squats or hold a plank for 5 minutes, and take note of what is going on. Your heart rate elevates, your breath becomes shallow, and your mind starts wandering. You begin thinking, *Why am I doing this? It hurts. This sucks, I'd like to quit now,* etc. You must control these thoughts and your emotions if you are to push through any type of adversity in life.

This is exactly the type of stuff I'm referring to as purposeful pain or suffering. You can absolutely grow grit and train your mental toughness by putting yourself in tough situations to see how your body and mind react. You are in control of the outcome. It's a simple decision: You can either choose to win or choose to fail.

MILESTONE CHALLENGES

In addition to my regular regime, I set challenges each month that would push my limits. At the beginning of each month, I would take a simulated PT test in boots and pants to see how I would score and notice where I might be improving or had some holes in my game.

February: 1,000 push-ups for time. This was awful. I tried doing sets of 20 every minute and burned out around the 250 or so mark. I quickly went down to 15, then 10, then 5. Final time: 1 hour and 15 minutes.

March: Hero WOD "Murph" for time with a (30-lb backpack). I'm pretty sure I ran more than the prescribed two miles, and at any rate, this workout is my favorite now as it always kicks my butt. Typically, I'll run the miles at an 8–9-minute pace and then partition the pull-ups, push-ups, and squats into 20 sets of 5–10–15. By partitioning and setting up the proper goal, I could normally get through that part in less than 25 minutes. My best overall time for Murph was 45 minutes (since then, it's now 35:46 at age 40).

April: 1,000 air squats. I didn't do this for time but to be very strict and deliberately slow, making sure I had full flexibility to go past the 90-degree mark with my knees and reach full extension at the top. Then I did a 3-mile easy run since I couldn't feel my legs. Wow, that was a terrible idea. Glad that one is over.

May: Twenty-four-hour walk. Yes, that's right. Walk for a solid day. Stop every hour to rest for 10 minutes, to eat, or hydrate. This might not sound hard but trust me, when you are walking solo in the middle of the night, tired with no one to talk to, it's amazing the thoughts that pop into your brain. This was actually one of my favorite workouts, looking back, because it really got me in tune with my internal dialogue. As I mentioned above, mastering this will allow you to break through most barriers in your life. Especially those where you feel you're alone and no one is coming to save you.

June: My best friend, a 20 plus year paratrooper from a long range surveillance unit in the Army, put my training to the test by guiding me on a 12-mile ruck with 40 lbs. I hadn't been that far yet or with that much weight. He pushed me and gave me some pointers on how to ruck—keep your weight high on your back if you can, use your hips to move, walk uphill, jog downhill, and go at a 50% jog when on flat surfaces. With his help, I was able to crush this milestone, and he told me if I can go 12 miles, then the rest is all mental. He was 100% spot-on. Thanks, JB!

After I checked the box on that final challenge, I felt that I had trained as hard as I possibly could, and I was 100% ready for whatever would face me. I knew I would get broken... that's the point. I had deliberately tried breaking myself on purpose over and over again for five solid months. I knew what it felt like, and I was also in tune with how my mind and body would respond. Bring on Kokoro... I am ready to meet myself for the first time!

PACK YOUR RUCKSACK

You don't rise to the occasion; you fall back to the level of your training.

"Rise to the occasion." Those simple words were printed on the front of thousands of NCAA men's basketball tournament T-shirts back in 2013. I remember the teams wearing them on the sidelines, and I thought it looked catchy, so I ordered one. My favorite basketball team, the

Indiana Hoosiers, had made it to the Sweet Sixteen. Indiana dominated the college basketball landscape that year, spending 10 weeks ranked #1 in the country, and all but two weeks in the top 5. The Hoosiers won the outright Big Ten regular-season title with a 14–4 record. Indiana went 7–1 against AP Top-25 teams during the season; no other Big Ten team had better than a .500 record in that category.

However, despite the impressive regular season, my beloved Hoosiers fell in the Sweet Sixteen for the second consecutive year, extending their championship drought to 26 seasons. Why? Why did they lose? I'm not a basketball coach and don't claim to be one, and I have absolutely no connection with the team or any insider information for that matter. But what I can tell you is derived from what I witnessed on television that day: their matchup with the Syracuse Orangemen, who absolutely destroyed them.

Syracuse was known for one thing that year, which was its defense. It was not just any defense; they were one of the few teams in the nation that runs what's called a full-court press. A full-court press is a defensive style in which the defense applies pressure to the full length of the court. While it does take a lot of effort, the full-court press can be very effective when used correctly. The opposing team can look disoriented if they have poor ball handling and will fatigue quicker with the constant pressure. And that's exactly what happened to my Hoosiers as they fell 61–50.

It was as if they'd never seen that type of defense before. It was hard to watch. They struggled to even get the ball up and down the court. Now I'm not saying they did or didn't practice for this type of defense, but whatever they did, it wasn't very effective. Styles usually make great games (and fights for that matter), and we just didn't match up well against that press. We got run out of the building. It was a joke.

There's a famous saying in the military: "You don't rise to the occasion; you fall back to the level of your training." That's why military training can be so hard and without excuses, because once training is over and you're doing it for real, the pressure gets ratcheted up. There is little room, if any, for error when human lives are on the line. When shit hits the fan and chaos consumes your environment, you will naturally fall back to your comfort zone and the techniques you've learned along the way. You don't just hope for the best or rely on some sort of magical elixir that will get you ready for whatever is thrown your way. You practice it over and over again until you can recall it at a subconscious level.

As my high school baseball coach once said, "Practice doesn't make perfect. Perfect practice makes perfect." And you don't just prepare for when things go right. You actually should plan to fail.

My friend Larry Yatch, retired Navy SEAL, runs the company SEAL Team Leaders. I had the privilege of taking one of his courses on tactical planning several years ago. What I learned completely changed how I thought about projects and solving problems.

To start with, when most people are faced with a problem to solve or a goal they wish to achieve, they immediately jump into thinking about the tactics and strategies to accomplish that task. Instead, try coming up with your desired end state, which is a clear description of the environment you wish to produce on successful completion of the project. It should answer questions like these:

- "Where do you want to go?"
- "What do you want to avoid?"
- "What does it feel and look like?"

Part of the planning is also centered around contingency planning, or in other words, planning to fail. You literally take your plan and purposely identify at least three conditions that could result in not meeting your desired end state. Then you plan how to solve those. This tactic works well because most plans have at least three ways they can fail, and if you spend time working through how to avoid, mitigate, or provide a backup plan, then you'll feel better prepared to execute your plan knowing that you've tested it to fail using three of the most common scenarios.

By consistently forming habits of deliberate practice and pressure testing them for when things go wrong, you can help to bulletproof your mission. "Rising to the occasion" is just an illusion.

P.S. I still have that T-shirt and keep it as a reminder of how not to approach things.

CHALLENGE

Plan to Fail.

I want you to take any plan you're currently working on, and poke holes in it. It could be a business you wish to launch, a training plan for your next marathon, a quarterly plan at work, etc.

First, identify the top three ways your plan won't work. Now I want you to figure out how to avoid each problem, mitigate it, and/or back it up. If you are having trouble finding three, get creative. If you really need inspiration, just think of the COVID-19 pandemic from 2020. No one planned for the world to be shut down, yet it happened. Most problems can be identified, and if you already know what they are, you can plan how to fix them in case they show their ugly heads.

NO GOING BACK
(THURSDAY,
JULY 23, 2015)

"You are about to embark upon the Great Crusade."

—GENERAL DWIGHT D. EISENHOWER
(D-DAY SPEECH)

The day had finally arrived for me to fly out to California. All of the training I had put my mind and body through for the previous six months was about to be tested. I felt ready. My mind was calm, and physically, I was in the best shape of my life. I couldn't have trained any more strenuously. I had put in the hard work. Failure was not an option. I woke up at around 5 a.m. and hopped into the shower.

After my shower, I looked at myself in the bathroom mirror. I had that look... you know the one. The look you have when you're getting ready to take a big test, play a big game, walk down the aisle (hopefully the one and only time), give a big presentation in front of a ton of people, experience the birth of your child, etc. It's that feeling that you're getting ready to experience one of the most pivotal moments of your life. You know what's about to go down, and you can't run from it. Why would you want to? All that's left now is to show up, put out, and have some fun.

It's times like these when I think back to when I was a new sales associate at a major medical company and participated in the most extreme scholastic training I've ever gone through. I'm not sure if it's true, but I have to believe it's the hardest corporate training you can find anywhere in the world.

It lasted six months and was the equivalent of getting an MBA or learning another language in that amount of time. At one point during that training, I lived out of a hotel in Minneapolis for a solid month because that is where that division of the company is headquartered. It was a hardcore schedule. Classes ran from 8:00– 5:00, Monday–Thursday with a test on Friday morning. If anyone scored a 90% or above, they passed. If they scored less than 90%, they lost their job right away.

I've seen more adults cry because they had just been fired than I cared to admit. This was not an episode of *The Apprentice*. It was real life. If someone didn't meet the standard, they got fired and sent home, simple as that. The reason for such an extreme is that this job meant that we would literally have someone's life in their hands. The standard was to be at the top of your game 100% of the time, no excuses.

It was the night before my first test, and I'd spent every hour of every day in class or studying. The only exception was to eat, sleep, shower, or get a quick workout in. I was beginning to feel the fear creeping in, and I couldn't shake it. It was starting to take hold of my mind, and my hands became cold and clammy as I paced back and forth across my hotel room unable to sleep. *Have I studied enough? I'm not as smart as most of the folks in the room. What if I fail and lose my job? I don't belong here. My wife is depending on me.*

I needed a pep talk and needed one badly, so I called my Dad as most young men might do in a time of crisis. He could sense the level of anxiety in my crackling voice, fully knowing the high stakes and what my fate would be if I didn't perform up to the standard. I'm sure I unloaded on him about how I didn't know if I could do it; I wasn't smart enough, gifted enough, talented enough . . . I don't remember everything we talked about, but I do remember what he told me after my ramblings.

Dad: Brad.

Brad: Yes, Dad?

Dad: How hard have you worked at being successful there?

Brad: I've never worked this hard before in my life, and I can't put forth any more effort.

Dad: Well, then, son, get some sleep, and when you wake up in the morning and look at yourself in the mirror, know that you gave this everything you had, and you put your heart and soul into it. Let the chips fall as they may, and at the end of the day, win or lose, you will have learned from it, and that makes you a winner.

Brad: Thanks for the pep talk, Dad.

I could have sworn I heard a microphone drop after that. That's exactly what I needed to hear. I went to bed, woke up, and crushed my first test with a 98%.

Those same thoughts and feelings from ten years prior ran through my mind along with my Dad's words of encouragement as I stared at another mirror looking at the man on the other side. As I was finishing getting ready, my wife was waking up. I could tell that she was scared for me. She'd seen the videos of what I was going to voluntarily put myself through and knew how committed I was to it. She probably still didn't understand why I was doing it, but she has always known that once I set my sights on something, I jump in with both feet. I don't halfway do anything I'm passionate about. I gave her a long kiss and a massive bear hug. I wanted to remember that feeling because before long, I'd be sitting in the cold Pacific Ocean freezing my baguettes off.

I told her I would call her Thursday evening after I reached California and got settled in, and once more Friday morning before I left for SEALFIT HQ. After that, she would not hear from me for the next 50–60 hours. I think that was the first time since we'd been married and living together that I wouldn't be talking to or texting my wife over a three-day period. I told her the only way I would not finish was if I were medically discharged or dead. Seriously, I said that. That's the attitude you have to have to make it through events like this. I gave my kids a kiss while they were sleeping, grabbed my backpack, and headed out the door. Similar to the Spartans of ancient Greece, I was either going to come back home carrying my shield *or on it.*

My flight arrived in San Diego around 12:30 PST. I proceeded to take an Uber to my buddy Adam's residence. Adam and his wife Steph lived in a place that overlooked the Pacific Ocean—simply beautiful and breathtaking—a far cry from the cornfields of the Midwest. I'd never been to Southern California before, and I was quickly becoming a fan. They both were still at work, so I spent some time getting used to my new surroundings.

Sun's out, guns out... I immediately changed into my swim trunks and took a stroll along the beach. Time to hop into the ocean. I sprinted out and dove in. *Holy crap, it's cold,* I thought to myself. The water wasn't as warm as the Gulf of Mexico, which is where I typically vacation in Florida. No wonder everyone swimming out there had a wetsuit on, except for me. I'm guessing the water temp was a warm 65 degrees.

I walked back to Adam and Steph's place a couple of hours later and took a selfie (I can count on one hand the number of times I've taken a selfie, by the way) and posted it on Facebook.

A stroll along the beach. Notice the steep shoreline.

The infamous FaceBook selfie, this will come back to haunt me.

I spent the next couple of hours sorting my gear, making sure to double and triple-check that I had everything and knew exactly in which compartment of my backpack each item was stored.

Adam and Steph got home shortly after, and I took another walk with Adam along the beach. Over the previous week or two, I had scaled my training back and mostly went on walks, short slow runs, or ruck marches. This two-mile walk on the beach was a perfect end to the intense training I had been doing for half a year to prepare for the world's toughest civilian training. When we got back to their place, I showed them videos posted on YouTube of prior classes going through different evolutions. Their jaws dropped in amazement. Steph said she thought I was there for a marathon or something. Not exactly!

After eating an amazing meal and loading up with carbs, I decided to take in one last view of the sunset and hit the sack. The three-hour time-zone change was starting to take effect, and I wanted to be completely rested since I was soon going to be awake for 50–60 hours straight without any sleep. I made one tiny mistake, though. Since I had been drinking water like it was nobody's business all day to stay well hydrated, I had to wake and pee every hour. I think it was a combination of nerves and all that water I had consumed. I slept terribly and never got more than an hour straight of sleep. Not exactly the way you want to start a weekend of sleep deprivation and other torture. Oh, well, just makes for a more interesting morning and story.

PACK YOUR RUCKSACK

"Anything worth doing is worth overdoing. Moderation is for cowards."

—LONE SURVIVOR (2013)

What's the hardest training you've ever gone through? Was it at work, or did you volunteer for something? How much time and effort did you dedicate to it? Was it enough, or looking back, do you wish you had spent more time preparing and studying and putting just a little more work in? What's one thing you've overdone in your own life?

That quote above could be my favorite line out of the movie, *Lone Survivor*. Alexander Ludwig plays Shane Patton, who is a newly minted SEAL or the "new guy" in Afghanistan. Up until that point, he hadn't been allowed to go on missions. He had one final test, an appearance before the kangaroo court, in which he'd need the thumbs-up from his teammates to push him through and deem him mission worthy. In front of his team, he had to be able to recite a version of the "Ballad of the Frogman." That's where he recited this line and delivered it to an audience of his peers before they unanimously voted to push him through. I remember hearing it for the first time, and it was one of those movie quotes that stuck in my head.

The year was 2009, and I was a new recruit working for one of the "Big 3" in the higher education publishing industry. I was transitioning careers and starting in a brand-new industry that I knew next to nothing about other than what my good friend Chris had told me over the years.

Chris and I went to high school together and were best buds, but after graduating and going off to college, our lives took different turns. We had lost touch with each other until a chance encounter at Sears Automotive (you remember those stores?), where we were both getting our company cars an oil change. It was like seeing a long-lost brother, and we picked up right where we'd left off.

We exchanged business cards and kept in touch over the phone and would even meet up for beers to talk about our work. Since we were both in sales, although the products and services were different, the stories and processes were very similar. We would help each other out and have ad hoc strategy sessions over cheap appetizers and beer at the local pubs in Indy. One day, I told him I had just been fired from my job in medical sales. This was three weeks before Christmas, and we had a child on the way.

He told me that at his company, there was a new position being created that I would be perfect for. I interviewed shortly after and won the job.

My very first day with the new company, in a new-to-me industry where I knew only one person, was at their national sales meeting. I'd never seen anything like it in my life. There were easily over a thousand of us who had invaded the Gaylord Texan Hotel, and I was truly impressed with not only the talent level but the culture of the company. Everyone was positive and eager to help one another out. That's hard to find today, especially with large companies. At the time, little did I know that I had joined the top dog, the number-one company in the industry, and they were proud of it too.

On the last day of the event, they held an awards ceremony that at the time I had never seen the likes of. It would remind you of a wedding reception. Everyone was dressed to the nines, filets were served with dinner, and they had an open bar and live band.

One by one, they introduced the top performers of the company and provided a PowerPoint presentation for each person. It showed their picture along with the dollar amount by which they had grown their sales territory beyond the annual goal. You could calculate in your head the amount of money they were going to be paid in commission. Six-figure bonuses were not uncommon... and as a soon-to-be new father, I quickly took notice.

After a couple of glasses of wine at dinner, I excused myself from my table and hit the bathroom. On the way, I ran into the president of our division, Brian. I introduced myself to him.

He asked what I thought of awards night, and I told him that I'd never seen anything like it before, and it was something truly special. He then told me that it all starts with talent, that they seek out the most talented people and hire them. That's why I was there. I'm sure my ego grew instantaneously with that comment.

I only had time for one question, so I asked him what his advice would be for someone just starting out—how do I end up on that stage?

He stopped dead in his tracks, looked me square in the eye, and said, "Most people, when they start something new, it can take a while for them to dip their toes in. Very few jump in the deep end and attack this job with everything they have. My advice is to jump in with everything you have. If not now, then when?"

His advice hit me like a Mike Tyson uppercut. I made it my mission to out-work my competition, and I was going to make a name for myself in this industry. I woke up early, stayed up late, and made sales calls into the evening. I hit the road before the sun was up and before my wife woke up for her job and most days, I wouldn't come home until it was dark. I was obsessed, bound and determined to become a top performer and cash a big payday.

By the time the year ended, management and product team leaders had noticed me. I was being looped into leadership positions within the company as well as higher-level internal strategy calls. As for the stage, I did walk across it during the next national sales meeting. I had finished the year as Rookie of the Year as well as a top performer in the company. You only get one chance to be Rookie of the Year, my manager told me as I stood up to walk across the stage in front of the entire company. And by the way, I did cash a nice bonus check, too, but that wouldn't have happened unless I did what some people would deem unnecessary. I overdid it!

CHALLENGE

Push It.

I'm not talking about the hit single by the American hip-hop girl group Salt-N-Pepa here, although they did have some jams. Can you answer this question? When's the last time you overdid anything? If you can't answer it, then you've probably been living in a world of mediocrity your whole life. Sure, you might be successful by society's standards, but only you know if you've been playing small ball or living a life of too much comfort.

This is your chance. Push your limits, see what you are capable of, and strive for excellence. My challenge to you here is to try something new and don't do it halfway or just meet some standard. Jump in with both feet, grab the bull by the horns, and dance with that big ugly.

If you fail, so what? That just means you grew a little along the way and learned something new that you can later teach someone else. But what if you actually go all-in for once in your life and succeed? What if...

05

READY. FIRE. AIM!
(FRIDAY, JULY 24, 2015)

Ready means preparation. Get yourself ready to do
something, then do it. If you screw up, you go back and
see what happened. What I call "aim" is hindsight—you
find out where you screwed up, and you can correct
it much easier. A lot of people would rather sit and
prepare. They can prepare all their life.

—BILL COOK

I woke up at 5:00 and hopped in the shower. After rinsing off, I made
sure to Vaseline every nook and cranny that could potentially chafe. I
knew I might not have the opportunity again for another 50 hours, and
chafing so badly that I might bleed was a real possibility so I didn't take
the precautions lightly. I meticulously took care of my feet by applying
body glide, moleskin, and duct tape, making sure to pay special attention
to any hotspots that I had already identified through my months of
running and rucking in boots. My last step was to place put a sock liner
over my duct tape dressing and then put on a pair of wool socks. And
not just any wool socks! My socks of choice were Vermont Darn Tough
Socks made right here in the USA. After doing some research, I learned

those are the preferred socks of most infantry units. If they work for our men and women in uniform, why wouldn't they work for me?

With my feet secure, I put on my black Battle Dress Uniform (BDU) style pants (BDUs are a camouflaged combat uniform) and then put on my white cotton T-shirt that had my last name stenciled on the front and back per SEALFIT protocol. I tucked in my shirt and threw my belt on. I even styled my hair. Last but not least, I put on my tan Oakley Light Assault boots, making sure they were on perfectly and the laces were double tied and tucked in.

The before picture.

Dressed to impress, I went into the kitchen and ate a breakfast that consisted of eggs, peanut butter on toast, and coffee. I wonder if this is what the Disciples felt like at the *Last Supper*. I made sure to enjoy every single bite because I didn't know when or if I'd be eating again. After saying my goodbyes to Steph and their daughter Maddie, Adam and I loaded my gear into the back of his SUV and took off from their place at 7:30.

The Warning Order said to be at SEALFI HQ at 0800 sharp, so I wanted to get there with some time to spare.

As we rolled up to HQ, I could see several of my new teammates in full uniform. Some were already stretching and running around the building while others were pacing nervously. We came to a stop outside the front entrance, and Adam helped me unload my gear. We said our goodbyes and I told him, "Well, I didn't get dressed up for nothing," channeling one of my favorite quotations from the movie *Braveheart*. In a scene before their first battle, Hamish, a lead character, asked William Wallace where he was going. The Scottish and British armies had just met for the first time on the battlefield, and neither side had made a move yet. Wallace said to Hamish, "I'm going to pick a fight."

Hamish then jokingly replied, "Well, looks like we didn't get dressed up for nothing."

My nerves were really starting to creep in. You know that feeling when you're about to get your rear end handed to you, and there's nothing you can do about it? That's what I was feeling. I noticed a large group of people, dressed in BDUs, lined up perfectly on the sidewalk outside the main entrance. A whiteboard at the front of the building said:

Kokoro 38 Welcome to the Party!

- Form up on the north sidewalk and wait for further instruction.
- Converse quietly.
- Have your ID card available.

- Stay off the Grinder.

Good Luck!

Welcome to the party.

Party? Good sense of humor. And what the hell is a grinder, anyway? I'm sure I'll find out soon enough. I asked the guy next to me where everyone had stowed their gear, and he told me to go around the back of the building and add it to the pile.

It had to be close to the 0800 start time, and I was cutting it close. I didn't know for sure because we weren't allowed to wear watches or bring cell phones. Looking around, I wondered if I was the oldest one there. I also noticed that I was one of the tallest as well. I'm 6'2" and typically hold my bodyweight around 205 lbs. Most of these guys were around 5'8"–5'10" with body weight in the range of 160–175.

I didn't see any ladies there, unfortunately. However, this crucible does bring out some very strong women. I overheard a coach say after the event that they've never had a woman voluntarily quit. Get medically discharged, yes, but never quit. This is a strong testament to the grit of women. In fact, nowadays, when people ask me who I think is the grittiest and toughest of people walking the planet, I have no doubt that it isn't a man. We men have a lot to learn from you ladies.

We stood there in line for several minutes, with the same look on our faces. Whether we wanted to admit it or not, everyone was scared, and fear was starting to grapple with everyone's minds. We were all looking at each other and sizing everyone up. Of course, these would be my teammates, but they would also be my competition.

My teammate on my right noticed something I was doing and immediately called me out on it. I had my hands in my pockets. He told me not to put my hands in my pockets, so I placed them on my hips. He told me not to do that either. I asked him what the proper hand placement was, and he said, "Either stand with your arms at your sides, or place your arms behind your back." He had been at the SEALFIT academy the week prior, so he had learned a thing or two about what to expect. The Kokoro Camp was his final test to graduate. Needless to say, I listened and thanked him for correcting me. I made a mental note to never cross my arms or put my hands in my pockets again.

Right then and there, I knew it was going to be the most difficult experience of my life both mentally and physically. Everything we thought we knew, we might as well throw out the window because the coaches were about to teach us a whole new way of doing things. Every single thing we were going to do or decision we were going to make would be evaluated, and if we weren't meeting their standards, we would surely know about it.

PACK YOUR RUCKSACK

Body language says a lot.

Fun fact: Did you know that up to 90% of communication comes from nonverbal cues? The 90% figure wasn't plucked out of thin air. It was Albert Mehrabian, a researcher of body language, who first broke down the components of a face-to-face conversation. People you come into contact with start judging you within seconds of meeting you. It really makes you think about how well you portray yourself in public and around your home, doesn't it? Do you look people in the eye, or do you look at the ground while walking on the sidewalk in a city, or coming out of your favorite coffee shop? How about your cell phone—are you constantly looking at the screen in public? Pay attention to your posture as well. Do you walk upright with your chest out and shoulders back, or are you slouched over? And what about your face—do you walk around with a frown, or do you smile a lot? Did you know you can smile with your eyes, too? Or perhaps you have been told you have a bad case of RBF (resting bitch face). As a kid, I didn't need my parents to say anything to let me know I was in trouble. All I needed was "the look." I find myself giving that same look to my own kids when they are out of line.

Sales could arguably be one of the toughest careers you can choose (everyone is in sales, I might add, whether they know it or not). To be great at sales, you have to be comfortable hearing the word *no* a lot and keep coming back for more. Sales can be broken into two main types—inside sales and outside sales. With outside sales, as the name suggests, folks will typically meet their clients face to face either at an office building or some sort of neutral location. You can tell a lot about someone within minutes of meeting them by paying attention to their body language or even how they have their office decorated. Often, simply being aware of your surroundings will give you the necessary information to start quickly building some sort of rapport with your prospects.

Inside sales is an entirely different animal. Rarely do you get to meet your customer face to face, although, with applications like Zoom and other web-based video conferencing tools, it is becoming more and more common. It's hard enough trying to sell something to someone in person that you just met, let alone someone you can't see and all you can do is talk to them over the phone.

I had an inside sales position for a marketing firm in Indianapolis several years ago. I sucked at it when I started. For every fifty calls on the phone, I might get five people to pick up, and out of those five people, I'd secure one appointment for my outside sales counterpart. My job was to get him good leads so he could go close them in person. The game was to make as many phone calls as we possibly could in the hours we were clocked in sitting in a cubicle. I had a performance evaluation with my manager about a month after starting, and needless to say, it wasn't stellar. I wasn't generating sales leads at the level the company wanted me to, and I was looking for any way I could get my numbers up.

My boss at the time told me something that to this day I still use. He said to smile and dial.

"Smile and dial?" I asked.

"Yes, pick up the phone, smile, and dial your prospects. Then if they answer or if you leave a voice mail, keep that smile on your face. People can feel your energy over the phone, and they can tell if you have a smile on your face."

To be honest, this advice sounded like something I should have learned in kindergarten. But I was desperate to prove I had what it took to keep my job. So I started smiling and dialing, and you know what? It actually freaking works! Soon I became one of the top inside sales reps in the company, and my numbers went from securing one appointment out of fifty calls to one out of twenty. I know it doesn't sound like much, but trust me, it adds up.

CHALLENGE

The Doorway Challenge.

I have a simple challenge for you. I'm not going to ask you to smile and dial for 24 hours, although, I guarantee if you do, you'll notice a difference in your conversations with your spouse, siblings, friends, coworkers, etc. I'm going to issue what I call the Doorway Challenge to you. I received this challenge from my good friend Larry Hagner, who runs the Dad Edge Podcast. It's a community of like-minded dads who seek to become the best version of themselves so they can be the best for their kids, spouse, and others.

The Doorway Challenge is simple. Any time you enter a doorway, whether it be in your house, office, coffee shop, gym, hotel, church, etc., you must walk through with positive body language. Make eye contact with everyone you see, and simply acknowledge them. Positive body language is standing or walking upright with your spine aligned, chin up, shoulders back, and a slight smile on your face (you don't have to overdo it here like the Joker from Batman or you might actually scare people).

Most of the time, they'll acknowledge you back, and if they don't, don't throw a fit. It's not about how many people you can get to smile back at you. This exercise is meant to teach you just how many times a day we have the opportunity to communicate without actually saying anything.

As a sidenote, after I made it home from Kokoro, I asked my best friend JB, (who is a paratrooper in the Army), why arm placement was such a major deal. He laughed. Arms crossed means you're in charge, and hands in your pockets is a sign of laziness. Roger that. Lesson learned.

06

EXTRA SAUCE

It's not the critic who counts; not the man who points out how the strong man stumbles, or where the doer of deeds could have done them better. The credit belongs to the man who's actually in the arena, whose face is marred by dust, sweat, and blood.

—THEODORE ROOSEVELT IN
THE MAN IN THE ARENA

Our instructions were to report to the office with a teammate and provide the staff with our driver's license and complete a "release of liability form." Simple, I thought. Time passed as I watched my new teammates venture off two-by-two as they went to the office never to return, and the line I was standing in started to dwindle. My mind started wandering. I thought, *Where is everyone going afterward? Are people getting beat down right now? Aw, man. I have to pee. Will I even be able to use the bathroom this weekend?* I could already tell that coffee at breakfast had been a mistake along with the two gallons of water I drank the day before.

About half of my class was left standing in line when one of the SEALFIT coaches appeared. He was about 5'9" and sported a beard with a slight gray patch in the middle. He wore a green camo beanie and was definitely looking for someone or something as he inspected our formation. We all stood at attention facing the building. He looked serious and didn't say a single word.

I caught a glimpse of him, and he looked slightly familiar like I'd met him somewhere or seen his picture online, but I quickly passed it off as pure coincidence. Was it a uniform inspection?

It's amazing where your mind wanders when you aren't in control. I could feel his presence, standing behind me, as I stood there being evaluated. I knew he was looking me up and down, and the hair on the back of my neck tingled.

The coach then reached around my torso and presented me with a piece of paper I recognized right away. It was the application I had submitted to be selected to come to Kokoro Camp. *This can't be good*, I immediately thought to myself.

The coach said, "Are you Brad Ritter?"

"Yes, sir."

He barked, "Do you know me?"

I didn't know what to do next. Was I even allowed to look at the guy? So I kindly asked, "Permission to turn around, sir?"

"Granted."

I slowly turned around not knowing who would be in my line of sight. His voice sounded familiar, and I had caught a glimpse of him earlier but didn't think I actually knew the man. As I turned around completely, I knew right away it was Coach Brad McLeod. Coach McLeod runs an amazing training site called SEALgrinderPT.com. I used his site to help train for the crucible. He posts a lot of YouTube videos as well, so I knew his voice and what he looked like without actually having met him. He's a stud and is well known for having completed BUDS (arguably the hardest military training in the world) twice and is constantly raising money for veterans through various endurance races.

But that wasn't the full story. Sure, I knew him from his website and his workouts that he posts daily, but how could he know me? There was something else. Allow me to introduce you to the power of social media. Remember the selfie I had taken the day before? You know, the one I posted to Facebook? It had a caption that went something like this, "Enjoying my last day of peace in California before all hell breaks loose tomorrow."

That night, my coworker Cindy replied to my post and said #BradMcLeod, you're in San Diego as well, right? He responded yes, and she proceeded to tell him that she works with me, and I'd be one of his students that weekend. Coach showed me the Facebook interaction on his phone and had me dead to rights. *Crap, this probably isn't going to end well*, I thought. *Last time I post a freaking selfie.*

"Yes, sir, I know of you."

Coach Brad then asked, "Do you think that's a good thing?"

"Probably not."

Then came the verdict: "*Extra Sauce* for you this weekend, Ritter."

Great, I thought. *I haven't been here more than 20 minutes, and I'm already f'ing up. I'm a marked man now. So much for being the gray man.*

Coach Brad dished out some sauce right then and there. "Get down in plank position."

I proceeded to engage in the lean-and-rest position, one that I would grow accustomed to the whole weekend. The lean-and- rest position is performed by engaging in a push-up position, with your arms extended, and holding that position while keeping your core tight. I held it for at least 60 seconds while my teammates stared. Coach Brad then took out his cell phone and made me smile as he snapped a picture. He relieved me of the punishment shortly after and told me to stand at ease. He left and walked into the compound but not before saying that he'd be waiting for me on the grinder.

Great. And what is this grinder thing I keep hearing about?

Side note: I have come to find out, the lady (Cindy) I worked with and Coach Brad went to the same high school in Florida and even attended prom together. What are the chances? Just goes to show you that everyone is connected somehow or some way, and that social media can get you into trouble.

The following picture was in my iPhone when I turned it on that following Sunday. Good times... I'll always owe you one, Cindy.

Shortly thereafter, my teammate and I proceeded into the office to hand our identification to the office manager. She asked for my wedding ring.

"My wedding ring?" I asked with uncertainty.

"Yes. We don't want you to lose it," she said.

Truth is, I hadn't taken that ring off in 10 years, and I couldn't get it off. Plus, I planned on looking at my ring to help get me through the dark times ahead when I started to question whether I could do it or not. I told her that it wouldn't come off, and she allowed me to keep it on. I signed the release of liability, which pretty much said I was signing my life away, and I was finally officially checked in.

I waited on my teammate, and we proceeded to walk to a room that the lady pointed us toward. It was my first look inside the complex. The complex reminded me of a fortress, with buildings on the outer perimeter and then a paved concrete floor at the center, complete with multiple racks and pull-up bars surrounding it. I passed a sign that said, "Stay off the grinder." Ah, so this is the infamous grinder. After I made it home, I looked up what the definition of a grinder is. Stew Smith wrote this in an article published on military.com (https://www.military.com/military-fitness/navy-special-operations/navy-seal-grinder-pt)

The definition of *grinder* is the concrete-asphalt area at BUD/S where the students do their calisthenics workouts. It is surrounded by pull-up bars, dip bars, and the offices of the instructors, training officer, and commanding officer. You have the constant feeling of always being watched while you are on the grinder. So, put out hard, count loud, and cheer your class through the workout, or you will wind up doing the workout "wet and sandy" or spend an hour in the lean-and-rest position!

My teammates and I made it into the room not knowing what was waiting for us. There was another sign posted with the following instructions:

- Fill two canteens with water, and square away your ruck (These rucks weren't even real rucks, just cheap pieces of black canvas.)

- Find a swim buddy.

- Memorize "Invictus" and the SEAL Code.

- Take five minutes, and focus on why you're here.

- Report to the grinder at 0900 sharp.

Pull up rigs, rucks, and canteens.

I proceeded to grab a black canvas ruck. A guy named Goodard, who was from Australia, was next to me, and we quickly decided to be swim buddies. I'm guessing he was 5'5" and 150 lbs. We resembled Danny DeVito and Arnold Schwarzenegger from the movie, *Twins*.

He had already been at SEALFIT HQ for a week attending a comprehensive academy.

At the academy, the coaches do deep-dive sessions on mental training and teach the tools needed to be successful. To cap off the week, Kokoro Camp is the final exam for the academy.

I was quickly intrigued and knew he had a lot of intel that I didn't, so I followed his lead. We both took two standard-issue olive drab canteens and filled them with water. I placed my canteens in the side pouches of the ruck, then read "Invictus" and the SEAL Code (see Appendix) and committed them to memory as best I could. I had been tipped off prior to the event and had been memorizing "Invictus," so I knew it by heart (and still do).

The SEAL Code was another story. Although it wasn't the full creed, it still has seven lines that I needed to memorize. That's a tall task when you're as nervous as you were on your wedding day and moving around frantically trying to get all your gear squared away. It was 0850, and with 10 minutes left before we were to report to the grinder as a class, a couple of SEALFIT coaches came in for a brief pep talk. I don't remember much from that conversation other than our class was standing in a makeshift formation listening to every word as if it were gospel. As we stood and directed our attention to the front of the room, we could see hanging on the wall pictures of each graduating class of Kokoro Camp that came before us. I visualized someday coming back and seeing my face in the picture of our graduating class. A coach addressed the class by saying if any of us were doubting our decision or commitment level, to speak now and DOR (drop on request). Heck, they would even pay us back the money we spent to come if we were already doubting ourselves. He waited to see if there were any takers. Each teammate did a quick left-to-right scan to see if anyone was already quitting. I just took a deep breath and thought, *It's game time—it's about to get real.*

Then he asked if anyone was going after a contract for Special Forces (SEAL, Ranger, MarSoc, etc.). The coach used a black permanent marker to put an X on the necks of those folks as they would be held to a slightly higher standard than the rest of us. The coach ended his briefing with the following advice. This is some of the best advice I've ever received in my life, and I have recited it on numerous occasions since then not only to myself but also to others. "Men, you will be successful this weekend if you do these three things and these three things only:

1. Breathe.
2. Think.
3. Execute.

No matter what you are asked to do, no matter how hard it gets, always fall back to these three things."

And like that, he was out. We were dismissed and asked to line up in formation on the grinder in five minutes.

PACK YOUR RUCKSACK

Breathe, think, and execute.

Three simple words, right? Here's the deal, though. If you actually follow that advice and take a breath (or several), think about what you're going to do next, and then finally execute on it, you'll be better positioned to make improved choices. The simple act of breathing can have a calming effect. It slows down your heart rate and soothes your parasympathetic nervous system. Not only that, but it also buys you valuable time before you rush into a bad decision or knee jerk reaction. With those precious seconds, you can use your mind to think rationally about your next course of action and examine the variables of the situation to analyze it and arrive at a sound conclusion. Once you've mentally made your decision, then you can act upon it.

I call this responding versus reacting, and there is a big difference, which I'll outline below in a parenting example. It may seem like breathing, thinking, and executing would take a lot of time, but with practice, you can learn to do all three simultaneously instead of in a matter of seconds. I encourage you to try this technique right away in your own life. I use it daily, and it's had a profound impact on my own decision-making process.

I'm not sure if you're lucky enough to have kids. They are not only the best gifts in the world but also are sometimes the most taxing. As of the time of this writing, my daughter Hallie is 10, and my son Brody is 7. My wife Leslie and I both have careers, and we're no different from you. We'll come home from work exhausted, often with plenty more work to catch up on at home. Sometimes it can be hard to make the switch from the role of a worker bee to a dad, but my process is that once I enter the house and the kids are home, I flip the switch and turn into Daddy. Work can wait. Now, this isn't true 100% of the time, but I've gotten good at turning work mode off and turning dad mode on.

Sometimes, you're so tired from the workday all you want to do is sit on the couch and do nothing. Inevitably, that's the exact time my son or daughter will come up to me and ask, "Dad, you want to play tag?" *Ugh* is typically my gut reaction. I used to tell them "no" quite often because I needed to focus on myself and not them (years ago, that would be to turn on the TV and watch the news, which let even more negativity into my mind—but that's another story).

Over the years, I've learned to subdue that first reaction, take one big breath, and then think before I answer. Now, I typically always answer yes when asked if I want to play, or at the very least tell them that we will a little later if something truly important has popped up that needs my attention. The simple act of taking a breath calms my nerves from the busy workday and gives me time to examine my thoughts. I immediately think about their needs and the fact that at some point, they won't want to play tag anymore with their dad, so I'd better take advantage of all the time I can get with them, no regrets.

Armed with that new thought process and some motivation, I make the split-second decision to play with them. And you know what? It actually refuels me in a way that sitting on a couch or chair wouldn't have. This is what I'm talking about when you look at reacting versus responding. The same goes for handling our discipline as well. Let's say your child is disobeying you. A common response is to yell, fly off the handle, or even get in their face to show them that you are the authority figure. Congrats, Mom and Dad. You may think you're winning the battle, but you could be losing the war. Instead of having a knee-jerk reaction, just simply try breathing before you act. Heck, I've even left the room to let nerves settle before dishing out the consequences. Often, if we react in the heat of the moment and in a very emotional state, we make decisions that we'll regret. Thinking before you act and responding instead of instantly reacting will help you become a superior version of yourself. Give it a try.

CHALLENGE

Authentic Listening.

This challenge is simple but hard to do. The next conversation you're in, take note of what's actually going on inside your head. This could be a chat with your kids, spouse, girlfriend/boyfriend, or coworker. It doesn't matter with whom. What does matter is whether you are actively listening. There's a big difference between listening to form an opinion and listening to understand.

Listening to form an opinion is easy. You may not even be fully engaged with the person communicating, and your mind starts to wander. You're thinking about the next thing you're going to say, or worse, completely tuned out and thinking about yourself and how you can one-up them.

Instead, just try being present without judging. Have some empathy. That's actively listening—being fully engaged without bias, seeking to connect with the other person. Pay attention to how much you talk as well. Chances are you're probably speaking too much and not asking enough questions. We were born with two ears and one mouth for a reason. Remember that ratio. Listen twice as much as you speak.

07

BREAKOUT... HOOYAH!

"You must be shapeless, formless, like water. When you pour water in a cup, it becomes the cup. When you pour water in a bottle, it becomes the bottle. When you pour water in a teapot, it becomes the teapot. Water can drip, and it can crash. Become like water, my friend."

— BRUCE LEE

Our class moved out onto the grinder and stood at attention, lined up in formation, or at least what we thought a formation ought to look like. There were 38 of us, so we formed five lines of seven or eight. We stood there waiting and then waited some more. There weren't any coaches to be seen. I really don't know how long we stood there. It seemed like we had been standing for an hour. Realistically, it was probably 15–20 minutes, but all we could do was just stand by, knowing that somewhere someone was looking our way and sizing us up.

Don't show any weaknesses, I said to myself as I paid extra attention to my posture and facial expressions. I stood straight and rolled my shoulders back, making sure my chest was out. I pointed my feet out at a 45-degree angle with my heels touching. My chin was horizontal, not tucked, as I stared out toward a building. I wasn't necessarily fixated on the building but instead let my mind focus and put myself in a meditative state. It was an out-of-body experience as I witnessed myself observing my thoughts and perception almost as if I were looking into a mirror. I wasn't sure whether to look mean or put a smile on my face, so I held a neutral lip position. I cupped my hands and let them dangle straight down the sides of my body.

Grinder formation.

It was so quiet we could hear a pin drop. In fact, I heard someone pass gas right behind me, no doubt a result of nerves and fear. Normally, this would have drawn some third-grade humor, and I most likely would have laughed, but I was so focused I didn't even smirk. Everyone was as quiet as could be as we awaited our fate. Not only was it peaceful but also downright scary. That was the moment I'd been waiting for my whole life.

Finally, after all of the waiting, all of the anxiety, all of the mental games, and all of the training, Commander Mark Divine himself appeared out of nowhere to address our class.

I'd seen him several times on his website and YouTube videos since I'd been following SEALFIT for about a year at that point. I have to admit I was in awe of the guy. He didn't know me from Adam, but he was one of my mentors. I knew his story and background, and when you actually see one of your mentors in person, that is a feeling you don't forget. I can't remember exactly what he said, but what I can tell you is that when he speaks, people listen.

He talked about how it was the cadres' intention that everyone graduate, but they hadn't had a single class accomplish the feat yet. (We were Class 38 at the time, and as of 2021, I believe there's about 60 or so.) He reminded us that we were participating in the hardest training in the world outside of actual military training. He reminded us that we paid good money to be there, and his staff would not mess around. This was the real deal. One of the last things I remember him saying is when you're down and out, when you're questioning why you're here, when you don't think you can move or perform another task, look at your teammate, and help them out. They are in the exact same scenario as you, and this training is designed to bring together true team spirit. Not the artificial teamwork that gets thrown around most corporate cultures and team locker rooms but a real team, where you'll put others before yourself.

What Coach Divine was referring to is honor. Or as my friend Larry Yatch from Sealed Mindset Leaders says, honor is oftentimes foreign to civilians and not used a lot, especially at work. That's because honor is living up to a code of behavior where the concerns of the whole team come before the concerns of the individual. Think about it. Outside of your family or a team sport, does honor play a major role in your life? How about at your place of employment? Probably not.

All of my attention had been on Cmdr. Divine, and I hadn't realized that while he was speaking, we were being surrounded by cadre/coaches. They were all physical specimens in their own right, and they all looked like they were there to hurt me. These men would be our teachers during the weekend, and I was sure we had a lot to learn. I estimated there was a ratio of one coach for every two to three students. Translation: There would be no room to hide.

The last thing I remember Cmdr. Divine doing was having us repeat several phrases after him, such as, "We do today what others won't so we can do tomorrow what others can't," and "Pain is weakness leaving the body." Then, he asked us all one final question. "Are you all ready for this?"

We all shouted in unison, "Hooyah!"

He then gave the go-ahead signal to the cadre, who were lined up all around us, and that's when all hell broke loose. Like sharks circling their prey, they knew there was fresh blood in the water.

I was swimming right in the middle of it.

SHARK ATTACK

The cadre busted loose on us immediately. There would be no warm-ups, no easing into it, no brief introductions. One of them had a megaphone and was delivering orders. The rest were attacking us by moving in and out of our pathetic formation and verbally abusing us, questioning us, making us do whatever they said.

I stood at attention and steadied myself as I hadn't been messed with yet, but I could see out of my peripheral vision my teammates to my left and right were already down in the lean-and- rest plank position while being yelled at. I was sure my turn would come soon enough.

To make it more fun, the cadre doused us with cold water from a hose or a bucket every chance they could get.

I was trying my best to pay attention to the leader of the cadres as he gave his orders over the megaphone, and we were supposed to be following along as a team. The pressure was so intense; our team couldn't even follow simple instructions like forming a single-file line and sounding off. Do you know how first-grade teachers have their kids count off to form groups? We could not even accomplish that simple task. It was a complete circus. I was doing my best to keep up with all the commands, but it was pure chaos everywhere I looked.

We did every kind of body-weight exercise one could think of: push-ups, planks, flutter kicks, mountain climbers, squats, duck walks, get on your back, feet, bellies—you name it, we did it. And it was endless. Within the first 10–20 minutes, I was already smoked, sweating, and having trouble keeping pace with the directions. I had just gotten up from the "Get on your feet, get on your belly, get on your back" routine when Coach Divine appeared in front of me.

A few brief seconds of the first shark attack.

"Are you ready for this, Ritter?"

"Hooyah, sir!" I replied.

"Have you trained hard for this?"

"Hooyah!" I replied.

"How have you trained?" he asked me.

I told him that I'd been following the SEALFIT OPWODS and SEALgrinderPT programming religiously for six months. He then chuckled, gave a smirk from his chiseled face, and said, "Well, Ritter, we'll soon see what you're made of," and moved on. The next three hours were a straight beatdown on the grinder.

There would be no quarter given; there would be no breaks. The cadre refers to this evolution as "Breakout" or a "Shark Attack." Its purpose is to simulate a real-deal firefight when there's pure chaos surrounding you and decisions must be made in split seconds. You must be able to communicate with your team. Once communication breaks down, the team breaks down. For us, it was training that we had paid for, but for those who deploy, it is literally a matter of life and death. We were getting our butts handed to us.

It was rough, to say the least, and I had underestimated the sheer magnitude of it all. Midway through this first evolution, I was the guest of honor at my own pity party. I got a little more attention because I wasn't keeping up with some of the exercises. Remember how I told you I drank coffee that morning with breakfast? Big mistake. I was dehydrated, and my stomach was cramping. During one of the flutter-kick sessions, a coach stood on top of my stomach to make sure my abs were engaged. I was having trouble keeping my feet up, and my core burned so hard that my legs were shaking as a bucket of ice water was tossed on my face. I had to be showing visual signs that I was hurting.

Then, as if on cue, I looked up at the sky as I was gasping for air, and a face appeared right above me. It was not the face of God. It was Coach Divine again. He had what looked like a bottle of Gatorade, and I was hurting bad, very dehydrated from coffee and all of the calisthenics. "Are you thirsty, Ritter?" Coach Divine asked.

"Hooyah!" I replied.

He then said, "Hydration is only for those putting out, and you are not putting out. Breathing through the resistance is the only way you're going to make it through this weekend."

I happened to be holding my breath while I was doing flutter kicks. He told me I wasn't gonna make it that weekend if I didn't learn how to breathe right. I'd be toast. Period. This was not the impression I intended to make in front of my mentor.

Ten minutes later, still lying on my back, I was performing flutter kicks and barely able to keep my feet off the ground. Coach McLeod appeared above me much in the same manner that Coach Divine had. He proceeded to pour what appeared to be an entire bottle of red Gatorade all over my shirt and face. I didn't care. I welcomed anything wet that could get some sort of saliva back into my mouth. Shortly after my first little drink in about three hours of calisthenics, the head cadre on the megaphone yelled at us to recover and hydrate. *Thank God that's over*, I remember thinking to myself.

We were given a brief rest and hydration break, which probably lasted all of five minutes. We were then instructed to line up in formation according to height and face the ocean. This is referred to as a height line. I was one of the tallest, so I took my spot about third or fourth from the end. I hadn't realized it yet, but we had already lost several teammates. I was so focused on myself I hadn't noticed they'd quit.

The cadre instructed us to look at the folks who had quit and yell, "Hooyah, DORs!" (Drop on Request)

We complied.

I wasn't sure whether to feel sorry for them or to use their decision to boost my own confidence. Looking back, I'd say it was a little bit of both. I'll go ahead and admit it here right now: I also thought about quitting. I was broken, and I hadn't even made it to the second evolution yet. But then something happened.

I started to use visualization techniques and thought about my wife and kids and why I was doing it. Wait a minute, what did that coach tell us to focus on in the briefing? Breathe—Think—Execute. And what did Coach Divine just tell me? I started to really concentrate on my breath, and you know what? It worked! I calmed myself down. *Hey, maybe there's something to this breathing thing! Pain is only temporary*, I thought, *and sooner or later this evolution will be over.*

That simple act of breathing and visualizing my "Why" started to turn everything around for me. I ended up surviving Breakout. That was the first micro goal that I'd set for myself prior to the event. I thought if I could make it through the initial onslaught, I could make it through the days' evolutions. But be careful what you wish for. You have no idea what's coming at you next.

The next evolution they hit us with was the PST. It's the exact same PST I mentioned previously in the training chapter, and I'd performed it on multiple occasions but never under these circumstances. Not only were we all already smoked from the three-hour-long beatdown on the grinder, but also the instructors were watching our every move. Only perfect reps counted!

We were to perform the PST with our swim buddy with strict instructions to shout out "no rep" if the form wasn't perfect. We were told this test was all about integrity, and if we get caught letting unsatisfactory reps go, or worse, lying, we'd join the Goon Squad. *The Goon Squad?* I thought. *What the hell is that?* I knew one thing: I didn't want to find out. To add even more pressure, if we didn't meet the minimum requirements of the PST, our weekend was over. We would be sent home right then and there. Thank you for showing up.

My swim buddy Goodard and I decided that he would lead off. First up were push-ups. In two minutes, Goodard performed 96 push-ups, which is simply outstanding. That Aussie could really move.

Then it was my turn. I reached 50 in no time, but then I hit the wall. My arms and chest were on fire, and I had about another minute to go. I broke the next reps down into sets of 10 and then 5, making sure to rest at the top and trying to catch my breath. With roughly 30 seconds left, I was so gassed and the lactic acid had built up so much in my arms and chest that I could only manage doing singles. In the end, I had done 76—not bad since the minimum was 50.

Next up were sit-ups. Sit-ups are to be performed Navy style. Goodard went first and busted out 79 sit-ups. I picked a pace I could maintain for the entire two minutes and ended up completing 73. I was feeling pretty good at that point.

Third up were air squats. Goodard did 84. Similar to the sit-ups, I picked a tempo I could maintain without stopping and managed to get 76. I felt great knowing that I averaged about 20–25 reps above the minimum standard on all three events so far, and although I wasn't blowing folks away with my scores, I definitely wasn't toward the bottom.

Next to last were pull-ups. Pull-ups were to be performed dead hang style. Dead hang means you grip the pull-up bar with your hands facing out, and hanging from the bar with your arms fully extended and feet off the ground, you pull yourself up and move your chin above the bar, and then return to the dead hang position. You must maintain full extension of your arms and absolutely no kipping or any type of movement from your legs is allowed. Repeat until failure. Once you hop off the bar, you are done.

Goodard hopped on the bar and only managed 10, barely making the minimum. I thought he would have blown that one away, but all the prior work must have weakened him some.

It was my turn. I approached the bar and jumped up, grabbing hold of it. I started repping them out, one (this isn't so bad), two (easy day), then three... (I can do ten no problem). Four... *I'm almost halfway there*, thought as my grip started to fail just a little.

Then all of a sudden, I heard a familiar voice. "Ritter, stop kipping." I didn't even have to look. It was Coach Divine. *Ah, crap, this is going to suck.* He made a beeline right for me and got directly in front of me. He asked Goodard how many I was on. Goodard replied with "Four."

"No way," said Coach Divine. "He's starting from zero."

From zero? There's no way, there's no possible way. I don't even get to hop off the bar to start over? This isn't fair. That was the fear wolf talking in my head. Guess what. Life isn't fair. We've all been there. It's that moment of self-doubt where you start questioning why bad things are happening to you, or "Why me?"

I couldn't quit. I had to harness my fear and turn it into aggression. I concentrated on my "Why." I started over as Coach Divine counted. "One, two, three, four." On my fifth rep, my legs were beginning to sway. I apparently have some sort of natural kip that Coach Divine immediately corrected.

"Cross your legs, Ritter," he said. Not only did it prevent me from swaying my legs and deter any sort of kipping from my shoulder, but it also made the last few pull-ups twice as difficult.

"I want at least five more perfect pull-ups," he instructed.

I proceeded with six, then seven. That was my breaking point. By my math, I had already done eleven pull-ups but still needed three more to hit the minimum mark or risk being sent home. My grip was shot, I couldn't feel my arms any longer, and my legs were crossed—a position I hadn't practiced at home. I hung in the dead hang position for a few seconds, trying to muster any remaining strength I had.

Then something happened that I can't quite explain. I scanned the area and saw several of my teammates struggling and putting out everything they had. I began smiling. I'm not sure why, but I smiled my way through the last three reps. Eight. *I got this.* Nine. *I barely made that one, and my arms are trembling. I need one more. No way am I coming off this bar. I've trained too damn hard for this, and I'm not going out on a freaking PT test.* I took one big breath, tightened my core, and thought about my wife and kids. It took everything I had to get my chin above the bar.

Coach Divine said, "That's ten, Ritter."

I dropped off the bar in absolute exhaustion. I couldn't feel my upper body any longer from the push-ups, sit-ups, squats, and those 14 pull-ups.

Coach Divine looked at me and said, "Ritter, you won't make it this weekend unless you're giving it your all, every time," and left. I thought about that statement for a few moments as I stood on the grinder awaiting the last test, which would be a one-mile timed run while we wore boots and long pants. *Am I prepared to give this weekend everything I have? I'm only a few hours into this thing and have a long way to go. Hell yes,* I thought. *It's going to take a lot more than that to get me to quit. I'm just getting started.*

The PT run was pretty basic. Participants have to run one mile in boots and BDU-style pants within the allotted time cap of 9:30. Relatively easy for most folks who are runners. Not so easy for someone who's been getting hammered for the past few hours, and can't feel their upper or lower body from all the work they've already put in.

We started as a group right outside of SEALFIT HQ and followed a preset path to a halfway mark indicated by one of the coaches. I made it back to HQ in 8:12, well under the allotted time, but far past the numbers I got while training at home.

There was a coach at the entrance calling out our times as we crossed the finish line. I finished somewhere in the middle of the pack and looked to get a breather, but we were not done running. In the center of the grinder, there was a circle of guys running together in unison. Nothing crazy, just a slight jog to keep moving. As each teammate finished, they would join the circle, and it became bigger and bigger.

There was a coach with a water hose lightly spraying us in the face as we jogged past. I welcomed it, since I was very thirsty. A nice spray to the face meant I could get a little hydration. I opened my mouth as the water splashed my face. PST complete.

ONE MORE THING

So far, we'd been beaten down on the grinder for a few hours in Breakout and had completed the PST. I was feeling good knowing that I took the first wave of punishment earlier, and while I didn't post the best numbers out of the group on the PST, I was somewhere in the middle.

We were instructed to form a height line again. Our orders were simple. The classmate to our left would be our new swim buddy for the rest of the weekend. My swim buddy would be O'Kipney. We were the same size and build, only I looked about ten years older. There's only one rule to remember about your swim buddy: wherever they go, you go. Never, ever be caught alone. No exceptions!

We then counted off and divided into seven boat crews of five men based on height. I was in boat crew number seven. We were the tallest of the bunch and stood at full attention on the grinder.

Coach Divine addressed the group. He spoke about how we would have to rely on each other to make it through the weekend. We would have to come together as a team. He also said that if we weren't willing to give it all, then we should not continue because we would not make it. I thought about that for split second and remembered why I was doing the camp. Coach Divine then asked for the class leader to come up front.

Class leader? Do we even have one of those? There was an awkward silence, and everyone was looking around at one another. It was an exercise in who would step up to lead. One of the lines of the SEAL Ethos is that "we expect to lead and be led. In the absence of orders, I will take charge, lead my teammates and accomplish the mission. I lead by example in all situations."

It was as if some gravitational force was coming down on me, and for whatever reason, I couldn't move. I could only stand there looking dumbfounded.

The coaches started ripping on us, "What, there's no leader? Who the hell is gonna lead this team of sorry asses?" The verbal abuse started ringing in pretty heavy.

Obviously, we weren't sure what to do, but one thing was for sure: we were going to pay for our lack of leadership. What ensued was another horrific round of more calisthenics. As if the three-hour beatdown and PST hadn't taken its toll, it was time to perform more movements. This time, however, it was a little different. The entire class had to perform only one movement at the same time and call out the number of reps. The movement would be burpees, and I hate burpees.

"How many burpees are we going to do?" shouted one of the coaches.

One of my classmates said 100, another said 200, and quickly it became a game of how many we all thought we could do as a team until we passed out.

"What about you, Ritter? How many do you think we should do?" "As many as you ask us to, Coach."

"Look at the big brain on Brad" shouted one of the cadre, channeling his inner Jules Winnfield from the movie *Pulp Fiction*. In that notorious scene, Jules is interrogating a character named Brett. Brett eats his Big Kahuna burger right in front of Jules. Jules (who is a hitman) asks Brett, "You know what they call a Quarter Pounder with cheese in France... A Royale with cheese. You know why they call it that?"

Brett replies, "Because of the metric system?"

Jules then replies, "Check out the big brain on Brad" (even though the character's name was Brett).

"That's right, class. The answer to how many of anything you will do here is 'All of them.'" He then proceeded to show us what a prescribed burpee looks like.

"One—start in the full squat position with your hands on the ground. Two—full extension and kick your legs out so you are in the lean-and-rest plank position. Three—perform a push-up with your chest hitting the deck. Four—push up from the ground so your back is in the lean-and-rest position. Five—jump your feet back into a full recovery squat, which was your starting position. Six—from the squatting position, you will stand up, jump, and clap above your head." Basically, all you did in steps three and four was a standard push-up. Those six movements constituted one rep of a standard burpee.

The hard part was that we were to perform the movement in unison, and our first attempt was terrible. Talk about getting frustrated.

The coaches said we would be there all day until we got it right, and I completely believed them. After about 30 minutes, our team finally was able to synchronize and perform 10 perfect 6-count standard burpees. Ten ended up being the magic number.

One of the coaches had been keeping track of all the reps we had done. He asked the team if anyone wanted to guess how many reps it took to push them out as a team. The number was 205. It took 205 attempts to get 10 perfect reps. We all felt pathetic and defeated.

We were ordered to form boat crews and await further instruction. One by one, multiple white church style vans began to roll up in front of us. And just like that, on to the next adventure.

PACK YOUR RUCKSACK

We expect to lead and be led.

I recently had the privilege of attending a workshop at Heroic Public Speaking in Lambertville, NJ, hosted by world-class master teachers Michael and Amy Port. When most people are asked what they are afraid of, public speaking is typically near the top. I knew this would be a once-in-a-lifetime sort of opportunity, so I quickly jumped at the chance to attend (thank you, Amber Vilhauer, for sponsoring me).

On the first day, I walked into their headquarters and was warmly greeted by both Michael and Amy before entering a lobby full of strangers. I don't have any problem mingling, so I quickly found myself chatting with some folks before the event started.

Once the program began, we took seats in a room that had an actual stage, lighting, cameras, and the whole enchilada. It was set up to replicate being on a stage and delivering a keynote in front of an audience. Everyone knew what we were there to do. After all, "public speaking" appeared on the sign by the front door of the building.

After some brief intros and a few lessons, Michael asked my class who would like to go up on stage and deliver a part of their speech. What do you suppose happened? Do you think everyone raised their hand with excitement, practically jumping out of their seats to go up in front of a room of strangers and be completely vulnerable?

It was quite the opposite. It was quiet. Some people looked at the floor, and others tried their hardest not to make eye contact with Michael as he literally walked the room row by row looking for his first volunteer.

My heart started pounding, I started getting the sweats, and my hands were becoming cold and clammy. I had the telltale signs of being scared. I remembered the feeling. It was the same feeling you would get when you were in school and the teacher asked if there were any questions, and you would get too scared to ask because you cared what others might think. Or that same feeling when you want to ask for a promotion at work, but when you are faced with the opportunity, your nerves get the better of you. Or perhaps you are at a conference, and the main speaker asks for a volunteer.

I had been in that position several times in my life up to that point. My usual response was to let fear prevent me from being the first one to raise his hand, volunteer, or speak up. After the lesson I learned during

Breakout, I wasn't going to let that happen any longer in my life. I swore to myself that when I get put in situations where I have the opportunity to lead, I'm going to do it. And if I feel nervous about something that I know is good for me, I'm definitely going to do it, no matter how scary the situation might be.

As Michael dissected the room, a few seconds had passed, and I slowly raised my hand to volunteer. I didn't really have a speech, although I'd been working on a brief intro to a possible keynote or TED talk in the future. I knew I was one of the greenest members of the class. Most of the people there, I could tell, either spoke for a living or did it quite often. But I didn't care.

Michael and Amy had created an environment that was meant to allow people to take chances, try new things, make big choices, and crush their fears (This was part of their HPS Pledge we recited to start each day). Michael looked at me and said, "It looks like we have our first volunteer."

I smiled and was getting ready to stand up and deliver on stage when Michael stopped me in my tracks. He then proceeded to tell a story about a recent professional basketball game he attended where he had the chance to sit near courtside. The game was close, and there were only a few seconds left. The visiting team had the possession arrow, were down by one point, and in a time out. Michael was so close he could hear the coach delivering his strategy for how he thought their team could win the game. What was interesting, he said, was that although all of the players were professionals and extremely talented to even be on the court, you could tell by their body language that most didn't want the ball in their hands. They didn't want the pressure or to be the final thing that everyone remembers when the game was over. All, that is, except for one player. One player looked at the coach and his teammates and said, "Give me the ball." In that instance, the leader showed up, put everyone else on their backs, and took charge.

I didn't actually get to go on stage after volunteering. In fact, Michael chose someone sitting right next to me to go up. But the lesson learned here is to be that one player who asks for the ball when the game is on the line. Or as the SEAL Code states, "In the absence of leadership, we will take charge, lead our teammates, and accomplish the mission."

Sidenote: If you are serious about your public speaking career, you need to check out HPS! (https://heroicpublicspeaking.com/) Again, special thanks to Amber Vilhauer, who gifted the experience to me (https://ambervilhauer.com/). She is the industry leader for websites, book launches, branding, and marketing.

CHALLENGE

Ready to Lead and Ready to Follow.

Have you been in situations where there was a void in leadership? I bet you have. What were the conditions, and what did you do? Did you step up and lead, be the first to go, or did you do nothing and wait for someone else? If you're in school, do you raise your hand to volunteer, and ask questions? At work on a conference call, are you the first one to ask a question instead of waiting for that dead, awkward silence? If you're a parent, do you take charge and coordinate a fun weekend for the family; or do you wait for someone else to do it? These are perfect times to step up and lead. Your challenge here is to identify all areas of your life where you are part of a team. Trust me, you are on way more teams than you think. Your family is a team, your friends and your coworkers are a team, there are sports teams you may be a part of, or the local CrossFit box, the band, any groups you might take part in.

Now analyze it further. Are you a leader, or are you a follower? It probably depends on the time and situation because the truth is, we should be constantly flip-flopping between leading and following. True, most teams have the so-called leader, but if that person has to lead every single time, I can tell you this: that is not a high-performing team. Something is wrong or missing. Maybe the leader is a complete micromanager who has to have his or her hand in everything you do and wants to take the credit for everything. Or, it could be that the team hasn't bought into the mission and they are just cashing a paycheck so to speak.

Take stock of your roles, and if you find yourself leading too much, it's time to learn how to follow, which is just as important a skill as leading. Regardless, I want you to analyze the teams you are a part of, and when the opportunity arises to step up and lead, do it. Take charge, volunteer, and don't second-guess yourself. As Mel Robbins says, "If you have an impulse to act, you must move on it within five seconds, or your brain will kill the idea." Try it. It works every time.

08

IT PAYS TO BE A WINNER

"If you want to go fast, go alone, but if you want to go far, go with others."

—AFRICAN PROVERB

We were loaded into the white vans according to boat crew, blindfolded, and instructed to stay awake and absolutely silent. Our driver had all the windows rolled up, and the heat was blasting full force. What kind of sadistic man does that? We started out on blacktop and after a significant amount of time had passed I could tell that the terrain had changed from asphalt to rocks.

We then came to a slow stop. I'm guessing I'd been sitting quietly, sweating in my thoughts, for about an hour. The driver asked us to take off the blindfolds. I couldn't wait to be able to see again. It took several seconds for my eyes to adjust to the sunlight. As we looked out of the windows in the van, our driver said, "This is going to be your new home for a while." The location was majestic. I had a view of a beautiful lake in front of me that was surrounded by mountains. It was like something off of a postcard. It was by far the most beautiful thing

I'd seen so far that weekend. Anything was better than being facedown on the cement grinder.

Another coach came by our van and opened the door. He instructed, "Get out and get wet."

We sprinted to the lake, and I have to admit, the cool water felt comforting after the hot van ride, almost like jumping in a pool on a nice summer day back home in Indiana.

We were instructed to form a line, wade in chest-deep, and await further instructions.

I really had to pee. It was perfect timing. I moved out to chest-deep water and took a nice, long leak. It felt great. In fact, as the warm urine made its way down my legs, I made a mental note of that in case I should need to warm up, even if just for a brief moment, later that weekend, if I ended up in the Pacific Ocean.

While still in formation, we stood in a horizontal line. I counted around 15 coaches on the beach.

They walked toward us and, when they were within shouting distance, we were told to look around the lake. "Take it in, boys. I promise you will explore every square inch of this lake and shoreline. Now, interlock arms, and when I tell you, hold your breath and go underwater. Do not come back up until at least 30 seconds have passed. If I see one head pop up before 30 seconds, you all will get beat down."

Great. Water is not my strong suit and is the ultimate equalizer for me. Sure, I can swim, if you count the swim lessons I took when I was a kid at the local YMCA. To be honest, I'm not very confident in the water, never have been, and I'm pretty lousy at holding my breath. Thirty seconds sounded like an eternity. Plus, it wasn't a pool; it was a murky lake, which added to my anxiety.

Three, two, one, and the order was given.

I went under with the rest of the class. I closed my eyes since it was pointless to open them given the water clarity. I began to count my own heartbeats to estimate 30 seconds. But I had a slight problem. Water was coming in through my nose and starting to trickle down my throat, or at least that's what it felt like. Plus my heart rate was elevated, so counting heartbeats probably wasn't the best indicator of time. I held on as long as possible and continued counting heartbeats until I reached 30. I popped my head up out of the water, and do you know what I saw?

Nothing... except the coaches.

No one else on my team popped their head up. I was the first one who broke the surface. My teammates were still under the water. I knew it wouldn't end well, and I got a sinking feeling in my chest. I had let my team down, and I was the weak link.

One of the coaches was immediately on me. "Ritter, you effed up, and now you and your entire team will pay the price because you can't hold your breath for thirty seconds."

"Sorry, guys," I mumbled to those close around me. That is a terrible feeling, knowing that you're the reason your team lost.

We were ordered to run out of the water and hit the sand. When I say hit the sand, that meant we were to lie facedown on the gravelly shore of the lake. Our instructions were simple. We were to low crawl from our area to another coach who was about 100 yards down the shore. Imagine there is barbed wire above you, so you must crawl on your arms and legs the entire distance without your butt being hiked up in the air. Your head needs to stay as close to the ground as possible—that's a low crawl.

Low crawl.

I was about halfway to the finish line when I noticed my arms were taking a beating. *Well, this isn't good*, I thought, but what else was I going to do but suck it up and finish? By the time I reached the coach, I was completely wiped out, arms and legs beat up by the terrain.

He took a look at the 10 or so of us who arrived before the rest of the others and said, "Pays to be a winner."

One of my teammates who had finished first was allowed to sit out the next race. Those of us left in the group were immediately sent back the way we came. This time, we had to perform a crab walk backward.

Since we were moving backward, we were blind to where we were going, and the result was that we were running into each other as some were quicker than others. We reached the goal line and again were hit with the same response.

"It pays to be a winner."

So our race leader would be pulled to the side for a breather, and the last three would join the Goon Squad.

I could see that my teammates in the Goon Squad were getting beat down hard with calisthenics and being forced to roll around all over the sand. That was not a fun place to be. I think it was meant to illustrate a point that was driven home all weekend. If you aren't giving it your all and start to take a break, you're history. There is no place to hide. That makes you really think hard about why you're there in the first place. They do what they can to break you down to see if you will quit.

If my memory serves me right, we performed 10 of these 100-yard-or-so "crawls." While I never came in first, I was never in the last three, so I avoided the Goon Squad. My arms looked like I had a severe case of psoriasis. They were red and had been cut up from scraping against the sandy shore, and I knew my legs were in about the same condition. The only things saving them were my cargo pants and the protective base layer I was wearing underneath. My stomach, chest, and back felt bruised up as if I'd been playing tackle football. I felt like a mess, and it was still day one, only about five hours into the camp. I'm guessing it was around 13:00 hours.

Are we having fun yet?

"Hydrate and fill up two canteens... one with water and the other with Gatorade. Drink them as quickly as possible, and await further instruction. You have ten minutes."

Something became apparent quickly... there was no way 35 people were going to fill up two canteens apiece in 10 minutes and drink them. By sheer luck, I was number two in line for Gatorade. When it was my turn, I filled up my canteen all the way and stepped out of the line. I drank approximately half and then located my swim buddy and gave him the rest since he was last in the hydration line.

"Line up," instructed one of the coaches.

We gathered back with our respective boat crews.

I wasn't thirsty, which was good, but I was starting to get very hungry.

"Look behind you."

We turned. A steep, rocky hill was in our view. It could have been a mountain to an Indiana boy like me.

"You will run in boat crews to the top of that hill, and once you see the coach standing at the top, you will run around him and double back all the way down to the finish line marked by the vans. You'll start as a team and finish as a team. The race is over when your last teammate has crossed the finish line. This is an all-out race, and remember, it pays to be a winner."

"One–two–three, get it!" shouted a nearby coach, and the race was on.

I went hot out of the gate, probably faster than I should have, but it was an all-out race, and quickly my team separated. Then, it was basically every man for himself.

The incline was steep and the footing slippery. We were running on dirt and shale, so we had to watch where we placed our feet, or we could easily trip and fall. I reached the top of the hill in less than 5 minutes.

A coach stood at the top waiting for us all to run around him and head back down the hill.

It ended up being the descent that gave me problems because the footing was so inconsistent. I was constantly fighting to get a secure foothold. At no time did I feel like I was on stable ground, and my body weight was carrying me down the mountain like a juggernaut. I had to constantly pull back on the reins to avoid running out of control and being injured. The part that sucked the most was that the tips of my toes were getting smashed at the front of my boots, and since they were still wet, it was only adding to the problem. I couldn't do anything about it except suck it up and continue down the hill.

I reached the finish line and immediately looked around for my teammates. My swim buddy had beaten me, and we linked up, cheering on our teammates. We still had three running down the mountain. The problem was, those three were bringing up the rear of the entire class.

Team one, referred to as the "Smurfs" due to their height, ended up finishing first. They all flew down the mountain and finished within 30 seconds of each other.

My worst fear had come true: my team finished last. Completely gassed, we all stood with our teams waiting for the coaches to hand out the rewards, and what was likely to be a punishment for us.

"Team one," one of the coaches shouted, "It pays to be a winner. You finished first, and your reward is that you get to sit out the remainder of this evolution. All of you other teams get ready because you're to run this again. And team seven (which was my team), do not let that happen again."

Again? To say I wasn't looking forward to the next round was an understatement.

Our teams lined up again. "One, two, three, bust 'em!" and we were off to the races for a second time. However, instead of every man running for themselves, we stayed together as a team to help set the pace and encourage each other. I happened to be leading the men, but a couple of minutes into the race, I looked behind. Some of our slower teammates were starting to fall back. I stopped running, waited for everyone to catch up, and off we went again.

Once we reached the top, we again waited on our slower teammates to catch up. We encouraged them to pick up the pace as we headed down the mountain. We finished as a team but were in second-to-last place. I wasn't happy about our showing, but at least we weren't bringing up the back of the pack again.

We lined up awaiting the coaches to reward and punish us. I could see team one sitting down enjoying a canteen of fuel and catching a breather.

"Team three, you were the winners of this race. Join team one. All you other sad pieces of **** get ready because we're doing this again."

This is really going to suck, I thought to myself. I was starting to get smoked, and my body was aching.

For the third time, we lined up. With only five teams remaining from the original seven, we were all about the same pace.

I remember that race being the most difficult. It's not because I was tired, hungry, battered, and bruised, but because doubt started creeping in. My mind was off wandering, thinking about how many more times we were going to have to run this damn hill, would it ever end, and what would happen if we finished in last place again? I looked at my swim buddy and teammates as we got to the starting line. Time to flip the switch, turn my negativity into positivity. "We're going to crush this race. This is when we shine," I told my boat crew.

"One, two, three, bust 'em," and just like that, we were off on our third race.

We stayed together as a team, and we put the slowest runner first so he could set the pace. Halfway up the hill, we were in the middle of the pack. I talked to my team one last time. "Are you guys tired of running?"

Each of them nodded their head.

"Well, let's win this. Stay in the middle of the pack till we get to the top, and then once we start the descent, let it fly, and give it everything you got. Don't hold anything back."

They nodded, and we proceeded as planned. Once again, we rounded the top of the hill and started our descent.

"Let's do it!" I yelled, and we all turned on the afterburners. I felt like I was literally flying. One small misstep and I'd be rolling down the hill, but I didn't care anymore. I wasn't going to run that hill again. *Almost there*, I thought, j*ust keep pushing, keep the pace, and we'll have this race secured.*

Then in an instant, the whole damn race came unraveled. I heard what sounded like a whitetail deer after it's been shot, starts to run, and immediately hits the ground. I looked back. It was my teammate. He must have tripped over a rock or something because he was lying face-first in the dirt.

Without hesitation, the four of us who remained upright rushed over to pick him up, dust him off, and encourage him to keep going.

Luckily, he was okay except for some minor scrapes. He got up like a possessed banshee, and with sheer guts and determination, he headed for the finish line.

Other teams had started to cross the finish line, but we didn't care. We were going to finish that race like it was our last. My team finally crossed the finish line. We finished in third place out of the five teams. Of course, we were mad that we hadn't won, especially after giving it everything we had, but we felt like winners because we were there for each other and literally picked up our teammate when he had fallen down. Something happens to your psyche when you make things about others and not about yourself. Our boat crew was becoming a tight unit.

We lined up again to await our fate from the coaches. This time though, I didn't care. I could run that hill all day if that's what they wanted. I was not going to quit on my teammates, and they weren't going to quit on me.

The cadres addressed us, "This evolution isn't just about winning, it's about the team. Team seven, you showed what that's all about by picking up a fallen comrade. That's what we were looking for here today. Now go grab lunch and change, you've got 20 minutes."

PACK YOUR RUCKSACK

Who's your buddy?

Boat crews, swim buddies, battle buddies, squads, units, teams— what's the significance? They are meant to teach you one thing. In military training, teamwork is taught very early on. No one makes it through training by themselves. You can be the most gifted athlete and an absolute PT stud, but if you are mentally and emotionally weak and can't become a team player, you aren't going to make it very far.

Life is the ultimate test of your training, so naturally, it is the ultimate team sport. No one is meant to do life alone. The idea that anyone is "self-made" is a complete lie. At some point, you *will* need some help. The question is, will your ego be so big you won't ask for it?

Go back to the last challenge I presented to you in Chapter 7, and look at the teams you are a part of in life. Now ask yourself, "Who is my swim buddy on that team?"

Although *Rambo* was a great movie, it's fake. There's no way one man is going to do all of that by himself.

When I ask my friends who serve what they love most about the military, it's the team, it's the people they get to work with. It's their buddies. If only I had a dollar for every time I went out with my friends and I heard the phrase, "This is my army buddy" when someone was being introduced. That means you're in, you're one of them, you have a similar mindset and beliefs, you're a part of the tribe, the brotherhood. You might not know what they do, but you know why they do it.

The point I'm trying to illustrate here is to be aware of the teams you are on in life, and pay particular attention to who your buddies are. But beware. Let this be a cautionary tale. Choose your buddies carefully. It's been said that you are the average of the five people you hang out with. That really makes you stop to think about who you should let into your inner circle and influence you. If you are reading this and you're in high school, then I want you to pay extra special attention here. Take it from me.

I hung around a tough crowd and did a lot of stupid things growing up. Now, it wasn't all bad, and most kids go through some sort of growing pains, but I can tell you without a doubt that the circle of friends I hung out with had a direct influence on who I was becoming as a man.

My dad used to tell me, "Son, if you wallow with the pigs long enough, you'll become one."

I never really knew the true meaning of that and used to pass it off as some sort of parental Jedi mind trick. Only years later did I truly understand what he was trying to teach me.

Out of the circle of friends I had in high school, I was the only one who went to and graduated from college. Look, college isn't for everyone, and I'd never put anyone down for not attending, but the last thing I wanted to do was to just get a job out of high school and be a tumblin' tumbleweed for the rest of my life. As some of my friends and I grew older, we were drifting apart. We just didn't have the same dreams, values, and purpose anymore. The final straw for me was when I got punched in the face, literally. My friends and I took a trip to Panama City, Florida, for Spring Break. Yes, there was drinking, drugs, girls, the whole deal, but one of my so-called friends sucker punched me in the face while high on who knows what, and I ended up spending the next few hours in the local hospital getting the flap of skin under my eye stitched up. He was wearing one of those gaudy class rings. I learned the hard way that those can do some damage.

That was it! When we got back home, I basically stopped hanging out with my "friends" and devoted my time to school. It was one of the toughest and best decisions I ever made. Too bad it took something like that to change my mindset. I did get a pretty cool scar under my eye, though. Every now and again I'll notice it when I look in the mirror, and it serves as a reminder to choose your buddies carefully.

CHALLENGE

Will You Play With Me?

Make a list of who your buddies currently are, and if you don't have one, find one. Do your buddies bring you up or put you down?

I heard a statistic the other day that made me stop and wonder. The average American hasn't made a new friend in five years. Five years? I'm not talking about a Facebook friend, a LinkedIn connection, or any of the social media outlets. I'm talking about a friend you actually spend some time with in person and experience life with together. You remember how easy it was when you were a kid. All you had to do was ride your bike down the street, knock on your neighbor's door, and ask if Johnny wanted to play. Somewhere near adulthood, we've lost those kindred spirits.

I challenge you to starve your fears, feed courage, and ask someone you feel a connection toward, "Do you want to be friends?" Chances are, they might be looking for someone too. As the famous author Seth Godin says, "People like us do things like this." Now go out and make some new friends.

09

A CONVERSATION
WITH GOD

"Greater love hath no man than this, that a man lay
down his life for his friends."

—JOHN 15:13-17

After a quick lunch consisting of an MRE we made a mad dash to change out of our gear and put on fresh clothes, we were to line up by boat crew facing the lake. (The initialism MRE stands for "meal ready to eat," which is a self- contained, individual field ration in lightweight packaging bought by the United States military for its service members to use in combat or other field conditions where organized food facilities are not available).

It was an awesome feeling changing into dry clothes. Somehow, I knew they probably wouldn't be that way for long, so I embraced the scenery, rejoiced in my fresh wool socks and dry clothes, and began to focus on my breathing.

"Gentleman, we have reviewed your PT scores, and you all suck. We're going to do it again. Those of you who are borderline, well, we'll have some extra treats for you at the end, so make sure you put out. Now let's warm back up. Follow me."

Fabulous. More running.

As we ended the three-mile warm-up run, we made our way back to the shore. Another coach, who had been waiting for us to return, asked if any of us was a baseball player. I immediately raised my hand. Truth be told, I hadn't touched a baseball in years, but I was pretty good in high school and was our pitching ace. The coach handed me a canteen that was full of liquid.

"Ritter, how far do you think you can throw this canteen into the lake?"

"I'm not sure, Coach. How far do you need me to?" I replied. "You see that orange buoy out there. Do you think you can toss this canteen past that?" he asked. "Hooyah!" I responded.

I took about five steps back from the shoreline, took a deep breath, and then proceeded to throw the canteen as far as I possibly could. Within a few seconds, the canteen had hit its mark—roughly 20 feet past the buoy. For a split second, I felt like I was a ballplayer again.

"Not bad," replied the coach. "Now, time for some fun. How long, do you think, would it take the entire class to swim out to the floating canteen and back to the shore?"

I had no idea. I quickly analyzed the distance and thought to myself, *twenty seconds to the canteen and twenty seconds back with a five- second buffer.* "Let's go with forty-five seconds."

"Are you sure?" Coach asked.

Before I could even answer, another teammate piped in quickly and said, "Coach, I believe we can do this quicker. Let's go with thirty seconds."

"Are you sure?" Coach asked him, and he quickly replied yes. "Okay, line up, and when I say bust em, you will have thirty seconds to be back here. I won't stop the watch until the last person hits the shore. Don't be late."

My class lined up at the shore, and within seconds, we were off. I made the turn around the buoy and followed some of the quicker swimmers to the beach. We stood up in the water and ran onto the sand close to where the coach was timing us. We cheered on our teammates who were swimming as fast as possible, not knowing how much time had elapsed or where we would finish. As our last teammate emerged from the water, stood up, and landed on the beach, the coach yelled the time: "Thirty-five seconds. You all lose. Face the water, lean-and-rest position."

Here we go, I thought to myself.

He continued, "If you can hold this position as a team for five minutes... you're done. If not, we'll do it again."

"Hooyah!" we all responded together.

The first minute was no problem. The second minute, not so bad. However, by the third, I began to shake. I focused on my breathing, taking deep inhales and exhales through my nose. I scanned the class. *So far so good.* The guys were in pain, but they seemed to be pushing through. I'm guessing by then we were somewhere between four and five minutes in when all of a sudden, I heard the coach yell, "Stop."

We all broke out of our stance and looked around.

"One of you couldn't put out, so now you all will pay the price, again. Five minutes on my mark."

We didn't even have a chance to recover! "Bust em."

We all got back into the lean-and-rest plank position again.

One minute passed, and I was shaking like a leaf. I started deep breathing again, and it calmed me, but I still couldn't control the shaking. Two more minutes went by, but it felt like ten. Then I heard a familiar voice say, "Stop."

We're never going to make it past this evolution as a team. Another teammate had broken early.

Coach ripped us a new one and said something to the effect of how did we expect to make it thru the weekend if we couldn't hold a simple five-minute plank together as a team. "Take your positions," the coach said.

We lined up for the third attempt.

"Go" he shouted, and we all conformed.

The exercise had quickly become a mental game... I knew it was going to be difficult for some of my teammates to make it without breaking. My arms were shaking from the get-go, so I closed my eyes, focused on my breathing, and visualized a happy place, my family, and my "Why." Then I heard something I hadn't heard before that broke my concentration.

My teammate started reciting a poem. And not just any poem, but "Invictus" (see Appendix).

The poem was near and dear to me. I had spent multiple hours back home training to commit it to memory, and each word had emotion tied to it.

The teammate said, "Out of the night which covers me." The rest of the class recited in unison:

Black as the pit from pole to pole I thank whatever gods may be For my unconquerable soul.

We then proceeded to recite the entire poem together as a team. Reciting these words out loud for all to hear instantly took the fear and doubt off of ourselves, and we focused that energy on each other. The words we recited became energy sparks. We must have recited that poem three times, and before we knew it, we all had held the plank for five minutes without breaking.

"Recover," the coach yelled.

As soon as he uttered the word, I dropped like a log onto the sand, face-first. I didn't care. I was just glad that the exercise was over.

PST 2.0

"Okay, lads, line up for your second PST."

We were told to link up with our swim buddy and perform the push-ups, sit-ups, and squats test to the standard of the original PST we took that morning. There was one caveat. The numbers we posted earlier in the day would be our baseline, and we had to fall within five reps of it, or else we would face possible discipline or expulsion from the program. Basically, we'd better put out and give it everything we had or risk going home. Even though I was physically exhausted, my mental game was still on point, and there was no way I wasn't going to perform well.

My swim buddy, Matt, and I linked up. Matt went first and posted an impressive 82 push-ups. Then it was my turn, and I scored a 75, which is one fewer than the 76 I posted that morning. *So far so good*, I thought.

It was time for the sit-ups. Again, Matt posted an impressive score of 80, and I turned in a score of 74, one more than my earlier 73.

Last but not least came the squats. Matt continued to crush his scores and posted an 80, while I gave it everything I had and managed a 72, just barely within the five-rep allowance of my prior score of 76. After squats, we were given a few minutes to recover. The cadres had a brief huddle, then addressed our team and pulled two individuals aside. They ordered the rest of us to move quickly to a pull-up rig we ran past during our warm-up run.

I'm not sure where my other two teammates were taken, but one thing I did know: they got beat down. I could hear them grunting in pain. I couldn't worry about them. They chose their own path and either didn't put out or were not prepared to begin with. On to the next evolution.

MURPH

We double-timed it to the pull-up rig approximately 300 meters away. The rig was an impressive sight. I wondered how long it took to build such a monstrosity of metal in the middle of nowhere. It was somewhere around 1700, and I figured we had just a couple of hours of daylight left in Day One.

One of the cadres stepped forward, and he was wearing a T-shirt with the name "Murph" on the front. My heart sank into my abdomen. *OMG, we're going to do Murph now.*

The coach read us the Medal of Honor citation awarded to Lt. Michael Murphy.:

LIEUTENANT MICHAEL P. MURPHY UNITED STATES NAVY

For service set forth in the following CITATION:

FOR CONSPICUOUS GALLANTRY AND INTREPIDITY AT THE RISK OF HIS LIFE ABOVE AND BEYOND THE CALL OF DUTY AS THE LEADER OF A SPECIAL RECONNAISSANCE ELEMENT WITH NAVAL SPECIAL WARFARE TASK UNIT IN AFGHANISTAN ON 27 AND 28 JUNE, 2005. WHILE LEADING A MISSION TO LOCATE A HIGH-LEVEL, ANTI- COALITION MILITIA LEADER, LIEUTENANT MURPHY DEMONSTRATED EXTRAORDINARY HEROISM IN THE FACE

OF GRAVE DANGER IN THE VICINITY OF ASADABAD, KONAR PROVINCE, AFGHANISTAN.

ON 28 JUNE, 2005, OPERATING IN AN EXTREMELY RUGGED ENEMY-CONTROLLED AREA, LIEUTENANT MURPHY'S TEAM WAS DISCOVERED BY ANTI-COALITION MILITIA SYMPATHIZERS, WHO REVEALED THEIR POSITION TO TALIBAN FIGHTERS. AS A RESULT, BETWEEN 30 AND 40 ENEMY FIGHTERS BESIEGED HIS FOUR-MEMBER TEAM. DEMONSTRATING EXCEPTIONAL RESOLVE, LIEUTENANT MURPHY VALIANTLY LED HIS MEN IN ENGAGING THE LARGE ENEMY FORCE. THE ENSUING FIERCE FIREFIGHT RESULTED IN NUMEROUS ENEMY CASUALTIES, AS WELL AS THE WOUNDING OF ALL FOUR MEMBERS OF THE TEAM. IGNORING HIS OWN WOUNDS AND DEMONSTRATING EXCEPTIONAL COMPOSURE, LIEUTENANT MURPHY CONTINUED TO LEAD AND ENCOURAGE HIS MEN.

WHEN THE PRIMARY COMMUNICATOR FELL, MORTALLY WOUNDED, LIEUTENANT MURPHY REPEATEDLY ATTEMPTED TO CALL FOR ASSISTANCE FOR HIS BELEAGUERED TEAMMATES. REALIZING THE IMPOSSIBILITY OF COMMUNICATING IN THE EXTREME TERRAIN, AND IN THE FACE OF ALMOST CERTAIN DEATH, HE FOUGHT HIS WAY INTO OPEN TERRAIN TO GAIN A BETTER POSITION TO TRANSMIT A CALL.

THIS DELIBERATE, HEROIC ACT DEPRIVED HIM OF COVER, EXPOSING HIM TO DIRECT ENEMY FIRE. FINALLY ACHIEVING CONTACT WITH HIS HEADQUARTERS, LIEUTENANT MURPHY MAINTAINED HIS EXPOSED POSITION WHILE HE PROVIDED HIS LOCATION AND REQUESTED IMMEDIATE SUPPORT FOR HIS TEAM. IN HIS FINAL ACT OF BRAVERY, HE CONTINUED TO ENGAGE THE ENEMY UNTIL HE WAS MORTALLY WOUNDED, GALLANTLY GIVING HIS LIFE FOR HIS COUNTRY AND FOR THE CAUSE OF FREEDOM.

BY HIS SELFLESS LEADERSHIP, COURAGEOUS ACTIONS, AND EXTRAORDINARY DEVOTION TO DUTY, LIEUTENANT

MURPHY REFLECTED GREAT CREDIT UPON HIMSELF AND
UPHELD THE HIGHEST TRADITIONS OF THE UNITED STATES
NAVAL SERVICE.

SIGNED GEORGE W. BUSH

As the coach read the citation, I couldn't help but visualize myself in that exact same situation facing unimaginable odds. What would I have done? Could I have led my men in that amount of chaos and almost certain death? Would I be willing to risk my own life so that my brothers could live? Thank God for those men and women who have taken the oath to fight and protect our country. After hearing the citation, one thing was made absolutely clear.

The evolution we were about to endure was much bigger than ourselves... it wasn't about doing a tough workout or completing the next evolution... we were doing this *for* Murph. Tonight, we weren't just doing another hard workout. We were honoring his memory. It also happened to be the second pass/fail evolution. The first was the PST, which proved we had the physical ability to even show up. It was time to test our resiliency.

"The Murph workout consists of a one-mile run, one hundred pull-ups, two hundred push-ups, and three hundred air squats followed by another one-mile run, all while wearing your ruck. This will be an individual contest, and it will be strictly pass/fail. You will have seventy minutes to perform Murph."

This was going to suck—big time! I felt pretty good going into it since Murph was one of my favorite workouts and I was very familiar with it. But—and this is a big but—I never dreamed of trying to perform it after getting beat down for nine hours prior. I joined a single-file line with the rest of my class.

We had been instructed to fill our own rucks with a sandbag equivalent to the 20-pound minimum load requirement of dirt to ensure we were performing to standard. The last thing I wanted to do was make my bag too light and risk being sent home on an infraction.

I filled my bag all the way. I'd done this workout several times before and had trained long enough to know what 20 pounds should feel like. As I loaded my sandbag into my ruck and secured it to my back, I knew I had fudged up. My pack had to be closer to 30–35 pounds, which is a big difference. To say the fear wolf was creeping in was an understatement. Had I just let my ego write a check my body couldn't cash? We would soon find out.

As I waited in line for the bag weigh-in, I started doubting myself. It's amazing how quickly your mind can turn negative. I focused again on my breathing, taking deep inhales and exhales through my nostrils. I then thought about home, specifically training to do this very workout in my neighborhood streets, local parks, and high school. My imagery of back-home training quickly vanished as one of the cadre greeted me to weigh my bag.

"Ritter, you got twenty pounds?"

"Hooyah, Coach."

He then lifted it and said, "Overachiever." He knew it was overweight. "Square away your ruck, and select a pull-up bar."

"Hooyah," I replied and jogged over to the pull-up rig.

I think it's fitting to mention here that these rucks weren't actual rucksacks. They were cheap pieces of black canvas shit without any padding. They were also hard to secure to your back, so your pack would constantly be shifting all around as you moved.

One of the cadre I hadn't seen before walked over to our group, and he took out a notebook and pen. He told us all that we would be using the honor system and reminded us that anyone caught cheating would be sent home immediately. "After you complete the one-mile run, you are to begin your twenty rounds of five pull-ups, ten push-ups, and fifteen air squats. At the end of each round, you will shout out your last name along with the round you've completed. If I don't mark you down, then it didn't happen, and you don't want to do any extra rounds, do you?"

We all jogged over to the starting station.

"On my mark, you'll have seventy minutes to complete Murph.

Are there any questions?"

There was complete silence for a few seconds.

"Alright, gentlemen, Bust 'em."

We all took off. I knew from previously performing this HERO WOD, if I went too hot out of the gate with the first one-mile run, I would be smoked, and the rest of the workout, I would be sucking air. My swim buddy had run out ahead of me, but he was still well within sight. My goal was to keep him within view since he was a better runner. We made the last turn of the first one-mile run and ran past an American flag hanging on a flagpole in the middle of nowhere.

Talk about inspiration. Nothing gets me going and lights me on fire like seeing Old Glory flying.

I could see that I was quickly approaching the pull-up rig. That was our starting point, and my swim buddy had just reached his pull-up station.

He would have a head start on me, but that was okay. I wanted to stay within a few minutes of him. It was time for the real fun to begin. I took a couple of breaths, and then I jumped up and grabbed the pull-up bar.

My first thought was that the load was extremely heavy. My arms were already beaten from the abuse earlier, and for the Murph, I had an extra 30 pounds on me. I completed my first five pull-ups, but it felt like ten. I released my hands and came off the bar. I couldn't believe how heavy the backpack felt. I couldn't worry about that. On to the push-ups. I proceeded to get into push-up position making sure my chest hit the dirt and that my arms were fully extended. I quickly made it to ten, and although it was heavy, it wasn't nearly as bad of a feeling as the pull-ups were. Finally, the last movement were the squats. *Man, these effing hurt, and I've just started.* All the running we had done had taken its toll on my legs. I'm a larger guy, typically in the Clydesdale division of most races, and with an extra 30 pounds, I was squatting around 230– 240 pounds every time I moved. I went slowly on the squats and managed to get 15 without breaking. "Ritter, one," I shouted and made sure the coach acknowledged me.

Only nineteen more rounds, I thought. I knew that my average pace to complete the WOD was around 42–45 minutes back home, but that was completely fresh and with 20 pounds of extra weight. The Murph at Kokoro Camp was going to give me a whole new level of pain. The next four rounds went relatively smoothly, although the pull-ups and squats were giving me grief. I could manage to catch my breath and recover a little on the push-ups.

I had made sure to yell out my rounds to the coach and had completed five rounds out of the twenty up to that point. "Ritter six, Ritter seven, Ritter eight," I yelled as I progressed through the workout. I was making my way, but in round nine, things started to change.

I started hurting severely. Not in just one place but everywhere. My body felt like one giant piñata that had been beaten to a pulp, and my energy was leaking out of my body just like candy. To add insult to injury, my ruck kept hitting me in the back of the head every rep when I performed a pull-up, which was causing some bruising.

I looked around and noticed the sun was starting to fade. The darkness of night was starting to set in. Doubts accosted me. *I mean, I haven't even made it through nightfall, and who knows what sadistic stuff they have planned for us.* As I started on my pull-ups, I looked around at my teammates. I remember thinking, *Well, if they are putting out, then I'm not going to just give up. Dig deep; I've done this workout before. Easy day.* Round ten was the halfway mark for me mentally. *If I can get this one done, then I'm halfway home. Only ten more rounds and a one- mile run left. By breaking down this workout into more manageable chunks, it becomes easier to digest.* Rounds 11–14 went relatively smoothly, but I noticed I was starting to break down. The pull-ups were becoming too much to bang out five in a row unbroken. The push-ups were taking their toll, and the squats seemed like it took forever to reach 15.

Before I finished my last air squat of the 15th round, one of my teammates yelled out, "Twenty" and took off for his last mile. *Are you serious?* I thought to myself, *This guy is a freaking machine. He's literally going to be done with the workout before I'm even done with all of my pull-ups.*

I started to doubt myself again. I felt like I was back in school taking a math test. Math was hard for me, and I had to study every day just to keep up with the other kids. During tests, there would always be kids who finished in half the time it took me. For a brief moment, I'd compare myself to those kids and start to get anxious. Those same feelings were with me at that moment during Murph. *But I always finished those math tests, and I'm going to finish this test now. I've got 70 minutes. Just keep going.* "Ritter fifteen," I shouted as I grimaced in pain.

"Fix your face" one of the cadre yelled at me. Amazing how turning a frown or a look of discomfort into a smile immediately changes things.

"Hooyah, Coach."

That same coach then shouted to the class that we had 30 minutes remaining. Even though I had a smile on my face, I was mad. I'm not even sure what I was angry at, but somehow, I had turned all of that pain and doubt into aggression. I grabbed the pull-up bar and banged out 5 straight, which I hadn't done in several rounds, along with 10 straight push-ups and 15 squats.

"Ritter sixteen," I yelled.

I completed rounds 17 and 18 with sheer guts, blood, sweat, and tears. The calluses on my hands opened up and became bloody.

My swim buddy was off on his final run.

I looked around. Again, I was right in the middle of the pack, never the fastest but never the slowest. Some of the first people to set off on their final mile run had returned, and I still had two more rounds to go before I could even attempt the run. *Just get these final two rounds done!*

"Ritter nineteen," I yelled.

"Last one, Ritter," the coach yelled back.

"Hooyah." *This is it, final round.* Without catching a breath, I hopped back on the pull-up bar. "Ritter twenty," I yelled. As I completed the 20 rounds, I felt like I had overcome a major obstacle at that camp. One of the coaches yelled to my class that we had 20 minutes left. *I got this*, I thought to myself. *Twenty minutes to run one mile, Easy Day!* It was dark, the sun had set, and I was alone, all by myself retracing the same steps I had taken earlier to complete the last mile.

Then about two minutes into the run, I developed the worst leg cramps I've ever felt in my life. They were the kind that instantly incapacitates you and leaves you paralyzed. You either have to let them work themselves out or beat them out because you aren't going anywhere until they subside. My jog slowly turned into a walk and then crawl. Every step I took was absolute pain.

Normally a one-mile run like that would be nothing more than a warm-up, but my time at Kokoro Camp could quickly be coming to an end if I couldn't finish that evolution. *There's no way I can make it to the finish line with my legs cramping this bad* . . . I mean, I was having a hard time even walking. I'd never experienced pain like that before. Was my body breaking down? My heart and mind wanted to keep going, but my legs weren't listening.

I started feeling sorry for myself, alone in the dark, in the middle of nowhere. I'm not going to lie. I was in tears (Yeah, I cry. Put on the right movie, and I weep) because I knew I had met my limit. My body just simply didn't have enough left in the tank. I resorted to my last option. I completely quit moving to see if that would help, but it didn't. *Time is ticking. What am I gonna do?* Finally, I asked God for help.

I hadn't talked to God for quite some time. I was raised Catholic and attended a Catholic grade school. I would go to church twice a week, and we even had a religion class. I attended a public high school, and as I got into sports and working on the weekends, I just didn't have the time (classic excuse) to make it to church. I became a "Chreaster"—a person who goes to church only on Christmas and Easter. I'm ashamed to admit it, but I don't even pray every day anymore. I don't really know why, but for now, let's call it laziness.

My conversation with God went something like this. "God, I know I haven't talked to you in a while, but I could really use your help right now. My body is battered, but I know I can keep going. All I'm asking for is that my legs stop cramping. Can you help me out? Thanks for listening."

Within a few seconds, you know what happened? Nothing. I still felt shredded. My legs were still cramping. Just because you pray doesn't mean God is going to answer according to *your* timeline. I had almost thrown in the towel. It was the second time I had really thought about quitting.

Suddenly, I heard something behind me. It was the distinct sound of rucksacks swinging and boots hitting the dirt. It was a couple of my teammates. They had just finished their 20 rounds and were off to finish their last mile when they ran into me. "Bros, I need some help. I want to finish, but my legs are giving out. Can you help me for a bit?"

"Hooyah, Ritter." Each put one of my arms around their shoulders so they could act like crutches. I slowed their pace down to a quick walk, but I was so excited to see someone and that they were willing to help me. We continued like that for what I'm guessing is about 100 yards. My internal dialogue started changing, too. I was starting to get positive again. I was thanking God for sending help.

Do you know what happened after that? I got my legs back. As quickly as my leg cramps appeared, they went away. I could put my full weight on my legs and jog like normal. I thanked my teammates multiple times and silently thanked God as well.

The three of us crossed the finish line together.

I had a newfound spirit and had overcome something that I'd thought for sure would expel me from the camp. I crossed the finish line at an even 59 minutes, which was eleven minutes under the time cap. I figured the last mile took me thirteen minutes or so to run. It was the first time in my life I'd been truly broken down, and I finally got to meet myself for the first time. That brought a huge smile to my face.

PACK YOUR RUCKSACK

Goals

Goal setting. It's one of the big four techniques of mental toughness that Mark Divine teaches in his Unbeatable Mind coaching academy. As the saying goes, "How do you eat an elephant? One bite at a time." Or, "The journey of a thousand miles starts with a single step."

Have you ever had a goal that you knew was good for you, but you gave up on it? We all probably have at one point or another. Now think back and ask yourself why that happened. Maybe you lost interest in it. Maybe people told you it couldn't be done, and you believed them instead of believing in yourself. Or maybe you didn't take the time to plan out an appropriate course of action.

Let's look at an example you are reading right now—this book. This is my first book. I have zero experience in writing, working with an editor, picking covers, doing a marketing launch, the list goes on. I bet I've spent somewhere around five years making this a reality. Five *long* years. Think about that.

When I first started writing, it was easy. I was excited. It was new, and I was motivated. But somewhere along the path, I lost the motivation. It became harder. It had grown old, and new things were popping up that piqued my curiosity and took my eyes off the prize. I took a break from the book one summer and didn't write a single word. Somewhere along the line, I got motivated again but needed to change my process.

My process before was just to sit down and write without any direction or goal. While that might be good for brainstorming, I knew I needed to hold myself accountable. This book was never going to become a reality if I didn't set proper goals. Instead, I could add it to the list of the many books that people have half- finished sitting on their hard drive or the cloud. Books that no one will ever read, that won't have the opportunity to impact other lives. In fact, I believe some of the best books ever written are literally sitting in a nightstand somewhere or locked up in the minds of authors who think they could never write a book.

Believe me, you can. It just takes discipline and goals. Goals are great and important, but you have to have a plan to get there. My plan became this. First, I created a spot in my house that was inviting, and I would report to that place early in the morning at 0430 or 0500 Monday–Friday before my wife and kids were up. This was my time—my time to write, my time to make my dream a reality. I then broke the book down into bite-sized chunks and committed to writing 500 words a day. Some days I would write more, but at a minimum, I had to write 500. Guess what. Within a year, I had about 120,000 words written, and my rough draft was finally complete. All of that because I had the discipline to wake up early and stick to a goal that was measurable and attainable. In the words of Lao Tzu, "Watch your thoughts for they become your words. Your words become actions. Your actions become habits and your habits become your character. Watch your character, for it becomes your destiny."

CHALLENGE

Target Selection.

I want you to sign up for something that pushes you out of your comfort zone and that you know would be good for you (since that's where the real growth happens). It could be your first 5K, a full marathon, a SEALFIT crucible, a Spartan, or GoRuck event; learning a new musical instrument or language, or getting an advanced degree or skill. The choice is up to you.

After signing up, I want you to plan out how you are going to accomplish this goal. Make sure it's realistic, measurable, and fits your mission. If you're writing a book, how many days a week, and how many words per day will you write? If you're running a marathon, how many miles a week do you plan on running, and when are you going to do it? If you are learning to play guitar, how many hours a day or week will you commit to practicing? One of the many things Mark Divine has taught me is how to properly select your targets, i.e. goals. You can do this quickly by running them through a model called FITS.

FITS:

Does your goal fit you and your team in terms of your skills, resources, time, and personality? Is it reasonable or a long shot? Will the return on your investment in time, resources, and energy be worth it for this goal, or should you be looking at a different goal with a higher return on investment?

IMPORTANCE:

Is this goal strategically important to achieve your mission or purpose? Will your mission fail if you do not achieve your goal? Is there another, more vital goal on which you should be directing your precious energy?

TIMING:

Is this the right time for this goal? What has to happen first for this goal to become a realistic achievement? Is there some other goal or target whose timing trumps this one?

SIMPLICITY:

Is this a KISS goal? Can you break the goal into smaller micro-goals, aka stepping-stones, to increase the simplicity and your chances of succeeding and gaining momentum toward actualizing your vision?

Finally, (and this is perhaps the most important) I want you to hold yourself accountable, or if that's potentially an issue, find someone who will. Tell your spouse, friends, parents, or coworkers so that they know what you are doing and more importantly, if they really care about you, they will ask how it's coming along. Ensure you have the proper feedback loops in place to receive your accountability. Now you've set yourself up for success. Just one thing left to do: Take massive action. Sign up and commit today!

GATES OF FIRE

"Fate whispers to the warrior, 'You can't withstand the storm.' The warrior whispers back, 'I am the storm.'"

—UNKNOWN

My team and I were smoked, and the coaches knew it. Nightfall was upon us, and we'd been functioning nonstop all day.

We were ushered up a small hill that had an oak tree perched on top, and we were ordered to sit underneath it.

The cadre headed our way, and there was a familiar silhouette wearing jeans and a polo leading them. The coaches toted boxes with unknown contents, and my mind began wondering what could be inside of them—ropes, weights, torture devices? The familiar silhouette was none other than Coach Divine, and that added an extra level of anxiety. I hadn't seen him since we were at HQ that morning when he poured red Gatorade on my face and stood on my stomach, questioning my work ethic.

"Are you guys hungry?" Coach Divine asked us. We responded with a loud "Hooyah."

The cadres then placed the boxes on the grass in front of us and instructed us to line up for MRE dispersion.

We were each handed one package, and we took our seats back under the oak tree. My class and I devoured our meals as if we hadn't eaten in days (it probably had been only six hours), but with the calories we were burning, it was impossible to eat too much. I've heard stories of real SEAL training where you burn on average 9,000–12,000 calories a day.

I was so hungry I didn't even bother looking at the packaging to see what I was about to tear into. It happened to be a bean- and-rice burrito, with peanut butter crackers, peaches, fruit bar, and pound cake along with salt/pepper, matches, toilet paper, and a heating device in case we wanted to use one. None of us did. There wasn't enough time for that crap.

It tasted amazing, and the dessert was an added bonus. Not exactly as good as my wife's homemade sugar cream pie, but at that point, I'd probably have eaten anything. To wash it all down, we filled one canteen with water and the other with Gatorade.

We'd been eating for about 5–10 minutes, talking among ourselves, when Coach Divine addressed us. He congratulated us for making it this far in the training and then proceeded to share a story from the book, *Gates of Fire*, which is about the Spartan King Leonidas and how he led 300 of his best-trained warriors against the Persian King Xerxes and his army of more than a million strong.

I don't remember everything Coach Divine told us, but he was essentially talking about our character and said if we cared enough for our teammates with everything we had, which he referred to as our Kokoro heart, then our team would be able to make it through the rest of the weekend.

The word *Kokoro* actually means, in translation, the blending of heart and mind into action. I would be caring more for my teammates than

I do for myself, and giving more of myself than I've ever given in my entire life.

Take your eyes off yourself and your own personal suffering, and focus on those around you.

He was making analogies between our crucible training and what the Spartans must have been thinking as they stared out at the invading army of Persians. After his speech, he brought us back to reality. "We tend to lose a lot of people the first night. The fact is, if you can make it through tonight, you'll likely make it the entire weekend. You're only ten hours into this thing, and we're going to bring the pain, but remember, make it to sunrise. Don't quit at night. If you have any doubts about whether or not you think you can make it, do yourself a favor and quit right now. We'll be getting back into the vans and going to an undisclosed location for the remainder of the night. If you quit there, you'll be there the entire night and well into the morning. We won't be bringing you back to HQ." Coach Divine then said that he hoped to see us all the next day and stood up abruptly. He then instructed us to somersault down the hill.

You read that right.

After eating and sitting for about 30 minutes, we had to roll head over heels down the hill. Our bodies rotated 360 degrees around a horizontal axis with our feet passing over our heads. Somebody even decided to land their size-12 boot on my nose while tumbling. If the somersaulting didn't wake me up, having my nose crushed and the sight of fresh blood sure did.

Once at the bottom of the hill, we all made a mad dash to the white 1 vans that had brought us to the lake.

I happened to see Coach McLeod walk by, and he asked, "Ritter, will I see you tomorrow morning?"

I replied, "Hooyah, Coach."

"We shall see, Ritter."

PACK YOUR RUCKSACK

It could always be worse.

We've all heard the saying, "It could always be worse." Who is the most resilient person you know? Resiliency is the ability to bounce back stronger and wiser after a setback. I want to tell you about the most resilient person I ever met.

This paragon of grit was born December 5, 1977, in Indianapolis, IN. She spent her childhood living in Detroit, MI, and finally settled down in Bloomington, IL. Grit loved animals and was especially fond of dogs, cats, cows, elephants, rabbits, and horses. Grit also loved sports and played softball and volleyball, skied, fished, and could target shoot. Perhaps Grit's most skilled sport was ice skating, where she was a member of Team Elan and won a silver medal at the International Precision Skating Championship in Helinski, Finland.

Grit knew the value of hard work and grew up with Midwestern values. Grit attended college at NIU and earned a degree in marketing. Grit worked many jobs including a stint at a dairy farm where she would milk cows twice a day, often in freezing temperatures.

Another job Grit held was on an all-male commercial painting crew where she would politely refuse help moving the full extension ladders. It's been rumored that the two owners of the painting company had bet each other on when she would quit. She did not. Eventually, Grit traded in the overalls for business attire and moved with her college sweetheart to the Big Apple in 2001, a few months prior to 9/11. Grit called me one day to see if I would accompany her on the big move as we drove from the Midwest to the Big City.

I helped move their belongings into a tiny fifth-floor walk- up in Brooklyn Heights. There was no doorman, the place was only 500 sq. ft., and all of this luxury only cost $1,250 a month rent in 2001. By comparison, $1,250 in Bloomington, IL, could get you a 4-bedroom townhouse. It was so small, I slept on the kitchen floor with my head by the refrigerator. At night, I would stand guard looking out for any cockroaches that would be encroaching into my territory. That was my first exposure to NYC, and it would leave a lasting impression on this suburban boy.

The first six months of living in NYC were very hard for Grit. She sold her car to help pay the rent. Most people take the subway into the city to work anyway, so she really didn't need it anymore. She stuck out like a sore toe. She's nice and friendly and spoke differently, and you just can't be that way in New York City, she told me. People would steal her cabs, and homeless people would walk up and touch her long blond hair.

In NYC, Grit was determined to "make it," and as the saying goes, if you can make it there, you can make it anywhere. After getting her feet wet and trying out a few jobs that did not suit her, she interviewed and landed a role at Chelsea Piers Sport and Entertainment Complex, where she excelled and quickly climbed to the ranks of Executive Assistant and Manager of the Human Resources Department at the New York and Connecticut locations. For over 15 years, Grit also served as the administrator of the Sky Rink Youth Scholarship Fund, something she was very passionate about. She loved her career and loved the people she worked with even more. That's what kept her and her family in NYC. Very few people can actually say they love their work.

But this isn't just a story about a Midwestern girl who moved to the Big Apple and thrived. The real story is about how she was able to endure life while being hit with some of the roughest adversity you could possibly imagine, the type of things you wouldn't wish upon your worst enemy.

Bringing children into the world was a monumental task. Grit had several miscarriages along the way and also dealt with the ups and downs of multiple IVF procedures. Then one day, she and her husband Jim were blessed with the ultimate gift: twins.

Joy quickly turned to tragedy however when at 21 weeks, they lost both of their twins and had to deliver them. Talk about a punch in the gut. But the experience would not define her, and she still endured the IVF procedures even after all the miscarriages and delivering stillborn twins.

Eventually, after five years of these ups and downs, their first child, Mason, was born. Grit's path was not easy or free from pain and hardship. But her resiliency gave her the two most precious things in her life: her two boys, Mason and Damon.

As if dealing with the roller coaster of fertility issues weren't enough, she would soon face a much tougher enemy. In 2014, just 4 months after giving birth to her second son, she found a lump in her breast while attending a friend's wedding in Mexico. She started an aggressive chemotherapy treatment right before Christmas with her final round ending in April.

Through tests, it was discovered that she carried the breast cancer gene, similar to her aunt, who had unfortunately passed away from breast cancer at age 57. Due to the fact that she was a carrier of the gene, she decided to have a double mastectomy a couple of months later along with breast reconstruction surgery.

After her surgery, she acquired an infection that put her back in the hospital, and to top it all off, a tissue expander that was implanted didn't work and needed replacing. What was supposed to *only* be two surgeries turned into four. After this was all done, she had radiation to minimize her cancer risk afterward.

Grit was cancer-free for two years, but then it came back with a vengeance. Cancer had metastasized to other areas of her body including the liver, bone, and spleen. She qualified for a new trial at NYU for a chemo and immunotherapy treatment. After three months of the trial, she noticed a slight haze in her vision. A brain MRI soon confirmed the worst: she had lesions on her brain. She underwent Gamma knife radiation treatments to eliminate the spots on her brain. Grit loved her work and the people she worked with so much that she was back to work a day after brain surgery. I mean really? That's freaking incredible.

Her dedication to her work was unparalleled, largely because she viewed her coworkers as family. A story that left me dumbfounded occurred about 10 days before she finally passed. Part of her job as head of Human Resources was to host award ceremonies for staff. There was a luncheon for 30–40 people lined up with speakers. This was *her* lunch, and she wanted to put it on, but she was also getting closer to her end of life. She had been dealing with all the side effects of being on powerful steroids, and her face was so puffy you wouldn't recognize her. She turned a blind eye to vanity and still showed up to the luncheon and didn't care what she looked like. These were *her* people, and she wanted to be with them. Talk about determination!

My last story that I'll share from her life shows you her character.

After work one evening, she and some of her coworkers stopped by a watering hole for some adult beverages. As the story goes, someone from the company had too much to drink and must have been making a fool of themselves. A small group congregated and stood around discussing what they should do . . . which was pretty much nothing at all. Grit did something uncommon. She found her coworker's bag, dug out her cell phone, and called her parents in the middle of the night while introducing herself as the Human Resources manager of Chelsea Piers. She calmly informed them that their daughter would not be coming home that night and would be okay and staying at a friend's house. Grit knew how to take care of business.

Even with the struggle of cancer and the terrible side effects of her treatments, she made time to put her family and friends first. Whether it was planning birthday parties or coming into town for a visit, she would have everything scheduled. She lived for her family and especially her two sons. Knowing that her days on this planet were numbered, she became determined to live long enough that her boys would remember her as their loving mother. Her advice to anyone fighting for their life is to never give up and keep fighting. A lot of this is your attitude, and you must be positive. It's easy to get consumed by the negativity, and it's okay to give yourself a little grace. But the trick is to pull yourself out of the negative space and get back in the fight.

Grit's name is Krista Jo Bugenhagen (Ritter was her maiden name). She was my cousin, a mother, a wife, a sister, a daughter, a friend, and many other things to many other people.

If you were lucky enough to know her, then you know how strong she was, and you would never know all of the adversity and pain she lived with day in and day out. I'd never seen or heard of someone who could remain so positive who had been dealt such a bad hand time and time again.

God called Krista home on December 13, 2018.

The challenges that Krista faced her last four years were difficult, but she faced them with grit, resiliency, and determination. Her faith, her family, and her friends gave her the strength to fight. As she would say, "You never know how strong you are until strong is the only thing you have left."

Her friend Debbie got to spend some precious moments with Krista during her last days. They talked a lot about her fears. Planning confirmations, birthday parties, her boys spending time with her brother Matt, and of course her parents and her husband Jim. As she listed out these things, what eventually came out was her fear of being forgotten. Not for what she was in the last years of her life, but for what she was for *all* the years of her life.

Krista, you may be gone, but your spirit lives on. It was an honor to know you, and you inspired more people than you'll ever know. *Legends never die.*

I want to share a poem that my cousin Angie shared with Krista because she exemplified the words. It's written by a cancer survivor named Mark Nepo, and it's entitled, "Free Fall."

> *If you have one hour of air and many hours to go, you must breathe slowly.*
> *If you have one arm's length and many things to care for, you must live freely.*
> *If you have one chance to know God and many doubts, you must set your heart on fire.*
> *We are blessed.*

Every day is a chance. We have two arms. Fear wastes air.

CHALLENGE

Find Your Energy Drinks.

Think about the last time you faced what seemed like impossible odds. You might have just lost your job. Maybe the economy is tanking, and you're wondering how you will feed your family, or perhaps you've even had to bury a loved one. Or maybe it's something smaller, such as being thrown an impossible task at work with an unfair deadline, and your job depends on it. Or maybe you're running your first race, and halfway through, you realize you haven't trained enough, and you start doubting whether you can do it. Who or what do you think of when adversity strikes? Now I want you to make a list of people you admire and who motivate you. Think about those who have been dealt a bad hand and yet they continue to get back up with a smile on their face time and time again. Visualize what they look like in those moments, their facial expressions, their never-quit spirit. I want you to ingrain these images in your mind so that when you face tough times, these thoughts, ideas, emotions, and pictures will help interdict any negative self-talk. These images are your energy drinks and will help you to keep going, stay in the fight, and never quit during your most trying times. Remember, it could always be worse.

11

THE LONGEST NIGHT

"If you're gonna fight, fight like you're the third monkey on the ramp to Noah's Ark . . . and brother it's starting to rain."

—SOME RANDOM T-SHIRT

My boat crew quickly took a roll call and proceeded to hop into the white vans for an unknown destination with no ETA. The ride was especially horrible. I don't think I'd ever been so tired or dirty and thrown into a moving vehicle. We probably drove for 30 minutes tops, and the driver yet again had the windows up and the heater cranked on full blast. We were told not to talk or to fall asleep.

I tried to cope by thinking about my family and what they might be doing right then, but before I could get too deep into my own mind, the vans pulled off onto a gravel road. It was dark outside, but the moon provided exceptional lighting. I could make out a huge mountain in front of us. The vans quickly came to a stop, and the driver gave us five minutes to grab our rucksacks and two canteens from the back of the van and then line up in our boat crews.

With all of us in formation, a new team of cadre were ready to greet us. I was just getting used to the voices, yelling, and personas of the day crew, and we were going to be introduced to a fresh, sadistic cadre of night crew coaches.

We're so screwed. I figured we would be scaling that huge mountain tonight, and my intuition was spot-on.

The orders were simple: we were to hike to the top and bottom of the mountain in ten hours. *Ten hours?!* I thought. I wondered how far we would be moving tonight. Oh, and one more thing, this was to be a silent hike—meaning no talking unless spoken to by a coach.

No time to worry about that because we were told to examine our packs and make sure our sandbags were filled to the top. We were to carry 35–40 pounds this go-around. Then, we made our way to the hydration station (which was the back of a pickup truck), where we were to fill one canteen with water and the other with Gatorade. Last but not least, we had to carry a weapon. Not a real weapon but a piece of PVC pipe that was filled with sand and capped on both ends. The pipe was to resemble a rifle and probably weighed 7 pounds. Lastly, we tied chem lights onto the backs of each other's packs so we could see one another. We were to report to the base of the mountain in our boat crews once we had all of our gear in check and await the start of what was sure to be the longest night of our lives.

Each boat crew had two cadres with them at the start. One would lead. The other would stay at the tail end of our team to make sure no one fell behind. It was pitch black, and all we could make out were the chem lights, the moon, and stars.

At five-minute intervals, each boat crew were released up the hill. My team would be the last to go. While we waited, the cadre assigned to our team chatted with us about how the training was going. They told us that we should dominate this evolution since we were the Clydesdales, meaning we were bigger and could carry more load in proportion to our body weight. We would also have longer strides than people on the smaller teams.

When we were released, the lead cadre took off, and I decided to follow right behind him, weapon in one hand, canteens in my cargo pockets, and 40 pounds of sand on my back.

It didn't take very long before I noticed something that would add a tremendous amount of difficulty to what was already a tough evolution. Not only would we be walking with weight at night, and it would be difficult to see to find our footing, but the entire way up was 100% elevation, meaning there would be no flat ground until we reached the top. To add insult to injury, the terrain was terrible. Rocks were everywhere, and the ground was very choppy with uneven dirt tracks. We really had to pay attention to how our feet landed with every step. It was a complete mind game, having to think about our footing every single step up the mountain. One wrong move, and we could easily twist an ankle or fall.

It didn't take long for me to lose my sense of time, and I was completely caught up in the moment. I remember walking, concentrating on my steps, and trying to keep a good pace with the cadre. I would often look around and see the city lights far off in the distance or gaze up in the sky at the moon and stars, wondering what my family might be doing.

Early into the ruck, we came upon a truck with its tailgate open. It was a hydration station, and we stopped to fill our canteens. We were informed that we were off-pace already, and if we hoped to climb up the mountain and back down by sunlight, we would need to move faster.

Here we go, I thought to myself, *time for real fun*. No more leisurely walking.

My team hightailed it out, and we could see another team in front of us, their chem lights in plain view.

Our cadre told us to fixate on them and to catch them. We double-timed it, and within 45 minutes, we had not only caught up to them, but we had passed them.

I have to admit, passing the other boat crew put a huge smile on my face, but I also started to notice a couple of guys on my team were having trouble keeping up. After we passed the other boat crew, our lead cadre instructed me to fall in at the back of the line and bring my two struggling teammates up to the front.

Ideally, when moving in packs, you want your slowest people up front and your strongest in the back. It's harder to keep up from the back, and wouldn't you know it, that's where I was heading. It was harder, much harder.

When bringing up the rear, it's easy to feel completely alone (even though I had a coach by my side). I started to get distracted. My feet were beginning to hurt, especially my toes. They were getting smashed into the front of my boots from the rocky terrain. My shoulders were going numb from the straps on my pack, my arms were wearing out from carrying a weapon, and my legs were starting to cramp up. *Wait a minute, is that a neon sign in front of us for the In and Out Burger?* I started hallucinating and noticing things that weren't there, especially random colors all over the place.

Focusing on my "Why" and concentrating on breathing quickly brought me back to reality. I smiled at different points, too. It is amazing what a smile can do to change your attitude. I would smile as if to tell my friends and family back home, "You wouldn't believe what I'm doing right now. Oh, what a story it'll make!" (Little did I know it actually would be a book years later.)

After a few more hours, I saw something else—it was more lights, people. *Am I imagining things again?* Nope. It was the second hydration station, and we had caught up to another team.

At that point of the night, everyone was smoked and running on fumes. We'd been beaten down all day. We'd paid tribute to Murph, and we were hiking all night. A new low point in morale was definitely upon us. It wasn't that we were being screamed at or going full speed. Just the opposite: we were slower-paced but knew we had a long way to go. People get that feeling when running a marathon or participating in some other endurance sport and ask themselves, "Is this ever going to end?" Getting caught up in your own head is so easy to do since there's plenty of time to think, and your mind wanders.

As we filled our canteens at the hydration station, coaches came up with lights and examined our faces, especially our eyes, to see how we were doing. Just like earlier that night at the first hydration station, our coaches told us to fixate on the chem lights in front of us and to catch the other team. This go-around would be different, though.

Two of the guys in my 7-man boat crew were mentally checking out. The coach had examined them, and they must have not looked good. They wanted to quit. My coaches were trying to rally my guys.

Now, I don't know why, but without hesitation, I interrupted the conversation. It went something like "Hey, guys, no one quits at night; you can make it to sunrise."

The coaches looked at me. I'm not sure if they were glad I said something, or if they were like *Ritter, shut up, and who asked you to speak,* but they asked my two teammates if they could walk without the extra weight.

They both nodded their heads.

Then one of the coaches looked at me and said, "Guess what, Ritter. You get to carry their shit! Grab one of your teammates, and meet back here ASAP."

I thought, *What the hell did I just get myself into?* but then quickly realized I was being asked because I was one of the stronger guys in the group, at least in this evolution.

I ran over to my other teammates. "Hey, guys, we got a couple of folks that need some help. Who will volunteer with me to carry an extra backpack and weapon for a while?"

With hesitation, someone stepped up to the plate. I placed my own rucksack on my back, grabbed my new one, and placed it around my chest and torso. I then grabbed two weapons, one for each hand. I looked at my teammate who had volunteered just as I had, and we both had the same expression on our faces like *This isn't going to end well.* No time to waste. If we were going to catch that other team, we needed to leave ASAP.

I'm estimating that I had at least 80 pounds of gear on. Every step I took, I swear, my calf muscles wanted to burn up and shrivel into nothing. Just as before, the slower guys in my team would be at the front (I hoped getting their second wind soon), and I was at the back with my other buddy, who was in just as much pain as I was. Time stood still. Every step I took, and I mean every single step, hurt like hell. The added weight really slowed me down; it was taking everything I had just to keep up.

One of the coaches asked if I was okay.

I replied with a Hooyah and then asked if he would reach in my cargo pants and grab my canteen and give me a drink. Since I was holding two weapons, I couldn't grab it and go.

He complied.

Then I remember seeing the summit. *Yes*! I thought. *We are almost to the top. That's quicker than I thought it would be.* Being that close to the top of the mountain gave me renewed energy, and I got stronger immediately with this newly found motivation.

As we drew closer to the summit, it seemed to drag on for days. *Shouldn't we be there by now?* I glanced over and asked my teammate. As we rounded the corner, defeat immediately was upon my face.

It was a false summit.

Oh, my God! I said to myself in anger. *Now I have false summits to deal with?* Failure—that's exactly what was starting to enter my mind. I didn't know how much longer I could hold on. I'd never been pushed this far physically and mentally, and the load I was carrying was really taking its toll on my body and psyche.

We continued the march up the mountain. I started hallucinating again, but this time instead of bright colors, I was seeing and hearing stuff that just wasn't there—bears, people, rocks, you name it. I was hurting bad but noticed a silhouette in front of me. I reached in my pocket for some money. I couldn't locate any, so I asked the coach next to me for a dollar.

"Ritter, what do you need a dollar for?"

"For the vending machine over there."

"Ritter, you're losing it. Better get yourself together."

Apparently, I thought I saw a snack shack up ahead and wanted to get a drink.

I kept walking. I saw more lights, and this time, those lights were real. It was another hydration station. I walked up and immediately tossed both packs and weapons on the ground, eager to refill my canteens. Taking 80 pounds of extra weight off feels amazing, and at that point, my shoulders were numb not only from the weight but from the shoulder straps cutting into my muscles, nerves, and tendons.

Wait a minute, what's this in my pocket? I reached into one of my cargo pockets, and there it was (no, it wasn't a dollar). Was I dreaming? What a sight for sore eyes. I had placed a protein bar and some energy gels in my pockets earlier in the day for a dire moment. Well, this was my moment. I gobbled down the protein bar and energy gel. I had two more gels left and purposely saved them for another time that I would surely need them that weekend. I instantly felt a little bit better and had an extra skip in my step.

I walked back over to my team. Everyone was quiet. Our two guys who were thinking about quitting were still on the verge, and we could tell that by their body language. I walked over to them and told them to hang on; we had to be close to the top, and to focus on their "Why."

"We'll carry your gear to the top for you," I told them. My buddy and I grabbed our double load and got ready for the rest of the climb. This part of the ruck was a little different. I knew what to expect from the extra weight, plus I had eaten a protein bar and an energy gel for a bonus.

We proceeded up the top of the mountain. That extra skip in my step vanished quickly. We had reached another freaking false summit. I felt like I was in the movie *Groundhog Day* where the main character, Phil Connors, played by Bill Murray, lives the same day over and over again. We would walk feverishly to what we thought was the top of the mountain only to be wrong. We encountered about ten false summits that night, each one its own painful reminder that it would surely be the longest night of our lives.

I was still at the back of the pack and could tell my pace was starting to slow. I asked the coach next to me if I could go to the front of the line so I could try to catch a break, and he nodded his head to signal "no problem." I sped up and took my spot at the front of our group, right behind the lead coach which gave me a little reprieve.

At this point in the night we had to be getting close to the top of the mountain, false summits and all. Somehow, we had caught up with the team in front of us. Both teams reached the next hydration station at the same time.

I dropped my load just like I had done before, but this time one of the coaches called me over. "Ritter, we're not going to make you carry a double load all night and punish you for some of your teammates not putting out. Go join that other team. They are faster than we are, and I don't want to ruin your experience here." "Hooyah," I replied and jogged over to join the other team. To be honest, I was relieved; I don't know how much longer I could have gone with the double load. I hustled over to join my new squad. After dropping 40-plus pounds, I felt like a new man.

The new boat crew I was a part of was great. Everyone was smiling and enjoying themselves, unlike the team I had previously been on. It's amazing what you can endure with a smile on your face. Within ten minutes, we could see the chem lights of the second-place team in front of us. One of the new coaches suggested that we should double-time our pace and catch them.

"Hooyah," we all replied, and we picked up the pace. In no time, we were passing the other team.

I was "in the zone" as some people might say, or in a state of flow. Although I was beaten, battered, and pushed farther than I ever thought possible, the evolution was starting to become sort of fun in a weird, demented way. By my calculation, we were in second place with only one more team to catch, and I could just barely make out a chem light from the person bringing up their rear. As we moved around the bend, we came upon another potential summit. Like the last, it was false. Instead of feeling rejected, I was pissed off and had turned my frustration into aggression. I turned to my new team and cadre and said, "Let's pass these punks." We all dug in deep, and with a reserve tank of premium gas, we made an all-out charge toward the team in front of us. Within minutes, not only did we catch up to them, but we also passed them. I don't think they could believe what they were seeing. Frankly, I don't know how we did it, either. We were in first place, and there was no way we were going to relinquish our position. Each person we passed gave us energy.

We kept the heat on for another couple of minutes to give some space between us and the second-place team. We slowed down to a walk, and all of us hydrated from our canteens. As we walked and were rejoicing in our small victory, we came across another bend on the mountain, and as we turned, we couldn't believe our eyes. "It's the damn summit!" Finally, after all of the marching, we had reached the top of the mountain.

There were a couple of coaches at the top wearing lights waiting for us. You wouldn't believe the instant joy that was on all of our faces. We'd done it! We had reached the top. We couldn't wait to take a much-needed breather, sit down, and get some more refreshments.

We decided to finish strong and slow jog to the coaches. Within minutes, we reached them. Surely, we were going to be rewarded. After all, it pays to be a winner, right? Joy quickly turned to instant heartache.

The coaches started yelling and ordered us not to rest but to run around them and head back down the mountain before the sun came up. I couldn't believe it. There would be no rest, no hydration, no reward.

Our gift for being the first team to reach the summit was that we were the first team to charge down the mountain. I mean, we didn't even get a chance to admire the view from the top. I was furious and dejected all at the same time. It was as if we had just crossed the finish line at a half-marathon race only for them to tell us to turn around and run it all over again.

I was toast, smoked, done, and felt like I had nothing in the tank. As my team and I made our way down the mountain, our two coaches told us that the race was still on, and there would be a reward for the first few who made it to the next checkpoint.

What happened next I simply couldn't believe. Instead of finishing as a team, we were ordered to charge down the mountain as fast as possible, every man for himself. After spending half the night climbing a mountain, it was a race to the bottom!

I charged down that mountain like a deranged lunatic, a man truly possessed, and I wasn't going to stop. I was using visualization techniques and imagined I was the mutant Wolverine from the X-Men series running down the mountain. If I had claws made of adamantium, they were out in full force. Saliva was erupting from my mouth with every exhale. I blew past my teammates and never saw them again. Each one I passed, I imagined taking their energy and life force with me.

The only thing I was focused on was finding the next checkpoint. Nothing else mattered. My toes were getting smashed in the front of my boots due to the downhill jog, and the rocky terrain sure didn't help. I didn't care. It was an all-out assault, and I had one thing on my mind—that damn checkpoint. I rounded a corner and saw what I thought I was looking for: the all-too- familiar white van.

"Ritter," one of the checkpoint cadre yelled at me, "nice work. It pays to be a winner. Put your rucksack in the back of the van."

"Hooyah," I yelled, rejoicing in my first-place finish. Not one of my teammates was in sight.

The entire weekend, I had been the gray man, so to speak— never first but never last, just sort of in the middle blending in. It felt good to be finishing first, and I couldn't wait to dump my ruck and weapon in the back of the van. I placed my hand on the back door and proceeded to open it when—pop, pop, pop, pop, pop—I was suddenly greeted by a coach in the back seat of the van shooting me with paintballs!

"You're dead, Ritter. Lie down on the ground, play dead, and wait for the rest of your class.

What the hell is going on? Was I hallucinating again? Not this time. My chest had neon green paint splattered all over and welts where I'd been hit. I did as instructed and played dead. "Coach, can a dead man have a drink from my canteen?" I was dying of thirst.

"Hooyah," he said. I sat on the ground, which was the first time I had sat down since the van ride over there. It felt amazing.

One by one, the rest of my team finished.

I watched a couple of them getting shot as well. It was hilarious to see their reactions and listen to their screams. I was laughing my butt off. I had lost all sense of time but knew that it was in the wee hours of the morning due to the tiny sliver of light protruding from the sky. I sat there for what seemed like an eternity, and I soaked up every moment of it. I began doing some basic stretching, butterflies, touching my toes, runner's stretches, etc. because I could feel my legs tightening up. I continued watching other teams finish and filling their canteens back up at the truck. I bet they were wondering why only a few of us were sitting on the ground covered in green paint. I was, too.

The cadre asked for a team leader, and someone volunteered. It was time for a roll call, which makes sense because we'd been broken into boat crews to start and then it had become an every- man-for-himself scenario. The class leader asked that all men sound off, but a coach next to me specifically told me not to say anything.

The class counted "One, two, three," and so on. The class reached the magical number 27. The class leader told the cadre that we had 27. The cadre asked how many did we start with?

He guessed: 30? 32? 31? He didn't know for sure.

The cadre lit him up in front of the class. "How can I expect you to lead a team if you don't even know how many are in your group? I ask again, how many did you start with? Get it right, or your whole class pays the price."

I don't even remember how many people we started with and had no clue how many were left. The new class leader didn't have a clue, either. When asked what his final answer was, he replied, "I don't know."

This really pissed off the cadre, and he continued to rip our leader a new one. "You started with thirty-five. Three of your teammates have already quit, and the other five are now dead. Here's what we're gonna do, class. Since you obviously can't count, we're gonna play a game. See your teammates on the ground? As a boat crew, you will carry your fallen teammate all the way down the mountain the rest of the night on those stretchers over there." I glanced over in the direction of the trucks, and sure enough, there lay several seven-foot-long military-grade drab olive gurneys (these are referred to as litters). One by one, each team walked over and grabbed a litter and then proceeded to make way toward a wounded or, in my case, "dead" teammate.

The Smurf boat crew somehow ended up standing next to me.

One of the coaches made a smart-aleck remark and said, "This will be fun, watching the smallest team carry one of the biggest dudes."

I started shuffling to move myself onto the stretcher.

A coach piped up and said, "Ritter, what the hell are you doing?

You're dead. Play dead."

So I complied and took my place on the ground and made sure not to move.

The Smurf crew placed their hands under my legs and torso and then picked me up. I could hear the fatigue in their voices—I was 200 pounds of dead weight. They gently placed me on the stretcher, if you call dropping me like a log "gentle." They tucked my ruck between my legs and placed all of the team's weapons, making a total of seven including my own, on top of me. That made for a total of about 300 pounds of dead weight with me, my ruck, and all the weapons.

"The boat crews are to make it down the mountain with their casualty and gear before sunup. As with anything, this is a race, and it pays to be a winner."

"Hooyah" everyone shouted in unison. "One–two–three, bust em!

My team picked me up, which must have been like deadlifting a Volkswagen Bug. Tired from the 13 or so miles we already rucked, they hoisted me above their heads and placed me on their shoulders. It was a rocky ride above their shoulders. But to my surprise, my team stabilized the litter, and my sudden fear of being thrown onto my head turned into nothing short of a Zen- like feeling.

I was lying on my back being carried like an Egyptian king. A calm came over me like I hadn't felt before. I began thinking about the weekend, the training I had put in, how far I'd come, all of the evolutions we'd been through up to that point, my class, the coaches. Everything hit me all at once. It was surreal. Had it all been a dream? It was like an out-of-body experience and hit me emotionally like I hadn't been hit in a very long time, if ever. I was completely consumed by the sheer magnitude of the moment.

While my team carried me, I gazed up at the sky and was lost in the moon and stars, wondering what Leslie, Hallie, and Brody were doing. I couldn't remember the last time I just looked up at the sky to watch the stars and moon without a care in the world. I used to love looking for shooting stars when I was a kid. *I could be anywhere in the world*, I thought, *and I'm right here, on some mountain I've never heard of with people I only just met several hours ago.* I was calm, present, and in a deep meditation-like trance.

My daydreaming was finally interrupted by someone shouting on a megaphone. I thought I was imagining things again, but my nightmare was true.

My team carried me to a landing zone and put me down. I rolled off the stretcher and stood up. I felt dizzy for a split second since I hadn't been on my feet for over an hour.

A white truck that had housed the litters in the bed had music playing from giant speakers.

The coach with the megaphone ordered us to stand in formation with our rucks on and our weapons in hand. Right there on the mountain, we were ordered to run in place with our weapons above our heads. Normally, this wouldn't have been a big deal, but we were all dog tired. We ran in place for 60 seconds at a time with a 30-second rest in between. It was terrible. I got to the point where I could hardly lift my feet.

Next, the song "Roxanne," by the band Police, came on the speakers. Each time we heard the name Roxanne, we had to do a burpee with our backpack and weapon. By the way, that's a total of 26, and we had to do them as fast as Sting would sing it. That is easier said than done. Apparently, my class couldn't keep up, so the instructors made us do it again, and again, and again until we got it right.

Last but not least, the Moby song "Flower" came on the speaker. I have to admit, I wasn't familiar with the song, but I can assure you I'll never forget it as long as I live. In it, the lead singer chants, "Bring Sally up and bring Sally down," and every time we heard that, we would perform an air squat with our weapon held above our head, and hold the squatting position until Moby said, "Bring Sally up." We performed these pause squats each and every time those words were cued up, which amounts to about 30 times—a complete killer. Those two songs will forever be etched in my memory, and even when I hear them on the radio or out and about with friends, it still brings a smile to my face.

After our calisthenics break, we got back to carrying our "casualties." The coaches told us that we would race (everything is a competition) down the mountain. This time, however, I would be replaced by someone else on my boat crew.

We started marching down the mountain. I could tell we were getting closer to the base, and we had to be getting close to our objective... the sun would be coming up soon.

Within minutes, my right shoulder had gone numb from carrying the litter. The metal pole was digging into my clavicle, and there was zero padding. It didn't matter. There was no padding to be found. I actually thought that carrying two rucksacks was easier than the gurney. It flat-out sucked. I was at the back of the stretcher, too, so I couldn't really see what was in front of me.

Pretty soon my team had to place our stretcher onto the ground and readjust. I couldn't wait to switch sides so I could get the feeling back in my shoulder. We repeated the maneuver of walking ten minutes or so and then placing the stretcher on the ground to readjust. The problem was, we were in last place, and the other teams were smoking us down the mountain. Could it be our weight?

I suggested that I stay back and carry all of the weapons down the hill while the team carried our casualty. I loaded up seven pieces of PVC pipe, which probably weighed 35 pounds or so. I carried them in the front rack position, and things were going pretty well, but my arms were quickly wearing out, and the pipes were getting hard to hold onto.

Within five minutes, I was toast and started dropping the weapons. I yelled at my team to hold up, and I quickly placed all of the weapons back on the stretcher and resumed my spot carrying the load. My idea of carrying the weapons separately turned out to be a terrible decision. We loaded the weapons back onto the stretcher with our casualty.

One of the coaches by our side told us we needed to pick up the pace and to not put the stretcher down on the ground anymore. Did I just hear him correctly? We can't place this stretcher down on the ground for the rest of the trip! How are we going to do this? Then it hit me: what we should have been doing was to have the men switch sides by walking under the stretcher as we carried it along. That way we'd never really stop and have to lift the wounded back up, which wastes valuable time and energy. It would be much quicker but would also involve more choreography. We could only have folks switch spots two at a time, and they would need to do it quickly so the others wouldn't drop the load. That also forced us to start communicating better as a team. We'd been relatively quiet for the most part unless someone spoke up about needing to switch sides.

We began communicating as a team and updating each other on how we were feeling, and if someone needed to switch out, they would just shout out the last name of the teammate they were switching with and get the job done on the fly. It was working like magic. Our pace had increased significantly, but we caught onto this trick too late.

As we inched closer to the base of the mountain, the sun started to poke its way over the horizon. It was a magnificent sight. The light bouncing off the clouds produced a hue of blues and pinks. With every step we took, we could feel the warm rays of the sun. It was poetry in motion to us and instantly gave our team a renewed sense of energy.

I did it! I remember thinking. I made it through the first day and got to see the sun come up, which was one of the goals I'd set for myself. My main goal, of course, was to complete the mission. But I had set two micro goals in between. The first was to take every bit of punishment the coaches could throw at me for the first few hours of Breakout. The second was to make it one full day, and I believed if I could make it 24 hours, then I could surely do another full day. I mean, what's another 24+ hours, right?

I had never pushed myself that far, and I was still rocking. Sure, I was tired, but I was mentally in the game, and that's what counts the most.

But back to reality.

We were only closing in on the halfway mark of the entire weekend, and we needed to finish this evolution strong. As we progressed, we could see the vans lined up alongside the truck, and all the other teams were waiting on us to finish.

We jogged up to the finish line and were relieved that the evolution was over. It had kicked our butts. We placed the litter down on the ground.

"Not so fast," said one of the coaches. "This was a team event, and your team finished last. There must be a punishment."

The wind was immediately taken out of my sails. I was thinking to myself, *What more could they possibly throw at us?*

The winning team was brought to the front of the class. On cue, they all said, "It pays to be a winner," and the rest of us could only watch as they got to sit down and start eating a nice breakfast of MREs. How demoralizing, but there wasn't any time to sulk about it since the next order was to pick our litters back up.

Just then, three people from my class stepped forward and quit right then and there. Two were from my original team, one of whose loads I had spent most of the night carrying.

I was livid. What a selfish thing to do. If they were going to quit, they could have at least done it 10 hours earlier, so I didn't have to carry their load all night. Those three teammates were escorted into one of the vans. I still couldn't believe what I was witnessing—to make it that far and quit after the sun comes up? Who does that?

With no time to worry about it, we immediately picked up our litter. We had another game to play. Relay races were up next.

All in all, we ended up rucking close to 26 miles that night. Plus my team had to play a few extra games of relay races with the litter, which was pretty terrible. My body was beaten up. But I looked around at the rest of my team. They were all in the same condition. *If they can do this, so can I.* I sat down next to my swim buddy O'Kipney. "What's up, brother? How was that night for you?"

"Terrible," he replied.

"Hooyah, brother... terrible." I opened my MRE and ate that sucker in like five minutes flat. I wondered what they had in store for us next.

PACK YOUR RUCKSACK

False summits are everywhere.

I'm not a rock climber, and I don't have access to mountains here in Indiana, but the psychological effects of false summits can be found everywhere in life. And the biggest ones are in our own heads.

Think back to situations you've encountered where you reached the pinnacle only to find out there was more, or even worse, that the view from the top wasn't what you thought it was supposed to be. Perhaps you've been in situations at work where you've chased a job title and finally climbed the corporate ladder only to find out that once you finally "made it" and got a seat at the table, then you couldn't believe what you saw when you peeked behind the curtain. Picture Dorothy from *The Wizard of Oz* when she finally sees behind the wizard's curtain only to learn the truth. Or maybe you've been chasing retirement, and you finally reach it but realize you haven't saved enough money or you're not able to do the things you thought you would be doing in your golden years. Could be that now that you are "retired" and not punching that time clock, you've lost your mission, your purpose, your identity, or maybe you've let your health go and you aren't physically able to participate in things you once thought fun.

I find that most of the peaks in life are never that high, and the valleys are never that low; but if you stop growing and learning, you are slowly dying. And if you think there's a magical wizard behind a curtain, and he's going to save you and give you direction, you are wrong. You have to put in the work and create good days that stack on top of other good days, and before you know it, you'll be living the life of your dreams. It's not about getting to a certain title, salary, or even a fancy getaway.

It's all about keeping your perspective and enjoying the ride. I was fortunate growing up that my parents took us to Florida for a week-long vacation almost every year. We couldn't afford to fly a family of six, so we would all hop in the van for the 18-hour ride and road trip down south on I-65. We couldn't wait to make it to Florida, to smell the ocean in the air and feel that warmth coming off the sun, and to indulge in the local seafood cuisine. Once we arrived, the week would feel like a couple of days. As the saying goes, time flies while you're having fun. In what seemed like no time at all, we would be back in the van making the dreaded road trip home, tired, sunburned, and left with only memories.

As I grew older, I came to enjoy the journey home almost as much as I enjoyed getting to the destination. The fact was, we would be back home in Indiana in no time and be left with only our memories as we slid back into the reality of life. Vacations were fantastic, but some of my most treasured memories were the trips to get there... singing Golden Oldies songs on the radio, playing games, and even experiencing the smells from the back seat. Vacations are great, but like promotions and mountains, they can lead to false summits.

CHALLENGE

Create Your IDEAL Day.

Ralph Waldo Emerson and Aerosmith's lead singer Steven Tyler once said, "Life is a journey, not a destination." The more I learn and study, the more I figure out that I don't know much. Funny, isn't it?

You can train yourself to be resistant to false summits and start enjoying the journey instead of the destination. If all you're living for is that next position, that next vacation, or that next big thing, you will likely be feeling empty inside once you get there. It's all about changing your mindset and shifting your perspective.

My challenge for you here is to start enjoying each day and not just measuring your life by all the things you've accomplished or where you are going next. Sure, those things will come as byproducts, but be careful: they may also be false summits in disguise.

I want you to create your ideal day. Days can change like the seasons. For instance, if you're a CPA, then you know during tax season, you need to allocate more hours to your profession. But all things being equal, what would your *ideal* day look like? Here's a guide for you to follow.

First, make a list of your non-negotiables and assign a time how much time you want to dedicate to each. Some of mine are the following:

- sleeping (7-8 hours)
- eating (2-3 hours depending on meal prep)
- family time (2 hours through the week, lots more on the weekend)
- self-care (morning/evening rituals, spot drills, journaling, training etc.) Varies. Morning routine is 30 mins to 2 hours.

These are the things you can't miss or, if you do, you'd better have a good reason as to why. I didn't put work on here because that can fluctuate depending on the day or week, season, economy, etc. Here's the other thing: I don't really take weekends off, although I try to make Sunday a fun day. I don't *try* to work on weekends, but there *are* situations in which I put in extra time on Saturdays and Sundays to catch up. But the rest of my nonnegotiables I hit every day without question, and that includes working out. If you're sore, try active recovery on the weekend and go for a walk or get a massage. No excuses.

Next, set up time parameters for each one of these. In other words, determine the amount of time will be dedicated to each nonnegotiable. As for the rest of the day, you can fill in the gaps with the following formula I came up with: I.D.E.A.L.

> **I**—Important items or ways you are improving yourself such
>
> as studying an online course, learning to play an instrument, etc.
>
> **D**— Dollars/Dinero. What's your job, career, and/or side hustle (Got to make that money to support your family.)
>
> **E**—Essential items such as sleeping, eating, training (Most
>
> likely, your nonnegotiables will fit here.)
>
> **A**—Adaptable or flex time for things that may pop up during the day like picking kids up from school or running to the grocery store
>
> **L**—Low-Key things like reading, writing, taking a nap, meditation, spot drills during the day, time to reflect and be in silence If you watch TV, the "L" could be a big one for you. Take note of how many hours you are in front of the TV or another screen such as computer, phone, or tablet.

Once you've identified all of your tasks, set up time parameters around these. Experiment with what is working and what isn't. Get rid of or reduce the things that aren't beneficial to you, and increase the time or create the windows of opportunity to work on yourself now that you have some extra time from the fat that has been cut.

Over time, you'll create your own IDEAL day.

Just think of what life could look like if you were able to stack IDEAL day after IDEAL day on top of each other. In a couple of weeks, you'd have some new habits and rituals. In a couple of months, you'd notice some big changes. In a year, people wouldn't recognize you . . . and neither would you.

12

WATER, THE GREAT EQUALIZER (SATURDAY, JULY 25, 2015)

"Victorious warriors win first and then go to war, while defeated warriors go to war first and then seek to win."

—SUN TZU

After a quick MRE breakfast, we were ordered back into the vans. My legs felt like Jell-O. We loaded our rucks and weapons into the back of a pickup truck. I was relieved to be shedding all that extra weight. The previous night had taken its toll on me. I'd never been pushed that far before, well past the brink, past the comfort zone. I mean come on. I hallucinated and tried to put money into a nonexistent vending machine—and I wasn't on any drugs. I was getting extremely tired. If I wasn't moving, I was having a hard time concentrating and keeping myself mentally in the game.

One by one, we climbed into the vans, and we all had the same look on our faces. It was the look of being beat down.

Our driver rolled up the windows and threw on the heater once again. "No talking," he said, "and if I see anyone fall asleep, you will pay."

Here we go, I thought. Within minutes, I felt my head drop, and I was asleep.

My buddy nudged me on the shoulder to keep me awake. My head popped up, and I looked around, dazed and confused. I'd stay sitting and alert for a few minutes and then boom, my head would drop like a bag of rocks, and I'd be out again.

My buddies around me would take turns nudging me to get me to wake up.

I'd never physically been so tired before. Everything I tried to do wouldn't work. I'd try concentrating on breathing, on my family, on my teammates, but nothing was working. I even slapped myself in the face several times but to no avail. I kept falling asleep and waking up with a gentle poke in the back or nudge on the shoulder. It was the closest thing to being a narcoleptic that I could think of. I just couldn't stay awake, no matter how hard I tried. I couldn't tell you how long the trip was or if we stopped anywhere. This part of the weekend was a complete blur.

When the van came to a stop, we were back at the lake retreat and ordered to immediately get wet, so we all double-timed it and jumped in the lake. (Later I would find out that this area of California was called Vail Lake near Temecula). It felt good to be back, but everyone had one thing on their minds: What the hell was coming at us next?

As the night crew vanished, a familiar group appeared. It was the day crew that beat our butts the day before. They approached us, and we awaited our fate. Calisthenics, getting wet and sandy, running our tails off, all of those thoughts had entered my mind.

The head cadre addressed us. "Men, congrats on making it this far... very few can say they have accomplished this. But we're only halfway. Go over to your PT gear and change into new shorts, shirts, and shoes. You have ten minutes."

I glanced over at Coach McLeod, and we made eye contact and exchanged a smile along with a head nod as if to say, "I'm still here" and "Glad to see you made it through the night, bro." That was one of my goals. I remembered him telling me the day before that he hoped to see me the next morning, and sure as sunrise, I was there.

I often wonder what his first impression of me was. A 30-something corporate America type shows up on the grinder with slicked-back hair, smiling all the time, and is going to try to make it through this training. "Good luck, son." I came to really admire that man over the course of the weekend.

Shortly after we put on clean clothes and tennis shoes, one of the coaches told us we had 30 seconds to report in formation and wait for further instruction. We frantically put our gear away and made our way to the field.

For formation, they wanted us to face the lake (we always had to face the nearest body of water) and stand in a height line.

After shuffling ourselves around like first graders, we proceeded to count off: 1, 2, 3... the last person in line said 27. Wow, we're down to 27, and we're only halfway through the training.

Another coach addressed us. "Class, time for a little morning PT run. We'll be running to an undisclosed location, distance unknown. Run together as a group, and keep no more than five feet between you and the person in front of you."

"Hooyah!" the class shouted in unison. We filed in behind the lead coach as he took off and led us down a dirt trail. We did our best to keep pace and ran in a two-by-two formation.

Fortunately, the lead coach wasn't on a mission to break any world records. It was one of those nice and easy paces one would do on a long, slow recovery run. The problem was, none of us knew how long we would be running or where to. Looking back at that run now, it's clear that it was just a way to keep us moving to the next big evolution.

My swim buddy and I glanced at each other, a slight smirk to indicate how proud we were that we were still there and that we were still in the fight.

I could tell it was going to be a hot day. It was early morning, and the temp was already very warm. The sun felt great, and I was absorbing the rays of sunshine on the back of my neck, arms, and legs. I figured we ran about six miles.

POOL COMPETENCY

We ran to where the trail ended, and we could see a small building lined with a black iron fence that surrounded a large concrete area and swimming pool.

A swimming pool, oh, my God! we're going to have to swim, I thought to myself. I'm not a good swimmer. Sure, I can swim to save my life, but I suck when it comes to swimming for stroke and holding my breath underwater. I just sort of jump in the water and do my own thing, the problem being I'm not efficient, and I end up wasting more energy than I need to. Which is exactly what was about to happen.

Talk about the fear dog entering your mind. Water is my great equalizer. I was already starting to psych myself out. I watched as the coaches took their strategic positions in the pool. Some were in the water. Others were patrolling the sides of the pool on the concrete deck.

The coach who led us on the run ordered us to strip down to our skivvies and toss all of our clothes into one massive pile.

We undressed as quickly as possible, taking off our shirts, shorts, socks, and tennis shoes, and then throwing them all together.

The coach then politely instructed us, "Now hit the effing pool.

Don't walk. Run!"

We converged on the side of the pool and stood on the deck at attention.

A familiar coach greeted us. This guy was hard as nails and didn't mess around. He had a bald head and one of those stares that went right through you. "Time for some pool confidence training, boys. Hope you like not being able to breathe. Partner up."

My heart sank. I took a big swallow of some saliva. In my mind, I was already defeated. I lost before that battle ever even began.

We quickly partnered with whoever was next to us. Once in the water, we were to perform the movement that was yelled at us. First, one partner goes, and when he hits the other side of the pool, the other goes. My partner took off freestyle down the pool. When he was close to the other side, the coach told me to take off. I hit it hard out of the gate, trying to be the first one down and show that I was a strong swimmer. That was a mistake.

As soon as I hit the other end, I got about three seconds of rest before being ordered to do another lap. This continued for 10 laps. I never really got a chance to catch my breath and recover, plus as you know if you've spent any time in the water, breathing can be difficult, and if you aren't a smooth swimmer, you exert a ton of extra energy.

Next up was something called the combat sidestroke. I had never heard of it. A coach gave us a quick demonstration.

Looks easy enough, I thought, and it probably is a great stroke to master, but as I took off down the pool, my coordination was off, and I wasn't gliding effortlessly. Unfortunately, there wasn't time to slow down and learn it; we were in a crash course. I struggled to find the correct form. By the time we got to the fifth lap, I was smoked and was bringing up the rear every time. Not only was it bad because I started to bring unwanted attention, being toward last place every time, but I also no longer had a few seconds to catch my breath. As soon as I touched the opposite wall, I had to immediately head back in the other direction. This was by far my worst evolution so far, but I wasn't going to give up. *Screw it! either they'll kick me out of the pool, or I'm going to pass out and sink to the bottom*, I thought to myself.

After ten laps of the combat sidestroke, we were ordered to dolphin kick underwater. Luckily for me, the bald coach from earlier was in the water right next to me.

"Ritter," he yelled, "why aren't you keeping up with the rest of your class?"

"Coach, I don't know how to dolphin kick," I replied. "Ritter, do you not know how to effing swim?"

"Not really."

He quickly showed me the movement. "Hands by your side with your feet together and using your hips to kick your legs and move like a dolphin."

"Hooyah," I responded. I was incredibly slow at it, and it didn't help that I started about 15–20 seconds behind my class. I was struggling big time just to keep up. I was starting to get passed by my stronger teammates.

Doubt really started entering my mind. Could I keep up? *I'm now a liability to my team.* For me, pool comp was the equivalent of running wind sprints without a break. Somehow, I made it through the dolphin kick laps (I think I did about 7 when everyone else did 10).

"Okay, class, now we're going to tie your hands behind your back and tie your ankles together, and you will swim underwater to the other side."

I'm sorry, what did you just say? Nope. Ain't gonna happen! Before I could mutter those words, the coach said that in BUD/S, that's what they make you do in drown proofing, but for our purposes, he wanted us to just hold our hands behind our backs and keep our feet together and swim underwater to the other side, only touching the surface to take a breath. "But do not release your hands and legs from being together, or you will pay."

As I put my hands behind my back and secured my legs together, I took a big sip of air and submerged underwater, managing to dolphin kick about halfway down the length of the Olympic-sized pool. I had sunk to the pool floor and was quickly running out of air. Not being able to use my arms and legs to propel myself to the surface, I relied on my natural buoyancy to send me to the top, albeit at a snail's pace.

I reached the surface and inhaled but ended up taking in a mouthful of water instead. I immediately stood up and started coughing uncontrollably. I was going to throw up but didn't want to do so in the pool. So I jumped out of the pool and ran over by a chain-link fence and proceeded to talk to some bushes. The bald coach sent another coach to check on me and make sure I wasn't throwing up blood. Fortunately, I wasn't, and the coach came by and asked me if I was okay.

I replied with a very weak "Hooyah" and sat there for a few minutes, trying to catch my breath. I felt like the wind had been knocked out of me.

This had been the only time during pool comp that I could catch my breath in the 30–40 minutes we'd been at it. Then the coach helped me up and walked me over to a parked vehicle where there was a Gatorade cooler. I filled up a canteen and took a couple of big swigs.

The coach looked at me and said, "You look fine. Now get back in the fight."

"Hooyah!" I said and ran back into the pool to join my class.

On my way back, I noticed something that I hadn't before.

There was a small group of five guys who were getting smoked on the deck by a couple of coaches. *Goon Squad*, I immediately thought. *Thank God I'm not there.*

I hopped back into the pool close to the lane my swim buddy was using and awaited further instruction.

"Now we want you to perform the 'lifesaving' swim."

I was thankful that it was demonstrated since I had never heard of or seen it.

"You grab your 'injured' buddy and place him over your shoulder faceup while one of your arms is under his armpit. Push your hip into his back, and start swimming a one-armed sidestroke. Basically, this is like the combat sidestroke except now you have the weight of your swim buddy on your side."

I loaded my swim buddy onto my side and proceeded down the pool. It was very hard, and I was terrible at it. Had that been a real lifesaving scenario, we both would have died. I was concentrating on saving my buddy's life and was practically drowning myself and him at the same time. Somehow, I made it to the other side of the pool.

We took turns performing this movement another three times. Each time I performed the movement, I did get a little better as I was starting to figure out how to situate my buddy and keep myself afloat at the same time.

Next up, instead of loading our buddies on our sides, they grabbed onto our feet so we could pull them while using only our arms to keep us all afloat. We repeated this movement about five more times. I was completely wiped out, and there was no end in sight.

Next, our class was ordered to start from the far side of the pool and swim underwater the entire length of the pool.

I can't do that on a good day let alone right now, I thought to myself. When it was my turn, I took a deep breath and pushed off the pool wall underwater, gliding as far as I could. I concentrated on being streamlined and gliding underwater, then repeating the motion. It didn't matter. At the first sign of my body telling me that I needed to breathe, I caved.

I was nowhere near the other side of the pool and popped my head up above the water. I'd only made it halfway and was the first one to break the surface. It was the second time during the weekend that I failed at a breath hold. Pathetic. And of course, the first person I saw as I broke the surface was the bald-headed coach. He's the one who busted my chops back at the lake the day prior. Apparently, he thought my performance was lackluster and enough was enough.

"Ritter, out of the pool and report to the Goon Squad." "Hooyah," I replied.

Strange as it might sound, I was glad to be out of there. I was exerting way too much energy just trying to keep up with the rest of my class.

I made my way over to the concrete deck at the side of the pool where two coaches were waiting for me to join a suck fest already in progress. I immediately joined in the fun, which at that point was flutter kicks.

What proceeded was the equivalent of our Breakout session when the journey first began Friday morning, only it was a condensed version made specifically for me and my five teammates. For the next 20–30 minutes, we were pushed nonstop with every calisthenics exercise imaginable as punishment for not being able to keep up with the team and being a liability.

I didn't care. I was happy as hell to be out of the pool. Burpees? *No problem.* Plank holds for minutes on end? *Bring it.* Hundreds of flutter kicks? *Easy day. Let's do it!* I was just glad to be out of the water.

Soon the rest of the class must have made the cadre happy because the swim lessons were over. They were relieved and ordered out of the pool.

We, on the other hand, continued with our punishment. We had to perform calisthenics for another 10 minutes while the rest of the class relaxed and rehydrated. After it was beaten into our heads that the Goon Squad was not a good place to be, we were allowed to join the rest of the class and hydrate.

I made my way toward the Gatorade counter, filled up my canteen, and began drinking when one of the cadres said, "Class, follow me, you're not done yet."

What?! I've barely had a drink and was starting to get my wind back from having the snot kicked out of me. Now what are we going to do?

YOU FAIL

We made our way back to a grassy knoll where earlier we had disrobed and thrown our clothes together in a huge pile. Our next instructions seemed like an impossible task at the time.

"Class, I want everyone to have their gear back on and squared away in five minutes. If even one of you has a uniform infraction, the whole class will pay. Understood?"

"Hooyah!" the class replied. "Get after it!"

And we were off. Now, the smart way to handle this task would have been to have a handful of us dive into the team gear and begin sorting it while calling out the names that should have been written on the gear, then pass the items out in an orderly fashion. This was a simple exercise in leadership. Who was going to take charge?

As I said, that would have been the smart way. Unfortunately for us, we didn't seem to be taking the hints that the cadre were throwing at us. The only way to make it thru the weekend would be to work as a team and not as individuals.

Instead of working together, everyone made a mad dash for the pile of gear and was hell-bent on finding their own stuff. The result was that most of us were lucky enough to find our shirts, but finding our socks and shoes... forget about it.

As the five-minute timer went off, only a handful of our team had their entire uniform squared away. The rest of us were done for. "You fail." The lead cadre took to the ground and got into push-up position, keeping his head up to see that we were following along. Not a word was said, and no orders were given. He then proceeded to do push-ups.

Were we supposed to follow along? The class all looked around at each other with a puzzled look not knowing exactly what we should be doing. After the coach made it to five, we all began doing push-ups along with him.

He stopped at 10, took to his knees, and just simply looked at us. Again, not a word was said.

After a few breaths, he went back into push-up position and started doing push-ups.

This time, we all joined in. We were all trying to keep up and follow along.

After another 10, the coach took to his knees again, looked at us, took a few breaths, and resumed push-ups again. This process took place for what I'm guessing had to be about an hour, and during that time, not a single word had been said. Somewhere around 200 push-ups, I broke and could no longer do a set of 10 straight through. I thought the hammer would be thrown down on me, but it never came. I looked around using my peripheral vision and could see my other teammates were all on the struggle bus with me. What's the point of this? To do push-ups until we break?

The lead coach just kept repeating the push up sequence and then taking a short break before starting over again.

Then something changed. Coach did nine push-ups for a few rounds, then eight, then seven, and so on. Thank God, because I could no longer perform the 10 straight. After several rounds of doing between five and seven push-up sets, the coach was decreasing the reps again, and we made it all the way down to sets of one rep. All that time, there wasn't a single word being spoken by anyone.

Finally, after what seemed like an eternity of doing push- ups, our class performed one push-up in complete unison to the coach's satisfaction.

"Well, it's about damn time," he said. "All I wanted was for the class to come together as a team and perform one push-up together. Instead of doing one, it took you all five hundred to get that point across. Learn from this."

LOW POINTS

After our lesson on teamwork, we were allowed to take a short break and hydrate. The coach who had led us on our morning PT run presented himself before us. "Time to head back to base camp," he said.

And just like that, we were off on another six-mile run. My mental state was at an all-time low. During that run, I was knee- deep in my own quicksand of negativity, and even though I was there with a team, I felt all alone.

It's hard to explain, and looking back, I don't think it was that big of a deal, but at the time, I was really struggling with my weaknesses and felt that I could be a liability to the team as the day wore on. I'd been in the Goon Squad, and I was beating myself up about it. I was starting to feel heavy fatigue setting in as well, and my hunger pains were being sent out to all corners of my body. Mentally, it was one of my lowest points of the weekend so far. I had a quick pep talk with myself and interdicted the negativity by telling myself, *Stop it, I got this, easy day! Look how far I've come.* I swore to myself I wouldn't let that happen again. I would not let fear take over my thoughts.

Once we arrived back at home base at Vail Lake, what greeted us was the one thing that makes everyone smile—*food!* Only it wasn't an MRE. It was *real* food! To my surprise, there was a taco bar awaiting my class set up underneath a shady tent. That was much needed and a blessing in disguise. Amazing what a little food combined with rest and relaxation does for the human psyche.

I felt myself getting stronger with each bite of food, and the pity party I was throwing myself vanished. I looked around at my team. Every one of us was experiencing the exact same thing, and it was up to each person to determine how he was going to respond to it. That's one of the very few things I still had control over—my choice.

You choose how to respond in any given situation. You choose to swallow your pride and ask for help or to suffer all alone. You choose whether you're going to put out and give it everything you have or leave a little in the tank. I decided, *From now on, I choose to be positive and to be the best teammate I can be. I choose to win*!

PACK YOUR RUCKSACK

First, win in your mind.

Winning in your mind is the first premise that Mark Divine teaches in his Unbeatable Mind Academy. Sounds easy enough, but it's not, and it requires you to look deep inside yourself and do the daily work needed to examine your mindset.

So how do you consistently practice winning in your mind?

Remember that morning ritual challenge I tossed your way? It starts there. Your morning sets the tone, and if you adopt some sort of meditation, sacred silence, or breathing practice, it will have a dramatic impact on your life. It is your time to go deep into your own mind and practice awareness, focus, being present, remaining calm, letting go, etc.

Focus on your mission of the day or the one thing you need to get done. Visualize yourself completing the most important tasks of the day. What does it look and feel like? What are the emotions associated with it? This is powerful stuff and takes a lifetime to master. But don't worry, I'll teach you a simple breathing practice that will cut your learning curve in half with the next challenge.

For some reason, meditation can have a stigma around it. It did for me, and I felt stupid when I first starting practicing. I had to experiment to figure out what worked for me. And after finding my rhythm and making it a consistent practice, I started noticing things, such as being more present around my family, not as quick to fire off with reactions, and even having a decrease in my high blood pressure. This whole breathing thing... it flat-out works.

What happens when negative thoughts enter your head, and your self-dialogue gets contaminated as it did to me in the pool? That's the real reason I failed that evolution. I could have kept up with the pace, but mentally I was sabotaging my own success.

We've all had situations like that in our lives, whether it be before a big game, asking someone out on a date, or getting ready to present to a client or audience. Our minds have the advantage over us and, if left unchecked, will be free to roam around all over the place. This has been referred to as your monkey mind.

Here's a tactic from Mark's teachings that will help you short- circuit your negative thought loops. It's called the WIRM. It stands for Witness, Interdict, Redirect, and Maintain.

- Witness your thoughts, and if negativity shows up, then,
- Interdict those thoughts with a Power Statement such as "Stop this," or "Not today."

- Redirect your thoughts to something positive such as your "Why" or purpose for being there and combine it with powerful imagery, something that motivates you.

- Maintain your new mental state with a jingle or mantra. I have several depending on the situation. It could be a few words or reciting a song/poem/etc.

CHALLENGE

Breath Work.

For this challenge, I want you to focus on your breath throughout the day. Take notice if you are breathing through your nose or your mouth. Are they deep breaths, or are you taking short, shallow breaths most of the time? Pay extra attention to your breathing when you are talking to someone, working, training, or playing a game. I find that when we start to feel stressed, our breathing is the first thing that alters, and we typically hold it and don't breathe at all, or we allow it to become very shallow.

This next part is for those who are new to meditation or don't have a consistent breath practice.

Introduce box breathing into your day. Box breathing is performed via the nose (no mouth breathing here) and is a practice where you inhale, hold, exhale, then hold for a certain amount of time. The standard is around five seconds, but if you need to decrease, that's okay. Just find something that works for you.

If you go with five seconds, the pattern looks like this:

Five seconds of inhaling, followed by a five-second hold, then exhale for five seconds, followed by a five-second hold. Remember this is all done through the nose. Repeat for at least five cycles at first. Once you get used to this pattern, experiment with the duration and length of the breath practice. I personally do this for between 10–20 minutes every day to start my morning.

Box breathing is definitely one of those things that needs to be practiced every day. You can also try using apps to help with the breath cycles and add different intentions during the practice. Unbeatable Mind has a great app that's actually called Box Breathing, and I highly recommend it.

Find what works for you. Box breathing has been my #1 secret weapon to managing stress in my life.

I challenge you to practice winning in your mind by box breathing for the next 30 days after you wake up as part of your morning ritual. Keep a journal handy for any thoughts and/or ideas that pop into your head. You'll thank me for this.

13

LOGS AND GAMES

"If you can't do the little things right, you will never do the big things right."

—WILLIAM H. MCRAVEN

After an amazing lunch, we were told to get into our boat crews. The directions were simple. We were to run over to a U-Haul truck, find a team log (picture a telephone pole that's about 10 feet long and weighs 300 pounds), carry that log back to the starting line, and await further instruction. We were given ten minutes to complete the task.

We quickly converged upon the U-Haul, and as you can imagine, it was chaotic. In reality, it didn't need to be. If we all worked as a team, we would have no problem making this time hack. The lessons I had learned previously were starting to kick in, and for some reason, part of the SEAL Creed entered my mind: "We expect to lead and be led. In the absence of orders, I will take charge, lead my teammates, and accomplish the mission. I lead by example in all situations."

We needed someone to lead the team. I quickly assumed the role. "Guys... guys... guys... listen up." I had their attention. "We all need to work together. I need a boat crew to hop into the U-Haul to help push the logs out, and another boat crew on the other end ready to receive them. The other crews will wait until it's their turn to pick up their team log. Once you have your log, wait until we're all set, and we'll move toward the finish line together as a class. Hooyah?"

"Hooyah!" was the response.

Alright, I thought to myself, *now let's get this show on the road.*

Within five minutes, as a team, we had all worked together, and each boat crew had their own log. It worked like clockwork. For the first time that weekend, I felt we were starting to come together as a unit.

You can do great things when you stop worrying about yourself and try to help those around you instead.

We all walked as quickly as possible with our 300-pound-plus logs toward the finish line, and the cadre gave us a grin.

"Very good. You finished this task in eight minutes flat. Great teamwork."

We were still holding the logs on our shoulders while the cadre continued, "Now for your next task. There is a course set up around the lake marked by orange cones. Your job is to carry your logs as a team around those cones. You will not be told how many laps, but this is a race, and it pays to be a winner. Questions?"

There were none. "Bust em!"

We were off.

As we walked with the log on our shoulders, my boat crew quickly discovered that this evolution was built for us. We were the largest guys there, so not only could we carry the heavy load efficiently, but we were also the tallest and could stride a farther distance with each step. I could feel and hear the other teams chasing us down, but that only fueled our engines and made us go quicker. As we made the turn for lap #2, Taco (one of the lead cadres) told us that we'd have to proceed around these cones another nine times for a total of ten laps.

"Ten laps? Are you freaking kidding me?" I said to the team. We all shook our heads with disgust.

One of my teammates yelled out, "There's no way, that's impossible."

Another one said, "We can't keep this pace up."

That's because we were already smoked from going hot out of the gate, and one lap was equal to about a mile. One mile is no problem unless, of course, you're under a 300-pound telephone pole.

We were starting to become a little unglued and worrying more about the end game versus the present.

"Let's just focus on this next lap and staying in first place," I said, trying to boost morale. "Remember, it pays to be a winner." As we made our way to the end of lap #2, we had a significant lead on the other teams. While that felt good, we were starting to slow down.

My legs felt heavy, like I was jogging in concrete cinder blocks, my shoulders were numb, and we had to switch positions under the log more frequently to reduce fatigue, similar to the litter races several hours prior.

Taco informed us that we had another eight laps to go, and he wanted to see if we could beat the pace that we had just set.

"Hooyah," we answered. As we closed in on our target, we shouted encouragement to each other. As we crossed the finish line first, Taco said, "Drop your log and relax, you're done. It pays to be a winner."

"Hell yes," I said to myself. As a team, we dropped the log and took seats on top of it, watching the other teams race.

One by one they'd trickle in, the look of disgust and pain all over their faces from the brutal evolution combined with seeing us relaxing and enjoying the moment. The last-place team ended up doing a total of five laps, which is half the distance that was originally told us. The evolution was about working as a team, putting out, and giving it everything you have despite seemingly impossible orders.

The cadre next informed the class that we would be playing some games.

We were once again broken into boat crews and watched as the cadre split up into their own teams and dispersed throughout the area. We had five boat crews of roughly five guys apiece. Each crew was sent to a different location. Once we completed the game/task, we would rotate so that every team would get a chance to have some "fun" at each game.

The games ranged from hide-and-seek with a sniper, to burnouts hanging on ropes and bars, to KIMs (Keep in Memory) games, and finally, we would all converge on the Murph rig and take it down bar by bar, screw by screw.

Our first game took place on the grounds of the True Grit Rack assembly where we performed Murph the day before. Our buy-in into the game (meaning what we had to do to start) was simple: 50 pull-ups, any way you can cut it.

My teammates and I took our spots underneath a pull-up bar of our choosing. The coach gave us all five minutes to complete the task. Once we finished, we stated our names and the number we did. "Ritter, fifty," I yelled out to the coach. I was the first one to finish and got a few minutes of rest while my team members completed their pull-ups.

True Grit Murph rig (site of Murph).
Blood, sweat, and tears were left here.

Our next exercise was to dead hang on the pull-up bar for as long as possible. The winner would sit out while the rest performed the same movement again, and then that winner would sit, and the rest would begin over and over and over again until only one of our teammates was left on the bar.

At first, it was peaceful, hanging there. I'd been practicing the move back home in my garage gym in Indiana. My daughter, Hallie, and I would take turns counting who could stay on the bar the longest. You'd be surprised how long a four-year-old child can hang on a bar. I looked up at the sky, saw a few birds flying overhead, and then looked around my periphery, where I could see my teammates hanging on for dear life.

Then the pain train started. My arms were tightening up, and my grip was weakening. I figured I must have been on about a minute. I closed my eyes so I could concentrate and not be distracted. I thought of Hallie, who loved to hang on that pull- up bar in her daddy's garage. One by one, my teammates dropped until it was between me and one other person. I could feel my fingers starting to slip, and once they started coming off the bar, I knew I was done. I dropped. *Ugh! I don't want to do this again*! My teammate who won stepped aside and took a seat.

The coach gave the rest of us no time to relax. We were back up on the bar within seconds.

My arms were already dead, and I was at a disadvantage since my other teammates had been resting while they watched the two of us battle it out. I also committed the cardinal sin when doing pull-ups or bar movements. I jumped weakly up to the bar and was holding on with my fingertips. I did not have a secure grip from the get-go. I couldn't believe it. I was starting to fall off, and it had only been 30 seconds. *Smash*, my boots hit the ground after I lost my grip.

I stood and watched as the rest of my teammates struggled, shook, and gyrated to maintain their grip. One by one, they fell off until we had our last man standing. Just like before, the winner got to join my other teammate, who was resting, and the three of us who were left had to jump back up on the bar.

I was ready. I had been resting, and the lactic acid that had built up in my arms had dissipated.

The coach instructed us to jump back up on the bar. This time, I had a fully secure grip complete with a slight smile. I knew I had the round won before it even started. I had won in my mind. Within 30 seconds, I was the last one holding on to the bar and had won that round. It was my turn to join my two other teammates for a little breather.

When we had one teammate left, our coach had a slight change of plans. He asked my remaining teammate how long he could hold on. He replied 30 seconds. "Tell you what," the coach explained. "I'll let you rest for the next two minutes, then you'll hop back on the bar. If you can hold yourself up there for 60 seconds, you'll be done, but if you fall off, I'm going to punish your teammates." Within an instant, we all were supporting our teammate and pumping him up. We also shared our words of wisdom, and mine was to just breathe through it. Two minutes quickly passed, and the coach called time.

On the count, my teammate jumped up on the bar, and our eyes fixed on him. Ten seconds went by quickly, and he was looking strong.

Another 10 went by, and we started cheering him on. "You got this. Easy day," we were all chanting.

He was at the halfway mark, and he started shaking. His face was getting red.

"Remember to breathe, you got this!" I yelled at him.

We didn't know how much time was left. The coach purposely wasn't giving us a countdown. "Come on! Yeah, yeah, yeah, you got this!" We were hollering, shouting, and doing everything we could to encourage him. "Keep going, keep going, and give it everything you got." *This is going to be close*, I was thinking to myself. After several more seconds, he finally lost his grip. His boots came crashing down on the ground.

The coach immediately asked him how he thought he did. My teammate replied, "I had to have gone sixty seconds."

"No," the coach replied, "you went seventy-five. You just proved to your body through your mind that you can push yourself farther than you ever thought." And with that, our pull- up game was done.

We cycled through the other "games," each one specifically designed to test us in a unique way. The stress level during game- time was low, and looking back, the cadre set this up on purpose to prepare us for what was going to happen next.

PACK YOUR RUCKSACK

Don't get treed by a chihuahua.

Leadership. Thousands upon thousands of books have been written on this topic. One of my favorite books ever written on leadership is by Pete Blaber entitled, The Mission, The Men, and Me. Pete was a former Delta Force commander and had taken part in some of the most dangerous, controversial, and significant military events of our time. While the book is mostly about his military action and life with Delta, its core message is mostly on leadership and what it takes to succeed in any endeavor.

One of his first points in the book is "Don't get treed by a chihuahua." An evolution that you must undertake to join Delta (or the Unit) is to hike the Appalachian Mountains with approximately 70 pounds of gear on your back for an unknown distance. It's commonly referred to as "the long walk." That distance is rumored to be 40–50 miles and needs to be completed in under 20 hours. I can tell you from personal experience, after completing a GoRuck Star Course event (https://www. goruck. com/star-course/) in 2019, that moving 50-plus miles even with about 25 pounds of gear on your back is excruciating. And I performed the task with two of my best friends on flat ground. I couldn't imagine having almost three times the weight, being on rocky terrain, and alone.

After the 15th hour of the long walk, Pete thought he was looking at what appeared to be a bear, which are native residents on the trail. His instincts told him to run, so he ran and jumped off a cliff and tumbled about a hundred feet. He was lucky to be alive, and fortunately, it wasn't a super-steep cliff. He glanced back in the direction of the bear, only to find out it was a pig!

What Pete is telling us here is to not get "treed" by losing touch with the reality of the situation. Getting treed can take the form of overreacting, cutting corners, or perhaps worst of all, not making any decision. Typically, this is a direct result of letting your emotions get to you.

During our log PT session, it would have been very easy for us to throw in the towel when we were told to move 10 laps or the equivalent of about 10 miles under the heavy load of the log. At first, we did overreact, but you just need to break down the situation into manageable bite-sized chunks. As it turned out, what we were told wasn't even true. It was a deception meant to get into our heads and get us to quit.

Likewise, not making any decision can be the worst decision of all. If we would have failed our time hack in getting those logs off the truck and squared away, it would have been because I failed as a leader to speak up. By not saying anything at all, I'd be holding back the team and not contributing. Not all of your ideas are going to be the best option, but what if you provide one that actually works? Don't be afraid to step forward to take charge. Speak your mind, and don't get treed by a chihuahua.

CHALLENGE

Crucial Conversations.

Where are you making mountains out of molehills in your life? I want you to identify a crucial conversation that you've been needing to get off your chest for a while now. This could be a talk with your boss, subordinate, spouse, kids, family, friends—it doesn't matter. The point here is that there is something to be said, and for some reason, you haven't faced it.

We all make excuses why. What if it ruins our relationship? It's not the right time. What if they get mad? But what if it allows your relationship to grow instead and reach a higher plateau? Think about your intentions and what your goal is by having this conversation. What is fear telling you to do? How does that make you feel?

Pay attention to your breathing, and if you are holding it, release. What images are you seeing? Reframe these images in a positive light. What possible good can come from it? If you need help, ask a swim buddy, friend, or loved one to listen to your conversation for feedback and advice.

Now, get it done!

CONTEMPLATION, PERSPIRATION, AND INSPIRATION

"It's not about how hard you hit, it's about how hard you can get hit and keep moving forward; how much you can take and keep moving forward. That's how winning is done!"

—ROCKY BALBOA

I swear the hardest part of this crucible is not knowing what you're going to be hit with next. It's the anticipation that can leave you with a sense of paralysis. When the mind is left unchecked, it can take you down some negative thought loops very quickly.

One by one, we were asked to grab our rucksacks from the night before and our "weapon," both of which were still lying in the giant pile that we had been instructed to place them in. We formed a single-file line and reported to the head cadre. I was standing somewhere near the middle of the pack and it appeared they were asking us the same question.

When my turn came, he looked me square in the eyes and asked, "Ritter, would you like to carry two weapons or two rucksacks back to the U-Haul truck?"

Knowing how far away the truck was and how heavy two rucks were from the prior evening, I immediately blurted out, "two weapons," without thinking.

"That's what I thought. Ritter, drop your ruck right here, and take your PVC pipe, and report over there for remediation."

Oh man, what did I just get myself into? I dropped my ruck, and with what felt like the walk of shame, I took my PVC weapon over to a small group of my classmates who had gathered on a grassy meadow. They were already lying facedown on the ground. I ran over and joined them by lying down and putting my face in the grass. We waited until all of the class had been sorted out, and it appeared that about half of us were about to meet the same fate.

A coach greeted our small group.

I didn't have a chance to look up, but it was clear that he was pissed. His instructions went something like this, "Because you aren't team players and chose the easiest path with less work, I'm going to PT you until you puke. I want you to push your weapon with your forehead all the way over to the U-Haul truck. Your hands are not permitted to touch the pipe. After you reach the truck, sprint back to the starting location."

What did he just say? That truck has to be at least a couple of football fields away. How am I supposed to push a 7-pound piece of PVC pipe through grass by only using my forehead? This was going to be a painful lesson.

"Three, two, one, bust em!"

At first, it was extremely awkward, and I was trying to figure out how I was going to push something without using my arms. I looked over at my teammates, and they were having just as much trouble. *Glad it isn't just me*, I said to myself.

I extended my arms out in a wide push-up position and used the toe box of my boots to help propel me forward in one fell swoop. It seemed to work, but I wasn't going very far. I could only manage to roll the pipe a couple of feet at a time. I had pushed the thing about 20 times, and I'd only gone about 10 yards. *Surely it pays to be a winner here.* I looked down at the ground, and I started getting in my own head and beating myself up for making a bad decision. The sun was searing my neck and giving me a sunburn. The temperature had to be in the 90s. And to add insult to injury, I was low crawling through a damn ant nest. They were all over my face and neck. *At least they weren't fire ants.*

I reverted to what I had learned on Friday: "Breathe, think, and execute." I had to control my physiology so I could control my psychology. I took a deep breath through my nose, exhaled out my mouth, and looked up.

I can't explain it, but the moment was surreal. A calmness I can't explain quickly came over me. I poked my head up, looked around, and took in the beautiful scenery—after all, we were still surrounded by mountains and a beautiful lake. The sun was shining, and the sky was a majestic blue. "It can always be worse," I mumbled to myself. In that pit of torment, I had managed to find peace and be present through breathing and positivity. Just then, like God reaching his hand out to help me, an orange butterfly landed on my weapon. What are the chances? I've heard butterflies can represent leaving your past behind and embracing the future but they are more symbolic in my family.

When I was in my teens, my grandma was living out her last days peacefully at my aunt and uncle's house. As my mom, dad, brothers, and sister were saying our last goodbyes, we all noticed a butterfly hanging outside the window of her bedroom.

My grandma noticed it, too, and although frail and on her deathbed, she managed to say, "I'll be that butterfly." It was a heartfelt moment and one that I'll never forget. Whenever I see butterflies now, I immediately think of her and know she is watching.

And wouldn't you know it, at one of the lowest points in my life, a butterfly just happened to be flying near me and decided to land on my weapon. That was all the motivation I needed.

In that moment, it all became one big mind game. I didn't care how long it took. I was going to roll my weapon all the way to the endpoint, and I was going to do it the fastest. I got mad. I channeled my inner Wolverine from the night before and started methodically pushing my weapon. Although the pace was slow, with each yard I became stronger and more focused. My anger had turned into determination. After what I'm guessing was close to 60 minutes of pushing, clawing, and chewing my way through, I was the first one to reach the truck.

I placed my weapon inside the truck and sprinted back to the starting line. Happy as hell that the hardest part was over, I raced back to the cadre with a grin on my face as I was the first one to report back. (Thanks, Grandma, for getting me through this one). *Surely it pays to be a winner here*, I thought.

My grin quickly turned to dismay as the cadre instructed me to pick up another weapon. His instructions were to bear crawl with one PVC pipe back down to the truck and sprint back. Orders are orders, and although I didn't like it, I sucked it up and grabbed another PVC pipe. I then lowered myself into a bear crawl position.

A bear crawl goes something like this: Crouch down with your hands in front of you approximately shoulder-width apart and feet behind you with hips up in the air (but not too high) and eyes forward. Crawl forward starting with your right hand and left foot followed by the left hand and right foot. Then repeat the process until you get to your desired destination.

Sound simple?

You're right. It is. But when you have to crawl a couple of hundred yards without your knees touching the ground, that's an entirely different story. Don't believe me? Right now, do this for me—drop this book and go out to your front or back yard and perform a bear crawl from one side to the other. Now imagine doing this for about 20–30 minutes with an extra seven pounds, and you'll get the idea.

This was going to be a modified type of crawl because I now had a "weapon" in my hand. I started with the weapon in my right hand and proceeded to crawl as far as I could. My left arm was supporting most of my weight, and I pushed until I couldn't feel it any longer. I then switched it up and placed the weapon in my left hand in order to give my left arm a break and put most of the stress on my right arm. This sucked badly. Several times, I just wanted to collapse face-first on the ground, but I couldn't let Grandma down.

I focused on the next five yards in front of me instead of the 100-plus yards remaining. I find this simple method of breaking a big gnarly goal down into bite-sized chunks to be truly beneficial.

Before I knew it, I was within a stone's throw of the finish line. I was excited. Not only did I achieve the goal, but also, I was the first one to do it, again. I sprinted back to the start line.

History has a way of repeating itself. This time, I didn't report to the cadre with a grin on my face. Instead, it was more of a "what else have you got for me" look. That tone was met with an equal and opposite reaction. The cadre pointed down at the ground in front of him. There were two weapons lying at his feet. "Ritter, grab those two effing weapons and bear crawl them to the truck and back ASAP."

"Hooyah," I responded and immediately grabbed them and turned in the direction of the truck. My body was numb. The muscles in my chest, arms, shoulders, upper back, abs, and legs were all screaming in pain. I took a deep breath and crouched down. I placed one weapon in my right hand and the other in my left. Just as I was ready to begin, something dawned on me: *I can use these PVC pipes to act like skis over the ground as I push with my legs.* Basically, this would look similar to a person pushing a sled, except I was the damn sled!

Guess what. It worked! The pipes were floating over the grass, and all I had to do was keep my arms extended and keep pumping my legs. I was flying, blowing past teammates who were still stuck with only one pipe. I had figured out the evolution. In record time, I reached the truck, threw my two weapons in the back, and sprinted back to the start line. Not knowing if I should smile or look pissed, I decided to have no expression at all.

"Ritter, you put out. Go up to the tent for some hydration." "Hooyah!" was my response. I was glad that one was over.

I walked over to a makeshift tent, which was basically a giant EZ-up that provided some shade from the hot sun that the cadre could kick back in and watch the debauchery unfold. On my way, I passed the other half of my class, many of whom were still getting their butts handed to them. It appeared, they had to carry four rucks (not two) at the same time about the same distance we had had to move the weapons. I'm not sure who had it harder, but I'd take being up on my feet any day over bear crawling.

I reported to the tent as instructed.

There were five coaches gathered around a cooler. They were in deep conversation and sitting on folding chairs. Among them was Taco. He saw me approach and asked what I was doing there, only it wasn't that nicely put.

I must have looked like a lost puppy dog, wandering. As I told him that I had finished with the weapon carry session and was instructed to report to the tent, he looked me up and down.

I thought I was going to get some extra sauce for interrupting whatever they had going on.

He then asked a few random questions like where I was from, what I do for a living, etc., small talk mostly. I told him and the other cadres a little about my background.

After about 5–10 minutes, another one of my classmates arrived. It was my swim buddy Matt. He was a sight for sore eyes. We'd been split up from the start of the games that occurred earlier in the day. We looked at each other and didn't need to say anything. It was the look of "you wouldn't believe what I just had to do."

Taco then instructed us to carry a cooler that was lying at the center of the tent all the way over to the U-Haul.

"Hooyah," we said. Matt took one side, and I took the other. I'm not sure what it was filled with, but it had to weigh at least 50 pounds. It was one of those party-size coolers that probably measured about three feet or so wide and a couple of feet tall. We moved a few feet and struggled with it, and I could tell Taco was looking at us.

What he said next I simply couldn't believe. He said we could drain out the excess water so it would lighten our load.

I couldn't believe what I was hearing and thought for a moment I must have misunderstood. *You want to make our jobs easier? With pleasure.*

We put the cooler down right where we stood, which was only a few feet away from the coaches, who continued to sit in their chairs and talk.

I unplugged the side drain of the cooler and watched all the water pour out. I should have been paying attention to where we placed the cooler because as luck would have it, a small pool of water was forming and heading right toward the coaches feet.

One of them had water almost touching his boots. He noticed it right when I did. "Ritter, if my boots get wet and dirty, I'm going to be upset."

I quickly thought about what to do. Matt and I turned the cooler so that the rest of the water would drain away from the leaders. But what about the small stream heading toward the coach? I didn't know what to do. I tried to gently place my boot close to his and push all of my weight down to redirect the stream of water. Bad move on my part. I pressed down with my boots and watched in horror as mud splashed all over the coach's boots.

He was pissed. I knew I'd messed up.

Sometimes you can talk your way out of certain situations. I had to try. I owned it, told him I was sorry and had screwed up, and offered to clean his boots. I even offered to lick the mud off if he wanted (true story). I was serious as a heart attack when I told him I'd lick his boots. At that point in the training, nothing else mattered.

He took one look at me and one look at his boots and told me to grab my buddy and get the hell out of there.

With that, I replied, "Hooyah" and quickly grabbed the cooler with Matt and we proceeded to the truck.

As we walked to the truck, we had a few minutes to catch up. We asked how each other was doing, and we were glad to see one another. We couldn't believe how far we'd made it, and wondered what was in store for us since we were over halfway done with the training.

When we reached the truck, we were greeted by another coach, who thanked us for carrying the load. He then told us we could pick out a drink and snack if we wanted.

Again, I couldn't believe what I was hearing. I guess it really does pay to be a winner. I figured out that Matt and I were the first ones to finish our jobs, and that was our reward. I picked out a Kill Cliff energy drink and an apple. Matt did the same.

We devoured our snacks in record time. The rest of our class was coming over to join us, so we quickly finished.

After we loaded all of our team gear into the U-Haul truck and played a game of tug of war with it, our time at Vail Lake was quickly coming to an end.

Something must have signaled the cadre that we were having too much fun. We were ordered to form up in our boat crews facing the lake. We'd done that routine so many times already that it only took a few seconds to get in our proper positions.

Taco approached us, and he looked sour. One by one, he closely examined each one of us for uniform infractions. He easily found infractions on every single teammate: untied boots or untucked laces, T-shirts not tucked in, belt buckle not in line with the navel, too much dirt on a uniform, you get the idea. In this particular kind of lineup, nobody wins, and everyone will be paying the piper. After our quick uniform inspection, those of us who were nailed with infractions, which was all of us, (mine was a dirty shirt) were told to report them once we got back to HQ. We were ordered back into the white vans with the same instructions as before. Only this time with the windows up and heat on, my driver told us that we could close our eyes if we wanted. *"Yes Sir!"*

I couldn't wait to close my eyes for some much-needed rest. Within seconds, I leaned my head against my buddy's shoulder, and I was out. I couldn't tell you what happened over the next 30 minutes to an hour since I was racked out, but what I can tell you is that I quickly awoke as were pulling into Headquarters. We were back where it all began. My brain was still in a fog, and drool was coming out of my mouth.

We hopped out of the vans. I wasn't worried about the next evolution, and my mind wasn't racing like before. My team and I had been through so much already, and I was so tired, it simply didn't matter. The cadre could literally tell me to do anything, and I would do it.

We stood in boat crew formation on the grinder and faced the ocean for further instructions. The cadres quickly were on us and ordered us to empty the contents of the U-Haul truck and report back to the grinder. We were dismissed and began working as a team to unload the contents.

There were logs (telephone poles), backpacks filled with sand, canteens, makeshift PVC weapons, etc. You name it, we unloaded it. Each item had a specific place where the cadre wanted us to place it all. As the saying goes, "Team gear first," meaning before you start to take care of yourself, you should focus your attention on getting your team's gear squared away first.

By that time, our names that we had written in black marker on duct tape and placed on the canteens were worn through, so we couldn't really tell where our canteens were anymore. After finishing up with the unloading process, we fell back into our boat crews, faced the ocean, and awaited further instructions.

The sun set for the second day, night was quickly approaching, and for a split second, I wondered what the cadre had in store for us. The previous night, we hiked up and down a mountain for 26 miles. What could be harder than that? Plenty! In a few hours, I was going to find out.

Taco approached our team one last time before his day squad retired for the evening and the night crew would begin punishing us. He asked how many of us had uniform infractions from earlier. About 15 of us raised our hands, which was over half of the remaining class.

"Well, the entire class has to pay. We're going to do eight-count bodybuilders together. How many are we going to do, class?"

We all answered in unison, "All of them!"

Here's how you perform a standard eight-count bodybuilder. First, begin in a standing position. The first count involves dropping to a squat position, with both your hands and feet touching the floor. For the second count, jump slightly and thrust your feet back so that you are in a plank position. The third and fourth counts involve a push-up: lower your body on count three, and raise it back to the plank position on count four. Counts five and six are also related, with count five involving kicking your legs apart so that your feet are spread and count six recovering from this back to the plank position. The seventh count returns you to the squat position with your hands and feet on the floor, after which you jump up for the eighth count and return to your original standing position.

Now, this exercise may sound easy enough, and it is for the first few reps, but try doing 100 in a row without rest, and tell me how you feel. That's exactly how many our class had to perform... 100 perfect 8-count bodybuilders. We were all pretty gassed after completing these and could barely stand. After the 8 counts our buy-out was 100 4-count flutter kicks which destroyed my core and hip flexors.

Flutter kicks.

After we were remediated, we were instructed to hydrate and change into new BDUs. "Hooyah," we replied.

Per SOP (standard operating procedure), it was timed, and we only had 10 minutes to complete the change out.

I rushed over to the canteens and grabbed the first one I could find. Not caring any longer about having my own personal canteen, I drank its contents not knowing what was in it. It tasted like Gatorade, and it was fabulous. I then ran over to a water cooler and filled my new canteen with water making sure to fill it to the top and quickly drank it down.

Next, I had to change out of my dirty uniform and place a brand-new one on with the little time remaining. Our backpacks that had all of our clothing and gear were placed into one big pile in a room that sits adjacent to the grinder. I walked into the room and quickly identified my camo assault pack that I had brought with me. I stripped down buck naked and took out a towel to wipe myself off with, making sure to wipe away any visible dirt and mud that had been caked on my skin underneath my clothing. One of my teammates saw me drying off my body and wiping away the blood, sweat, and tears from the events earlier and asked if he could borrow my towel. "Have at it, bro," I said and tossed it over to him.

I reached into my bag and pulled out a container of Vaseline and proceeded to dip my hand in the jar and cake my body, particularly the areas where the sun doesn't shine, with one of the best substances known to man. Chaffing in any area is bad enough, but downstairs, it's a recipe for disaster, and the last thing I wanted to have to do is drop on request because of monkey butt or worse.

Next, I grabbed a pair of leggings and tossed them on, then took a look at my feet, which were actually holding up quite nicely—not a blister in sight, I might add. I quickly applied some body glide all over my feet and then placed on a pair of poly liners covered with my always dependable Darn Tough wool socks. After getting my base layers on, I finished up the change-out and threw on some brand-new black cargo pants and a perfectly white T-shirt with my last name stenciled on the front and back. Last but not least, I threw on my belt and laced up my boots, and not a moment too soon. Time was quickly winding down.

While I was focusing on my own needs and getting my new uniform on and attending to my feet, I wondered where my towel had gone. It had conveniently made its way across the room. Apparently, I was the only one who had brought a towel to wipe off with.

One of my teammates threw it back to me, and I placed it in my backpack. I also tossed one protein bar and a couple of energy gels into my cargo pants. These treats really came in handy for me the day before. Outside food was forbidden, but it was a risk I was willing to take. My team and I walked out of the gear room and took our positions on the grinder awaiting further instruction.

We were lined up on the grinder, facing the ocean and in our boat crew formation. Night was upon us, and it felt rewarding to be in clean clothes. It's amazing what fresh clothes can do for your attitude. Sure, my team and I had been through a ton already, but we had a renewed sense of purpose, and we could feel the energy around us even though no one was talking as we were waiting for whatever was about to hit us next.

After a few minutes of waiting anxiously in formation, we were greeted by the night shift cadres. I'm sure the coaches were well fed, rested, and ready to dish out some punishment.

We were ready for whatever was going to be thrown our way.

PACK YOUR RUCKSACK

Adapt and Overcome

In a sales career, you're going to hear the word *no* an awful lot. After spending a few years in the copier industry earning my stripes, I had my eyes on starting a new career in the medical sales field. Those of you who have interviewed for jobs while also working know this is the equivalent of working two jobs at the same time. Not to mention being a skilled tactician at not tipping off your current employer as to what you are doing outside of the office. By day, I was the ideal employee, closing deals, filling out expense reports, and drinking the company KoolAid. At night, I was a man possessed, scouting Monster.com for job applications and working with sales recruiters to get lined up with interviews. It took me about nine months to finally be placed into an entry-level role in the medical sales industry. Nine long months of interviewing. During that time, I kid you not, I had over 100 interviews with dozens of companies. I had earned a master's degree in interviewing as well as the art of deception in not being detected by my employer.

Along the way, I started to take notice of my experience in interviewing. Time and time again, I would make it past the first or second round of interviews, but I would constantly finish in second place. As my recruiter told me, "You are the bridesmaid and never the bride." I wondered why that was and started to analyze what my mistakes could be.

Did I have a resume? Check.

Did I do some background research on the company? Check.

Did I follow up afterward with the interviewer? Check.

Something else had to be missing. What else could I possibly do? Plenty, as it turned out. These types of things are expected and merely the ante or buy-in. I had avoided the hard job.

The hard job in interviewing is reaching out to prior employees of the company to get an inside track on exactly what you would be doing and why they left. The hard job is contacting your prospect's current customers and having them give you the scoop on the company's technology and what their experience is overall. The hard job is contacting an existing employee and asking if you can ride along with them for a day to experience what they do day in and day out to see if it's something you would like to do. The hard job is putting together a 30-, 60-, or 90-day plan for your new boss regarding how you would attack your new territory. The hard job involves going deeper than you've ever gone, doing things a little differently, and when you start to get uncomfortable or the fear wolf appears, performing the task anyway. Put yourself out there and show your authenticity. Don't be afraid to fail. That's the hard job. Do today what others won't!

The next time when I interviewed, I *did* my homework. I mean I really did my homework. I contacted former and current employees, talked to several hospitals and doctors about the company's products, and put together a monthly plan detailing the way I would go about bringing in new revenue. I closed the meeting with senior leaders I met by asking if there was any reason they couldn't see me on their team. I followed up with handwritten letters thanking them for their time. I did the hard job, and as a result, I earned the reward and landed my first gig in an industry I was stoked to be in.

CHALLENGE

Do Hard Stuff.

Embrace the suck. I encourage you to find something to do that sucks but is also good for you and do it every day. Finding something that fits this description is relative depending on who you are and how you are wired. It could be waking up early, taking a cold shower, intermittent fasting, reading that book or article you've been putting off, running when the weather isn't so nice, going to bed early, journaling, etc. You'll know you've selected the right target when that inner voice says, "I don't want to," "I'm tired," "I'll do it tomorrow." Interdict that thought loop, and stop it dead in its tracks. The point is to do something like this every day so you build up your tolerance for hard things. Over time, these hard things won't be hard anymore and will become your new SOP. You might even find that you like doing it.

Now turn your attention to a job you've been putting off because it is hard and sucks. It could be at work, such as volunteering for a project that you know is not going to be fun. It could be a house project such as decluttering your basement storage area, or it could be getting your financial life in order by sitting down and going through your taxes and cash flow statements. It really doesn't matter. The point here is that you should do the hard job, lean into your discomfort, and grow from it. Make a habit of *"doing hard stuff."* As my friend Jim Brault says, "Easy Makes Us Weak." (Check out his book with the same title.)

LOG PT

"Teamwork is not a preference; it's a requirement."

—JOHN WOODEN

The next thing thrown our way was log PT. Log PT is perhaps one of the most demanding and at the same time one of the easiest evolutions I've ever had the pleasure of experiencing.

That's because log PT is all about teamwork. We would be tested on how easily we could follow simple instructions and function together as one unit. Each log weighed about 250–300 pounds and stood about 7 feet on end, which sounds like a ton, but if you're a 5–6-man group working in unison, each person is really only carrying 50– 60 pounds. If, however, one or more of your teammates wasn't putting out and carrying their share of the load, the whole team would know because the weight would increase drastically for everyone else.

The cadre split up so that we had a minimum of a 2:1 ratio between coaches and teams. There was the lead instructor, who would give the orders to everyone, and then the assistant instructors would monitor how we were reacting to the orders and correct our positions. Evolutions with logs are technique intensive. Everything needed to be done at the same time the same way, or else the log would break us. For the next two hours, we proceeded to do various exercises with the log such as:

- Overhead press: While standing and with arms fully extended and the weight of the log on our joints, we were to hold the log in place for as long as the instructors said to. Typically, it was 30–60 seconds.

- Overhead squat: Same technique as the press mentioned above but while also squatting.

- Bicep curls: Starting with the log pressed against our chest and our arms underneath carrying it, lower the log by straightening our arms and perform a curl.

- Good morning: Perform a bicep curl and keep the log against your chest and bend forward at the waist. Return to starting position. This kills the lower back and hamstrings.

- Sit-ups: Lying flat on the ground with the log on our chest, we had to perform a sit-up with our arms bracing the log.

- Shoulder presses: Move the log overhead from one shoulder to the other. This was done several times in a row.

- Bench press: Lie flat with the log on our chest and at the same time perform one chest press. Special note here: The guys on the outside had another job, and that was to try to keep the log centered and stabilized. I just so happened to be on an end and had the extra responsibility. It was difficult. This was the only movement where we almost dropped the log, and that would have been a very bad thing because it would have landed on our chests or our faces.

- Balance: As a team, we were to stand on top of the log and not fall off. We could place our arms around each other for stability. The knots on the wood didn't make it very easy at times.

I think you get the idea. Log PT is designed to teach you one thing: The only way to make it through is by working as a team. Although our class didn't lose any teammates during that evolution, we did have several instances where teammates weren't putting out, which caused the log to drop. Not a good thing, and thank God it wasn't my boat crew.

Those individuals who couldn't work together had to join the Goon Squad, which involved several chaotic callisthenic sessions. I don't know exactly what they were doing because I was focusing on the task at hand, but what I can tell you is I heard several of them grunting and moaning, then one of the coaches told them to shut their mouths and keep their noises inside or else they'd get PT'd harder. I made note of that observation and labeled it as *suffering in silence*. I was quite proud of how my boat crew performed. We seemed to be working as a real team.

After our introduction to log PT, we were all pretty tired from the constant repetition of moving the log and listening carefully to detailed instructions. We were allowed to get some hydration, which involved lining up at a big orange cooler and filling our canteens (or whoever's canteen you happened to be holding at the time) with water.

Shortly after, we were ordered to pair up with our swim buddies. Matt and I quickly located each other and stood shoulder to shoulder awaiting the next set of instructions. Nightfall was upon us, and the floodlights from HQ cast a spotlight on my class. I gave him a slight smirk as to mean, "Brother, we're still standing." The cadre must have felt sorry for us... either that or they were letting us recover before the real fun started that night because the next movement was something I'd never expected.

We were ordered to turn and face our swim buddies and slow dance. That's right, at around 1900 on a Saturday night in California with some random stranger I hadn't met until that weekend, there I was, arms locked and slow dancing on a concrete floor in the open SoCal air.

At first, it was extremely awkward. Music was being piped in over a speaker, and the song of choice was "November Rain," by Guns 'N' Roses. I heard someone chuckle behind me, and the cadre ordered us not to smile or laugh and to take the task seriously. I looked into Matt's eyes, and he looked into mine. As we swayed back and forth like an awkward eighth-grade couple at a school dance, the cadre began preparing us for the night with a pep talk.

"Many of you still standing won't make it through tonight. If you thought last night was hard, tonight will leave you crying for your mommy."

They had my attention. I maintained my focus on Matt's eyes. Sometimes you can talk to someone without saying anything; you can just feel the emotion and have a shared language without opening your mouth. At that exact moment, we both told each other that we wouldn't quit on one another. I can't explain it other than it's something that's forged through shared adversity. After the song was over, we stood still, no more swaying, but we were holding each other, not knowing what we would be doing next.

PACK YOUR RUCKSACK

Live with honor on and off the battlefield.

Perhaps you've seen the movie Blackhawk Down, which is about The Battle of Mogadishu. There's a great line near the end of the movie where one of the main characters gets asked why he is going back to the fight when they just took some heavy losses and injuries after intense urban warfare.

Eversmann: "You're going back in?"

Hoot: "There's still men out there. When I get home, people will ask me, 'Hey Hoot, why do ya do it, man? Why? You just some war junkie?' Ya know what I'll say? I won't say a [expletive] word. Why? They won't understand. They won't understand why we do it. They won't understand that it's about the men next to you, and that's it. That's all it is."

Or perhaps you've seen one of my favorite movies, *Tombstone*, where Doc Holliday gets asked why he's still fighting while slowly dying from tuberculosis.

Turtle Creek Jack Johnson: "Doc, you ought to be in bed, what the hell you doing this for anyway?"

Doc: "Wyatt Earp is my friend."

Turtle Creek Jack Johnson: "Hell, I got lots of friends."

Doc: "I don't."

What's my point? It's not about how many friends you have, the number of likes, thumbs-up, or views on your social media posts. Deep down, it's about the quality of those friends. The ones who have your back no matter what. The kind that you can call in the middle of the night and know they'd drop everything to help you in a moment of crisis. Those are real friends. That's real brotherhood or sisterhood. Sometimes these are friends you've known almost your entire life. Other times, they are random people that you meet during a crisis, crucible, or extraordinary event where you are thrown into it, and your bonds are forged through pain.

If you're lucky, you might have a few people who meet this distinction of being a real friend. What about the rest of humanity? Are you supposed to abandon them? Not at all; in fact, just the opposite. We should all strive to take care of one another. Sure, there are some bad apples out there, some truly evil people. But I believe that most of us like to help others and want to when we can.

That's living with honor on the battlefield that is life. Honor is putting other people's needs before your own.

CHALLENGE

Pay It Forward.

I want you to pick out a random stranger, a neighbor, or someone you don't know at all, and do something for them. This could be anything—from buying coffee for the next person in line to inviting an elderly man at a restaurant to sit down with your family for dinner. All it takes is one random act of kindness to change that person's day, and potentially the day of any folks that person comes into contact with if the person pays forward the favor. Heck, you don't even need to leave your house for this challenge. You could even send someone a text thanking them or just to say you are thinking about them.

It's easy to think about yourself first. It's much harder to put yourself second or even last and allow others to go before you.

Those of you who lived through 9/11 (September 11, 2001) know how terrible a day that was. But I'll never forget the American spirit that thrived the next day on 9/12 after the deadliest terrorist attack in human history. No one cared what you looked like, what your skin color was, where you came from, or what language you spoke. If you were a human being, then you mattered.

It's the same sort of thing I've witnessed during the COVID-19 pandemic of 2020. I've seen neighbors checking in with one another just to help out and see if they need anything. Why does it take an event of such magnitude as 9/11 or pandemic to slap us in the face and make us realize what's truly important in life? We should make random acts of kindness and gratitude a part of our daily practice. This is your opportunity to start right here, right now.

SURF'S UP!

"There's a storm inside of us . . . A burning, a river, a drive, an unrelenting desire to push yourself harder and further than anyone could think possible. Pushing ourselves into those cold dark corners where the bad things live, where the bad things fight . . . No matter how much it hurts, how dark it gets, how far you fall . . . You Are Never Out of The Fight."

—LONE SURVIVOR

The music cut, and the lead cadre shouted from the loudspeaker, "Hit the surf!"

My class stood there for a moment contemplating exactly what we just heard. We shuffled toward the entryway of the grinder inside of HQ, a familiar place I hadn't seen since I began the crucible. That was the spot where my journey began about 36 hours earlier as we had lined up along the sidewalk, and Coach McLeod told me that I would be getting "extra sauce."

The lead cadre yelled again. "Don't walk... *run*. Move with purpose!"

We hightailed it to the street not knowing exactly where we were going and hoping that someone in front of the class was leading us where we needed to be.

We ran down the mean streets of Encintas, CA, (I say this jokingly. It seemed to be a fairly quiet surf town with a yoga studio on every other corner) and down a steep flight of wooden stairs from the street to the beach, toward the ocean, where we could see several coaches waiting for us.

Each one had a flashlight. Once we reached them, we all stood at attention in a small group. The lead cadre addressed us. "Tonight, you're going to get a lesson on surf torture."

Surf torture? That does not sound pleasant.

Without any wasted time, we were following direct orders and immediately formed a line parallel to the shore. The next set of instructions went something like this:

"About-face."

My team faced the ocean. We stared out at the black abyss with its three- to five-foot waves. *Oh boy, this is going to be fun.*

"Forward march."

We slowly walked into the ocean. The first few steps in weren't bad, but when the water hit my calves, I could feel the cold of the Pacific. *I'm guessing the water temp is in the sixties. Okay, now the water is up to my knees. Exactly how far are we going out?* I wondered.

"Stop."

Thank God!

My class stopped all at once. The water was just above my knees but below my waist.

We looked to our left and right, all wondering the same thing: *What in the world are we about to do next?*

"Lock arms."

We locked arms tightly knowing all too well that the ocean was going to be our home for the foreseeable future.

I securely locked in with my swim buddy to my right and my other teammate to my left.

"Take seats."

Slowly, as a team, we sat on the ocean floor. The water was up to my collarbones, and it was frigid. *Just exactly how long are we going to be sitting here?*

The only ambient light was that of the half-moon shining down on us along with the flashlights that were beaming in our direction. We proceeded to stare out at the waves that were heading right for us. The first wave hit us like a Mike Tyson uppercut and we tried to hold our ground. I held my breath as my head crashed backward as if I had just been punched in the face. I almost lost my grip with my teammates on either side of me but somehow managed to hold on for dear life.

Some of my other teammates weren't so lucky.

The first wave had done its job and broke our chain. Our class was separated into two groups. Feverishly, my teammates hustled to get connected again with their arms but couldn't manage to do so before the second wave came in.

Again, all I could manage to do was hold my breath as the wave broke on my head and concentrate on holding on to my buddies.

Between waves, I could hear my teammates working together to try to relink the chain. They were successful.

After a few doses of the waves hitting me in the face, I was starting to get used to the cadence. After all, I could look out and see the waves coming at me under the light of the moon and then prepare myself for each hit. I'm not sure what was starting to suck more, getting hit repeatedly or being in the cold water. Each element was starting to take a toll on me, mentally and physically. I can remember talking to my swim buddy between sets, asking if he was okay, how long we'd have to do it for, how cold he was, etc. Looking back, I think that was what got me through the evolution. The more I paid attention to him, the less I felt sorry for myself.

After about twenty minutes, we were ordered to stand. The order was hard to hear over the sound of the crashing waves. Plus, getting hit by waves left me a bit disoriented with water filling my ears. I had a difficult time even standing up and had to rely on my buddy to help pick me up to my feet.

"Sugar cookie" was the next command. I hit the beach and rolled around as my swim buddy and I took turns covering each other head to toe with sand.

"Line up for inspection."

My team formed a line facing the ocean. One by one, the cadre walked up and down our line as they meticulously beamed their flashlights on us, looking for any signs of exposed skin or clothing. I stood there staring at the ocean and trembling from being cold. Did I have enough sand on myself? Did I make sure to get it everywhere? I was about to find out. I was next up as the cadre first shined his light in my eyes, I'm guessing to make sure I was still with it.

He then shined them on my boots, working his way up my legs onto my torso, shoulders, and head. "Turn around," he told me, and I pulled an about-face. As he finished his inspection of my body, he then focused on the tops of my shoulders.

"What's this," he asked me. "It's my shoulder," I replied.

"I know that, dipshit, so where's the sand?" I didn't know what to say.

"Hit the surf."

Apparently, as I was feverishly rolling in the sand and smearing it all over my hair, face, torso, and legs, I had forgotten to get it on the top of my shoulders.

These cadre are professionals. They know where to look for even the smallest infraction.

I ran back into the ocean and joined some other less-fortunate souls who had made a similar mistake, and we took seats on the ocean floor. I linked up with them, took a seat next to my teammate on the left side of the chain, and tightly held his left arm with my right arm.

The first wave hit me, which I was prepared for. What I hadn't prepared for was being alone on my left side. Since I was only holding on to the chain with one arm, the undertow was trying to take me out to sea. It was a constant, relentless battle, fighting like mad to keep my right arm secured to my teammate. After one wave would hit me, I'd use my left arm to dig into the ocean floor and reposition myself as close to my teammate as possible.

The lesson learned on surf torture is to try not to be on the end of the chain. You are much safer with teammates on both sides of you.

After about ten minutes, we were ordered to again stand, hit the beach, and make a sugar cookie.

I hadn't been paying attention to the rest of the class members, who must have passed inspection. They were made to keep standing in formation watching us get beat up by the waves. Every single one of them was shivering. I'm not sure which position would have been worse, ours or theirs. Yes, the ocean was freezing, but standing on the beach soaked from head to toe with the wind hitting you in the face isn't much fun either.

The good news was I did indeed pass inspection that time. The bad news was we were all going back into the ocean. Once the order was given again to form up, my heart sank. Getting beat up by the ocean is not fun and being wet, cold, and sandy is just plain miserable.

THE DARK ABYSS

The cadre had us walk to the shoreline where the waves washed up and eventually retreated back into the abyss. That was our new home.

We were ordered to lie down and to make sure the back of our heads touched the sand. We were in about six inches of water, the area where the whitewash rolls in from the surf. I had positioned myself somewhere in the middle of the pack. All together as a team, we linked arms again, took seats, and laid down on our backs.

Lying down was nice, but the fear and anticipation of waves crashing over my face was not. As I could hear the waves getting closer and closer, I would try to guess when each one would come crashing over me. I'd poke my head up to see the dark object heading my way, and at that moment, I'd hold my breath. However, if you hold it too soon, you might run out of air; too late, and you'd be swallowing water and coughing up a lung.

My natural reaction was to just lift my head up so I could see when the waves would hit. That would allow me the perfect time to hold my breath. Alas, it was not meant to be. Every time I tried that tactic, a cadre would shine their light on me and gently remind me—usually with a boot to my forehead—to keep my head down. I really struggled.

I'm not sure how long we laid there. It had to have been 10– 15 minutes, but it seemed like an hour. The only thing I could concentrate on was holding on to my teammates so we didn't get swept out into the ocean. I listened for the waves so I knew when to hold my breath. I swallowed more ocean water during that brief period than I probably have in my entire life. To make matters worse, I had sand in my ear canals. It was already hard enough to listen to the cadre's instructions with the roar of the ocean, but the sand in my ears made it even harder.

Finally, the "recover" order must have been given because I felt my teammates start to pull me up. I couldn't hear a thing. I needed help just getting back up on my feet. Once I was standing, I slowly walked with my class to the cadre. They didn't say anything and just made us stand there, shivering. Finally, one of them spoke up. "Boys, we've just started, and we will be doing this all night.

Any of you want a cup of coffee and a donut? Quit right now, and we'll take care of you."

While the thought of a donut did sound appetizing, and the feeling of drinking a warm cup of coffee would have been heaven, none of my class took the bait. We had already been through so much. No way were we quitting.

A coach made one final push and asked, "Anyone? Anyone at all? Alright, since you all think you have what it takes, walk backward."

Together, my team slowly walked backward with our arms still linked. We were all shivering, and it helped to feel the man next to us going through the same suck as we were. We marched back until the cadre told us to take seats.

This time, instead of lying down and facing the waves, we were lying down facing toward the beach. It absolutely sucked and was also a bit scary. We wouldn't be able to see the waves before they came crashing down on us.

This new position added a whole new dimension to the evolution. Funny how time washes away when all you are trying to do is breathe and keep from drowning.

The only way I got through the evolution was by being attached to my teammates and just shutting my eyes and going with the flow. What I mean by this is actually closing my eyes (it was dark anyway) and listening for cues on when the waves might hit me, and timing my breath along with each set. It became a game, and as time passed, I was able to get into a state of flow. I resisted the initial reaction of fighting the situation and started to accept it by feeling my way through it.

THIS TOO SHALL PASS

As you can imagine, we all were freezing after the grueling surf torture session. We were treated to a series of "beach games." Trust me, this wasn't volleyball but more physical endurance fun aimed at warming us back up so they could keep sending us back in the water all night. After the beach games, we were all tired, and what better way to wake up a class than to perform more surf conditioning? We were instructed to hit the surf and remain in the water until the sun came up.

That had to be a joke. No way they could keep us in there that long. After all, it was early evening, and the sun wouldn't be up for several more hours.

As a class, we took a seat in the ocean and laid our heads back on the sand. *Well, this is it, make or break time.* Minutes passed, and with each one, I could feel my body temperature dropping ever so slightly.

More minutes went by. I was so cold that my testicles had shriveled up into my stomach. Self-doubt, fear, and anxiety started creeping into my mind. And then it hit me.

I had a sudden urge to pee. I let it fly, and if only for a few brief seconds, I could feel the warm liquid spill out onto my groin and legs. I couldn't have cared less. Even just for those few seconds, I was warm, and it reminded me that yes, even this too shall pass. I started talking to my teammates more, focusing my attention on others. This led to someone breaking into a song, and before we knew it, we were all singing. Morale was building with each chorus, but more importantly, our minds were being taken off of how cold it was. Our team was forging, and we were continuing down the path of becoming a tight unit.

After a while, the cadre came into the water and flashed their lights on each of our faces. I made sure to look mean and alert. Then we received the order we had been waiting on.

"Hit the beach, and sugar cookie."

We quickly got to our feet as best we could. It took me a few seconds to get my footing and reorient myself. Once I recalibrated, I sprinted to the beach with the rest of my teammates and dove headfirst into the sand. We took turns rubbing sand all over each other's back and anywhere we saw wasn't covered.

"Form up" was the next command.

We formed a horizontal line facing the ocean. Shivering and covered with sand from head to toe, we waited for inspection.

There was no inspection. The cadre must have seen what they were looking for. Instead, we were asked a question.

"Who is hungry?" "Hooyah!" we all shouted. "Form up."

We could see the cadre counting paces in the sand as they walked away from us holding MRE boxes. Once they reached their destination, 50 yards away, we could see them burying our MREs in the sand. This would be no ordinary dinner. As with every evolution, even this late-night dinner would be a race.

On the count of three, my entire team sprinted toward the cadre and began searching in the sand for the buried MREs. They were quickly found, and unfortunately, I wasn't one of the lucky recipients. It looked like they had only buried five meals.

The cadre moved down the beach to begin burying more food. This was no longer a game to me. I was starving, tired, and covered with sand. I needed that food and was going to do everything I could to get my hands on one of those MREs.

Again, on the count of three, we sprinted toward the cadre and dove onto the sand. Out of the corner of my eye, I saw that all-too-familiar brown package. I reached for it but was too slow. One of my teammates dove on top of it and secured it for himself. *I'm going to have to go all-out, or I won't be eating*, I said to myself.

There were about 15 of us left, and the cadre told us this was going to be the last race. We had no idea how many MREs remained. I didn't care. I was going to get my hands on one. On the count of three, I sprinted as hard as I possibly could toward the cadre. I dove, head first, Pete Rose style into the first MRE I saw. But there was nothing there. My mind was playing tricks on me.

Then I noticed something out of the corner of my eye. One of the cadre placed a meal at his feet. It wasn't buried in the sand and was sticking out like a sore thumb. I made a beeline right for it, but so did one of my teammates. Clearly, it was a game of who wanted it more. With every ounce of energy I had left, I dove on to the instructor's boot and snatched the MRE. I was elated and joined the rest of my class members, who were sitting in a circle on the sand and eating their MREs.

I wasn't sure how much time we had, so I didn't waste any of it. I didn't even look to see what I was eating. It was food, and more importantly, it was carbs, which I needed badly. I happened to look back at my teammates who weren't so lucky and were coming back empty-handed. For them, there would be no dinner. I was about halfway through my MRE and saw one of them. I handed the rest of my package to him. "Here you go."

He gave me a heartfelt "Thank you."

I looked around at my team. More guys were doing the same thing, sharing what they could with the others who didn't get a meal. That could have easily been me. Little did I know, that would be the last MRE I would eat during the weekend. My class showed real honor at that moment, and I was proud to be a part of it.

PACK YOUR RUCKSACK

Anticipation

Surf torture isn't a very demanding physical evolution, but it does test your breaking point by using the cold. And it's not really the cold water of the Pacific that gets you (although it's close to 60 degrees). It's when the instructors pull you out and have you line up and face the ocean. You just stand there, completely soaked and disoriented, wearing your white T-shirt as the wind begins to break through your skin and muscles until it literally chills you to the bone.

The instructors know this, and for that reason, there wasn't a lot of yelling. Mother nature would take care of it for them. Instead, they looked for people who were shivering or jackhammering and simply walked up to them in a calm voice and asked if they would like to quit and get warm. Perhaps a warm blanket, coffee, or donuts could entice us, so they would show us those as well.

I just wanted to get warm. All I wanted to do was PT, but that would warm us up, and they knew it.

These coaches were masters at their craft. By using a combination of air and water temperature along with a hypothermia chart, they knew the time limit that we could be allowed in the water and exposed to the cold before warming us up with more calisthenics. Yes, it was the anticipation within that evolution that did the most damage. When would we be allowed to move again? When would we be going back in the water, and for how long? It was the consistency of not knowing that made the event a true test of will and spirit. You can practice this at home, and I'll show you how.

CHALLENGE

Get Comfortable Being Uncomfortable.

It's been said that comfort is a slow death. Now, I'm not suggesting you should go to the ocean and practice surf torture by yourself. That would be stupid (you should always take a swim buddy with you during water-based exercises). But what I am saying here is that you should try to make yourself uncomfortable every day.

What you'll find is that, at first, the simple act of being uncomfortable won't be very pleasant at all. But over time, your body will adapt because it will know what to expect, and what you're doing won't bother you as much as it previously did. Sure, it might still suck, but not as bad as it once did. And who knows, gradually, you might actually learn to enjoy it.

I want you to use cold water for this next challenge. I challenge you for the next two weeks to take a cold shower. Now you don't have to start off with a freezing cold shower every morning unless you're that type of person that likes to jump right in. If you are, then, by all means, do it.

Start off with micro-goals. Start with a warm shower, and then end your session with 10 seconds of cold, then 20, then 40. Pretty soon, you'll get to the point where you can be in for minutes at a time without it really having much effect.

Why the cold water, you might ask? I can't think of many other everyday items that are readily available to us that will instantly take your breath away and also play psychological games with your mind due to the anticipation of it.

Breath control is the first place to start when it comes to building mental toughness and emotional resiliency. You'll immediately start to hyperventilate, and you'll need to focus on your breath to make it through this challenge. Control your physiology, and you'll control your psychology. If you can control yourself in extreme situations like cold water or weather, you can use these same tactics and strategies when you feel nervous and anxious. This could be a big presentation, speech, test, you name it...there are many applications.

17

THE WALK FOR LIFE

"To each there comes in their lifetime a special moment when they are figuratively tapped on the shoulder and offered the chance to do a very special thing, unique to them and fitted to their talents. What a tragedy if that moment finds them unprepared or unqualified for that which could have been their finest hour."

—SIR WINSTON CHURCHILL

This entire weekend had been long periods of intense physicality and chaos followed by brief moments of calm. It was one big roller coaster ride of emotions, with no end in sight. What I did know for sure was that I was far past the halfway mark and deep into my second night. Things were going pretty well, or at least I thought so. Our late-night snack was over, and we were greeted by the cadre and informed of our next evolution. The setup was simple; however, the task would prove to be one of the most difficult things I've ever had to do in my life.

We walked from the beach, up the stairs, and onto the side street that ran adjacent to the ocean. It's a beautiful and picturesque spot that overlooks the beaches of Encinitas. It was still very dark. I'm guessing it to be somewhere around zero dark thirty.

We were ordered to quickly form a height line, and we took our places on a sidewalk across from a yoga studio.

One of the coaches opened the tailgate of a nearby pickup truck. The bed was full of rocks. Not just any rocks but big, nasty, heavy rocks. Some were smooth and others were jagged. Some were round and others were long and skinny.

The cadre selected rocks from the truck and placed them at our feet. When my rock was placed at my feet, the cadre told me that they had saved the largest, nastiest rock they could find for me. Something about needing a little extra sauce that weekend (thank you, Coach Brad McLeod).

We were briefed on the night's evolution. "On my signal, you are to lift your rocks and carry them by any means necessary. You will keep pace with the leader, and you will not drop your rock. And one more thing; you will be walking for a very long time. Do not let the rock hit the ground, or you will pay."

With that, we were given the signal to hoist our rocks. I squatted down and wrapped my arms around the small boulder at my feet and slowly stood up. There was no way I could hold the thing up very long. I held it with both arms in front of my chest and pressed it against my body.

One by one, we moved out from the sidewalk and started to follow the cadre. Destination unknown, time unspecified.

We walked down the stairs to the beach. The stairs were slick, so we really had to watch our footing for fear of slipping and cracking our heads open. Once we reached the beach, we headed south. It was hard to see the terrain in front of us in the dark. We were practically walking blind, and I was feeling out my surroundings with my boots. The beach wasn't very smooth, and there were peaks and valleys scattered all over. I cautiously moved forward paying close attention to where I would step next.

One thing was for sure: my rock was heavy. I switched holding positions often. Sometimes, I'd have both arms around it pressing its jagged edges into my torso. I'd also carry it like a running back does a football, holding it against my side with one arm. My favorite way was switching it from right shoulder to left shoulder, sort of like a rapper walking around with a 1980s-style boombox.

I'd try anything and everything to keep my rock from hitting the ground. It was a constant battle. I guessed that the rock weighed around 50 pounds. That's a quarter of my body weight.

Anytime we passed a flight of stairs, we had to walk up to the top and back down. As I grew increasingly tired, my coordination was starting to falter, and I almost tripped a few times.

Hours went by. I could feel doubt starting to creep into my mind. My upper body was numb with pain. I was in another bad spot mentally, and what's worse, I was also starting to hallucinate again. Those familiar colors and bright lights were making their way into my peripheral vision. I was having difficulty walking a straight line, especially on the beach, which is about as uneven a walking surface as there is.

Then it happened.

Walking with the rock pinned to my right shoulder, I stepped into a hole with my left foot. I didn't see it coming, but I sure felt it. I fell face-first onto the beach. My rock came crashing down on the back of my head. Dazed, confused, and seeing stars, I quickly hopped up onto all fours to assess the situation. I looked down at the sand and the big blunt object that had just smacked the crap out of my head. I took my right hand and rubbed the spot where I'd been hit. It was warm and wet. *I'm bleeding!* For a split second, I wanted to throw in the towel. I was beyond tired, hallucinating, bleeding, and possibly concussed.

I remember one of my teammates behind me who saw the whole thing asking, "Ritter, Ritter, are you okay, man? Can you get up?" Time stood still. At that very moment, I had two choices.

Lie down and quit, or stand back up, lift my rock, and keep on walking. I looked at my blood-covered hand again, only this time, there would be no pity party. My eyes widened and became more focused. I got mad—fuming mad. There's something about the sight of your own blood that can instantly put you in a different mental state. The pain went away, and some sort of newfound strength came over me.

I stood up, hoisted the rock back to my right shoulder, and began walking. That time, however, I wasn't sleepwalking. I was walking with a purpose, with attitude, and I was back in the game mentally.

My teammates behind me were telling me about how hard I hit the ground and how they heard the rock hit my skull.

I laughed it off, which is something I commonly do when things get bad. I can usually find the humor in any situation. Even stuff like this.

We kept walking south, making sure to ascend and descend each flight of stairs we passed.

The energy I had been gifted by the rock crashing down on my skull slowly wore away. I needed another motivator and was frantically searching my memory, to no avail. The pain train was taking its toll again. I wasn't sure if I truly had anything left.

We came across another set of stairs, and what happened next saved my bacon.

The cadre gave us a chance to rest. The only catch was that we couldn't let our rock hit the ground.

We all took seats, and I placed my rock on top of my legs. It felt so good to finally sit down and have the weight of the rock being supported by my legs instead of by my arms.

What really saved me, though, was that the cadre asked if anyone wanted to change out their rock with another teammate. He told us this would be the one and only opportunity to do so. I knew what I needed to do. But could I? As funny as that sounds, I didn't want to be the first and only one to have to switch out rocks because it was too heavy. What would my teammates think? I'd look like the weak link. What if no one would trade with me? All of those seeds of doubt entered my mind. Then, after several seconds of negative vibes racing through my head, I gave myself the internal "screw it" and said, "Coach, I'd like to trade out my rock."

"Why, Ritter?" the coach responded.

I was brutally honest. "Because it's the biggest mofo here, and I don't think I can carry it any longer."

"Alright, Ritter." Coach then asked my class who would like to switch rocks with me. Seconds went by that seemed like minutes. No one seemed very eager to want to trade places with me. And why would they? They probably had a pretty good thing going if their rock was only half the size of mine.

When I thought all seemed lost, a voice spoke up and offered to trade his rock with my own. It was my boy Goddard, saving my tail once again and coming to the rescue.

We quickly switched our rocks, which was somewhat difficult since we couldn't let them hit the ground. I gave him my jagged mini boulder, and he gave me his rock. My new rock was an instant relief. It was round and smooth and weighed only 25–30 pounds. I knew I could carry that baby all night.

He, on the other hand, instantly knew what he was in for. If my rock was a quarter of my body weight, it would be closer to a third of his.

I saw his face when he felt the full weight of what I had been lugging around all night, as if to say, "Holy cow, man, this is horrible," and "Why did I offer to switch rocks?"

The cadre ordered us all back to our feet and up the stairs. After walking at least another hour, we came to what appeared to be a lagoon with some sort of jetty on the other side. I thought we may have reached our final destination. I was wrong.

We had to cross the lagoon while lifting our rocks over our heads. Water came up waist-high for me, probably chest-high for the Smurfs in our class. Each step we took had to be well calculated since we didn't know what we might be walking on. And no one wanted to drop their rock there. Chances were that the person wouldn't be getting it back since it would be submerged, and that would surely bring a beatdown.

One by one, my class reached the jetty, which was made up of the very rocks we were carrying.

The cadre then spoke to us about how the rocks we had been carrying were to symbolize all the baggage we had in life. The stress, hardships, and pain. It could be the death of a loved one, a nightmare boss, or just our own self-doubt and limiting beliefs. None of that matters at this moment. After he was finished with his speech, he ordered us to drop the rocks onto the jetty in unison. I can still hear those rocks smashing the jetty. What a beautiful sound! It was a welcome sound of relief: No more rocks to carry. We cracked smiles. The sun hadn't come up yet, but the sky was starting to lighten up. We had done it. We had carried our rocks almost all night.

Or had we?

Cadre addressed us again. "You're only halfway there, boys.

Grab another rock."

You've got to be kidding me, I thought to myself.

We were instructed to grab a rock that represented us, but this time there was a twist.

"You're not allowed to switch out with anyone at any time for any reason. Pick too small of a rock, and you're looking for the easy way out. Select too large of a rock, and that means your ego is getting in the way."

I took inventory of the rocks that lay around me. Most were smooth from being exposed to Mother Ocean as her waves had eroded most of the surfaces over the years. But there was one that stuck out. Dark with sediment, it looked like the old soul of the bunch. It had a perfect combination of smooth and jagged edges. I hoisted it. I guessed it to be 35–40 pounds. Perfect. Not too light, and not too heavy, with lots of imperfections, but definitely a challenge. I was ready. This was my rock. There were many like it, but this one was mine. My rock is my best friend. It is my soul. I must master it as I must master my life.

With our new rocks in hand, we backtracked, retracing the same terrain. Each passing minute, the sky was starting to make way for morning light. That became my new motivator: To make it to sunrise.

As we doubled back, it was interesting to see how different everything looked in daylight versus in complete darkness. The staircases we climbed weren't as steep and scary looking. The beach wasn't nearly as rough. We could see the pitfalls that were in front of us. Although my arms, shoulders, and torso were numb with pain, the evolution was a little easier on the way back. We knew the terrain. We could see where we were going, and we knew the distance we had left (we hoped).

By the time the walk ended, I wanted to be leading the pack, and I also didn't want to let any of my teammates quit. I punched it into high gear, walking with an upbeat tempo. Anytime I strolled by one of my teammates, I'd ask the same question, "Hey brother, how are you feeling?"

The answer was almost always, "I'm doing okay" or "I'm fine" but they would grimace with pain and exhaustion.

Then I'd tell them to look me in the eye. "Hey, man, we're in effing California. Looking good, feeling good, ought to be in Hollywood?"

That would usually crack a smile, which is sometimes all that's needed. As with an earlier lesson I called "Fixing Your Face," you can deter pain by smiling your way through it and introducing the power of positivity.

I must have caught the eye of one of the cadre, as they asked me to double-time it to the front of the pack and lead the class. I obliged. Over the course of the night, I had successfully managed to go from the back of the class all the way to being the pack leader. I treated it like a race, and each person who was in front of me became my target.

There were two cadre at the very front who had been leading us most of the night. I walked up beside them and matched them step for step. We spent most of our time talking about life. They were most interested in why I chose to attend the camp.

I explained my "Why," and then I asked them about their careers as Frogmen. You want to know what the common connection was? A sense of belonging, to be part of a select tribe and brotherhood, and the excitement of pushing yourself beyond anything you thought possible. That's part of the reason I was there, too.

I could tell the sun would be rising soon. Ahead about half a mile was the first staircase we descended to start the whole thing. The cadre told me to finish strong and head for the staircase. Once I reached it, I could rest, but I needed to keep the rock off the ground.

"Hooyah!" I replied. I'd done it. I managed to go from the back of the pack all the way to the front. I watched as the rest of my classmates strolled in.

When my teammates reached the staircase, we did a quick roll call to make sure we hadn't lost anyone. We started with 27, and that's exactly how many we would finish with. Once we were accounted for, we were instructed to climb our last flight of stairs with rocks in hand.

After our ascent up the stairs we ditched our rocks and were told to report to the sidewalk that ran adjacent to the beach, and to face the ocean. As if it had been ordered, the sun began rising over the horizon. What a beautiful sight. The bright orange glow hit the water and reflected off. The warm rays of sunshine bounced off my face and arms. It was an incredible feeling, and we all just stood there taking it in for the next few minutes. I'd been up for over 48 hours straight and knew the end was in sight. But I was sure the last day wouldn't disappoint, and as you'll read, it didn't.

PACK YOUR RUCKSACK

Taking Souls

In his 2018 book, Can't Hurt Me, David Goggins, who, at the time of this writing, is the only man in history to complete elite training as a Navy SEAL, Army Ranger, and Air Force Tactical Air Controller, and is also considered to be one of the world's top endurance athletes, has a chapter that I absolutely love. It's chapter number four, and it's titled "Taking Souls."

Basically what Mr. Goggins is saying is that by "taking someone's soul," you've gained the tactical advantage. It's a tactic for finding your own reserve power and a second wind. This can be used in a physical competition, on the job in your career—practically anywhere. And it's pretty easy to employ, too, since it's mental, and the people you're interacting with probably won't even know you're doing it.

Let's say you're in a race, and you feel yourself starting to lag behind the race leader or the person you are keeping pace with. Instincts might tell you to back off and try to regain some strength/stamina to make a move later. But using the "taking souls" tactic does the opposite. Instead of throttling back, you kick your motor into high gear and pass the race leader or pacesetter. As you pass them, you can feel their look of disgust and anguish as you trot by. You've taken their energy or "soul" in this case, and it fuels your fire. *How can they be this fast?* they'll start to wonder.

You just did two things there. First, you took the lead or are at least in front of the pacesetter you were following. There's a mindset change when you are leading instead of following, plus you took their energy. Second, you just planted a huge seed of doubt in their minds. Getting passed by makes you really question if you have what it takes to keep up. You either find your reserve tank or simply back off. Most folks will back off. By the time they feel up to it, you are long gone and out of sight. Always remember that it's easier to keep up than to catch up.

Or perhaps you have a sales job, and the company posts rankings every week, month, quarter, etc. Do you think they do this by accident? It's all psychological, seeing your name in the rankings. Are you in the top 10%, or are you the gray person somewhere in the messy middle? Or, worse, are you at the bottom? I've been in all three scenarios in my sales career due to various reasons and excuses. Regardless, there's no worse feeling than seeing your name at the bottom of a stack ranking.

Conversely, seeing your name at the top of the list is incredibly satisfying as well. You learn to crave that feeling and keep pushing to maintain your spot as the top dog. This usually requires doing things just a little bit differently or putting in just a little bit of extra work compared to your teammates.

Maybe you wake up earlier and stay up later than everyone else. Perhaps you make that extra call when everyone else is calling it quits for the day. Or maybe you put in the extra time and study your industry and competition. Whatever the case, if you're in the top 10%, you are taking souls here, too.

Perhaps your intention isn't to deliberately go out and kick your teammates' butts, but trust me, that's definitely how it's perceived by people who are not in the top spot. When they're not on the leader-board, they'll start questioning how they do things and compare themselves to you. "Taking souls" works anywhere there is competition, whether friendly or serious.

CHALLENGE

Be Great at Something.

Make a list of all the competitive settings you're involved in. Some examples from my own life are my career, authorship, coaching, PT, Tae Kwon Do, and yes, even parenting is a competition at times.

Now pick one.

Figure out your strengths and weaknesses.

I challenge you to achieve greatness by employing the "taking souls" technique that Mr. Goggins has branded, or to simply find the calculated advantage that will take you from where you are now to greatness.

Don't be afraid to ask for help. Find someone you look up to—a mentor, coach, or someone you know who is rocking at the very thing you wish to be great at—and ask for help. Guess what. People actually like helping other people. You just need to swallow your pride and ask. Had I not checked my ego and switched out rocks, I probably would have failed that evolution.

18

SPRING CLEANING

"Never tell people how to do things. Tell them what to do, and they will surprise you with their ingenuity."

–GEORGE S. PATTON

After the cadre graciously let us take in a sunrise, our reality quickly set in. "Report on the grinder in formation, you have two minutes."

Oh, great, here we go again.

We sprinted toward HQ. Upon reaching the grinder, we all took our spots in our boat crews and made sure to face the ocean. We had done this so many times over the course of the weekend that this simple but sometimes frantic order had become routine. Everyone knew their place in line.

After waiting patiently for a few minutes, we were greeted by the day crew. We were instructed to get in two teams—A and B. Two team leaders were selected by the cadre, and they had to be someone who hadn't led before.

One of the individuals selected was one I had come to know fairly well because he was in my boat crew. Although we could work together, I didn't care for him too much. Just something about the way he carried himself. When things were stressful, he was the type of leader who was quick to blame everyone—everyone except himself. And if you ever offered advice, it was never taken. He had to be the source of the solution. In other words, he didn't know how to follow. I'll affectionately refer to him as "Squirrel" in this section. I call him Squirrel because that's how he acts when things don't go according to plan: squirrely.

Squirrel was the A team leader, while the other elected leader led the B team. Each leader got to handpick his team.

This felt like junior high all over again when playing basketball and selecting shirts versus skins. I was never the first one picked and was typically somewhere near the middle to last. I was hoping for B team from the get-go. Alas, it wasn't meant to be.

With about six guys left waiting to see which team they'd hop on, Squirrel announced my name. I reluctantly ran over to join him and the rest of my new team.

Once my class was broken down into two teams, we were given our assignment. This was a timed evolution, and as always, it paid to be a winner. The team leader got to select which "mission" their team would be taking on.

Mission number one was to clean the weight room. Adjacent to the grinder was a small but suitable CrossFit area. There were multiple dumbbells, barbells, bumper plates, medicine balls, kettlebells, you name it. Tons of gear. The mission was to take every single piece of equipment outside onto the grinder, clean the floor, and then place all of the equipment back where it belonged. The time cap was 90 minutes.

Mission number two was to do the same thing in the gear room. The gear room is where we all huddled up before the weekend started. All of our belongings were in there, and it was pretty dirty from my entire class changing in and out of our wet and sandy PT gear. The same time cap of 90 minutes applied.

Squirrel got to pick first, and without hesitation selected the second mission, cleaning the gear room. Not that it matters, but I would have gone with the weight room if for no other reason than the fact that sand is hard as hell to clean up, and there was a ton of it on the rubber mat flooring in the gear room. But hey, I'm not here to be a Monday morning quarterback. Both tasks would surely suck in their own right.

And so it was settled. Team A would clean the gear room, and team B would clean the weight room. The cadre started the stopwatch, and we were off.

The A team descended into the gear room. What an amazing mess. Gear was thrown everywhere. The floor consisted of 4×8 sheets of rubber matting, which were completely sand-caked in every crack.

Squirrel began barking out orders. "You six, start taking the gear outside, and the rest of you take the mats outside and clean them, once the gear is off of them."

Roger that. I started humping gear outside the door and placing pieces on the grinder.

One thing was apparent as I was making the trips in and out of the gear room to the grinder: there were tons of gear, and sand was being dragged everywhere. I could see the B team on the far end of the complex, hustling and moving all the items from the weight room onto the other side of the grinder as well. The race was on.

After my sixth or seventh trip into the gear room, I could see a couple of people were just standing around, not really doing anything but trying to act like they were busy. A couple of the coaches happened to peek their heads in as well. They were pissed off and immediately snatched them out of the room for a reprimand.

Those two guys also happened to be the weakest links the entire weekend. They were constantly in the Goon Squad and were consistently just barely making the standard. Not a good place to be. I watched as they were escorted out to the grinder and immediately were placed on the pull-up bar. I heard one of the cadres tell them that they would be taking the PT test all over again, and if they missed the standard by even one rep, they would be done with training. Could you imagine, making it this far only to potentially be sent home at that moment near the end due to a lack in judgment?

My team was down by two guys, but I couldn't worry about them. We had our own stuff to deal with. The other folks on my team who were cleaning the gear room floor were busy mopping the rubber mats. Another cadre saw what they were doing and immediately halted the work.

"What the f*** are you doing?" asked the cadre.

"Cleaning the floor" One of my teammates answered.

"Not like that. Take each mat individually outside of the room, hose them off, and then dry them before replacing them back in the room. Oh yeah, one more thing, keep track of where each mat belongs. These fit together like a puzzle, and if you put one in the wrong spot, it will throw off everything."

Well, this mission just became twice as difficult. The 4×8 rubber mats were pretty heavy and needed to be escorted out by teams of two. To make matters even worse, we needed a system to keep track of where each one went.

Squirrel was lost and didn't know what to do. We asked him what he wanted us to do next and even offered suggestions. He didn't know. There was no system in place, and we were flying by the seat of our pants.

I asked him if I could partner up and begin taking the mats outside to clean them, and he okayed it. We just needed a way to keep track of where each mat went. I quickly added up how many mats there were. I think I counted close to 20. I did the quick math. If it took five minutes to take each one out, clean it, and then dry it, that would be 100 minutes, plus we had already wasted about 10 minutes. There would be no way we could get the task done in the 90-minute time cap. Talk about a mission that was doomed from the start. But that was the idea. It wasn't about getting the job done in the time allotment. It was about how we would respond to stress and work through seemingly impossible problems as a team.

My teammate and I began taking the mats outside of the room. There was a hose on the back side of the facility, and we stacked each mat up against the side of the building and hosed each one off. One of us would hose the mat while the other went by and cleaned them off with a towel. The system was working until I walked back into the room to grab another towel, since the one I was using was soaked.

I walked into the gear room, which was vacant at the moment, and at the exact same time, another cadre popped in. There were four of us caught in an empty room.

He asked me, "What are you doing?"

I told him, "I've been cleaning the mats with this white towel that is now soaked, and I'm looking for a replacement."

"What about the other three?"

Two of them had mops, and the other, well that was Squirrel in his "management" position.

The cadre ripped into Squirrel because he wasn't leading by example, and his entire team was working hard except for him.

"Have you even been outside of this room to see what all is going on?"

"No," Squirrel replied.

"Well, let me tell you. You guys are way behind and getting your ass kicked by B team. Better step it up, or you'll be paying. Follow me outside."

As the cadre took a step back, he must have hit a puddle of water on the floor and lost his footing. He almost fell but caught his balance at the very last second. He was pissed. "Who the f*** has been mopping this section?"

We all turned toward my two teammates with the mops in hand. One of them raised their hand.

"You are relieved. Ritter, do you know how to mop?"

"Hooyah," I replied.

"Show me."

I quickly snatched the mop and began cleaning the floor.

"When were you born, Ritter?"

"Seventy-nine," I replied.

I was a child of the seventies (barely), something I'm proud of (not that I had a choice). We're the generation that grew up with black and white television, payphones, and typewriters and witnessed the technological marvels that we have today firsthand. We are the bridge between the Baby Boomers and the Millennials.

"Ritter, do you know who Adam Sandler is?"

"Hooyah," I replied.

"He had a song about mopping, do you remember it?"

Wow, I can't believe a CD I used to listen to that made me laugh during my teenage years was going to have a profound impact on the dilemma I was facing.

"Hooyah, Coach."

I remembered the song. The song was from Adam Sandler's hit album, *They're All Gonna Laugh at You*, and the title was affectionately called, "The Beating of a High School Janitor."

"Let's hear it," said the cadre.

I thought to myself, *This is either going to work out very well or I am going to get the hell beaten out of me.* Here goes nothing. And so I began singing the following: "*Mop, mop, mop all day long; mop, mop, mop while I sing this song. Gonna wax that floor gonna make it shine, gonna take off the spray paint with turpentine.*"

"That's hilarious, Ritter, f****** hilarious. You just got mopping duty for the entire room. I want you to mop this floor clean and sing that song until I come back in here and tell you to shut the f*** up. Hooyah?"

"Hooyah!" I replied back. And with that, I began mopping the entire floor while singing that song over and over and over again. With the gear room empty, I found myself alone mopping a dirty floor and singing that stupid song. And you know what? I loved every minute of it. I got to be alone with my own thoughts and was responsible for myself and myself only. I could hear the chaos outside with the cadre yelling and people running around like chickens with their heads cut off.

I was happy to be inside doing that monotonous task. Not that it was beneath me—quite the opposite. I was pretty banged up from the weekend, and everything was starting to take its toll. I could sense my response time, whether to a verbal command or physical activity, slowing by just a hair. Sometimes that's the difference between winning or losing, life or death. I embraced the time by myself to focus on my one thing, my "why" for being at the camp. That and of course doing a great job mopping. Whether my team won or lost the race didn't really matter to me. I was sure we would be getting beat down anyway.

About 20 minutes went by, and I had the floor looking spick and span. I left my mop and water bucket and ventured outside. I could see my two slacker teammates from earlier getting hammered on the pull-up bar and grinder, and not just by one coach. They had an entire team of cadre surrounding them, just like a shark attack. These two had been going at it the entire time? I thought, *That is unbelievable. I know they haven't been up to standard this weekend and were hanging on by a thread, but good for them. They aren't going to quit.* As I took my first steps on the grinder and scanned the place, I could tell there was no way we'd accomplish our mission in time.

Team B looked like they were almost finished, and we still had every mat outside of the gear room drying on the grinder. We began placing the mats back inside, making sure to pay attention to how they were supposed to fit. Whoever was in charge of that messed up because no one knew where the pieces went back. It was completely cattywampus. We looked like we were trying to solve a jigsaw puzzle, and our puzzle pieces were 40-pound black 4×8 mats. Not a good place to be. It didn't matter. About 10 minutes passed, and B team's leader reported to the cadre that they were done.

We paused as the cadre inspected their room. The report came back, "All clear. B team is the winner." They were instructed to help us figure out the mess we had made with the mats. And to add insult to injury, Squirrel was relieved of his duties, and B team's leader was in charge. Under new leadership and with the extra manpower, it didn't take very long at all to get all the mats inside the room and squared away.

The B team leader was the polar opposite of the A team leader, everything from his demeanor to how he gave out orders. Mostly, though, he kept constant communication with us and listened to our suggestions and/or problems. His was a far cry from the "my way or the highway" approach of Squirrel. Our last task was to then take all the gear and place it back inside. We had finally finished, but well past the 90-minute time cap.

"B team, you won. You can sit down and hydrate. A team, you lose. Time to pay."

Our punishment was to clean the entire grinder with a small push broom and toothbrushes. That's right, toothbrushes. And not just any brush, but the really cheap and crappy kind. I grabbed a red toothbrush and went to work. There were about 100 of these 12×12 cement squares that made up the grinder floor. Each square had its own joints surrounding it, and inside of those joints were all the dirt and debris that had been acquired over the weekend. The task sucked, and all eyes were on us to make sure we were moving with purpose and efficiency.

As we moved from tile to tile cleaning each joint, someone with the push broom would come in behind us to sweep it all up.

I was literally cleaning on my hands and knees, which hurt from all the abuse they'd taken up to that point. My knees were swollen from all of the running, squats, rucking, you name it. Kneeling on the hard cement was pure torture. The B team was enjoying their reward of some much-needed R&R, and as they sat down on their folding chairs and drank from canteens, they watched us work like a chain gang.

As we picked away the debris with our toothbrushes, I also had time to reflect on why we were in that position. It came down to one thing and one thing only: a failure in leadership.

PACK YOUR RUCKSACK

An exercise in leadership

There's a saying in BUDS that goes like this, "There's no such thing as a bad boat crew, just a bad boat crew leader." An experiment that is commonly performed is to take the first and last place boat crews and switch out the boat crew leader during evolutions. This allows the last-place crew to have the first-place leader and conversely, the first-place crew to have the last-place leader in command. A couple of things typically happen. As with any change in leadership, there's a new style or way of doing things, which will immediately affect the culture of the team. If the culture is impacted positively, the team will gel quickly and act as one. If the culture is impacted negatively, there will be no team, and performance will erode over time. What do you think typically happens? If you guessed that the last place team starts to perform better and rise to the top, you are correct. Consequently, the first- place team armed with their Squirrel leader typically starts to falter, and their performance drops.

You see this a lot in sports, in particular at the professional level. Head coaching positions are hard to come by, and if you are one of the select few in this role, you are typically on a short leash. Your job as a coach is to build a winning program and represent the school or league accordingly. At the end of the year, the numbers speak for themselves. No matter what, there are teams with winning and losing records, but only one true champion. And at the end of the year, it's a whirlwind of how quickly coaches are picked, plucked, and enticed to jump ship from one team to another.

In the NFL, it's even got its own name; it's called Black Monday. And every year, without fail, it leaves several head coaches without a job as others are brought in to fill their role and establish a new culture. Is it fair? Maybe, maybe not. I think there can be exceptions, but if your team isn't performing the way you want, it's on you as the leader. You own that.

CHALLENGE

Move On.

Examine your own life for a moment. Go back to the exercise I had you do earlier, where you identified all the teams you are a part of. In that exercise, you were to also label your role on the team, whether you were the leader, follower, manager, etc.

Now I want you to think back to a time in your life where you were on a team and you and the leader didn't see eye to eye. Get real. Who was actually at fault? Was it solely on the leader, or did you have a hand in making the situation worse? Rarely can the blame be 100% on the leader; however, the buck does stop at the top.

What could you have done differently during that time to have a better outcome?

What did you learn?

What mistakes did you make along the way?

It's important to write these down so you are not trapped in an endless loop of making the same mistakes over and over again. Finally, and this is going to take some courage and possibly seem awkward: I want you to reach out to that person and thank them. Maybe you didn't end on good terms, but who cares? If you are (or were) a direct report to them, they had a hand in hiring you and wanted you on their team. Somewhere along the path, things got blurry. That's how life goes. Nothing is black and white, and most of the time, we live in the gray area.

By stepping up and acknowledging them, you will have done some work on your own emotional baggage (which is typically the most challenging to deal with, I might add). We learn more from the things we fail at than the things we get right. Make it right, then move on.

19

DOUBLING DOWN

"Give a man a fish and feed him for the day, teach a man
to fish and feed him for a lifetime."

—AN OLD PROVERB

THE OLD 96ER

After our spring-cleaning session was over, I heard one of the cadresmention something about Sunday morning breakfast. Breakfast? No way I had heard that right, but sure as sunrise, they asked us if we were hungry and wanted breakfast. There had to be a catch or part of some cruel joke. But they were serious. "Hooyah," we all fired back.

"Well then, follow us." They led us on a leisurely walk a couple of blocks down the road.

We walked the mean streets of Encinitas like zombies, beaten up and battered, complete with our dirty PT clothes. I'm sure we all smelled ripe, too. We were approaching a full 48 hours of no sleep, zero showers, and more PT than I can recall doing in a month, let alone two days.

As the coaches led us down the sidewalk to a location unknown to us, we passed locals and saw the looks on their faces. It was priceless. Everyone could tell we weren't from around there and stuck out like a sore thumb. The locals mostly wore flip flops, yoga pants, workout gear, and swim attire. We, on the other hand, had on combat boots, BDU pants, and dirty white T-shirts with our names stenciled on them. The cadres were the pied pipers, and we were the rats being led out of the city.

After about a ten minute walk, we were in front of a restaurant called The Potato Shack. We marched into a back room, where we had private seating. The place smelled amazing, and we immediately took our seats. My teammates and I were segregated from the coaches as well as the other patrons.

Within minutes, every staff member in the place started hustling food to each one of us. We had hot plates of hash browns, eggs, bacon, and pancakes with warm syrup and butter. To top it all off, we also had coffee, water, and orange juice to wash it all down. I was in heaven, or so I thought.

There was one small problem. I wasn't hungry. I'm not sure if it was all the training we had completed up to that point, being tired and sleep-deprived, or a combination of both, but I knew it wasn't a good sign. If a person loses their appetite, generally something is wrong, and in extreme cases of overtraining, this can occur. Yeah, I guess you could say I probably qualified as an extreme case.

Despite that fact, I knew I needed the calories and had to force myself to eat. Have you ever had to force-feed yourself? Not fun, especially when you have two huge plates of food staring back at you. Truthfully, I would have been content just sipping on some coffee and water.

One of the cadre walked past our table. I was taking my time, looking around the room and taking in the moment as I sipped from my coffee mug. I hadn't touched my food yet.

"You all have ten minutes to eat, and you must eat everything on your plate. If you don't eat everything, you'll get some special treatment outside."

I gulped and knew what that meant. *Either I force-feed myself all of this food or suffer the consequences.* I scanned the room.

Everyone else seemed to be hungry and was gorging themselves.

Time for me to suck it up. I switched from coffee to water and began force-feeding my plate of eggs, hash browns, and bacon. This actually went down fairly quickly and easily, but I was full and still had a huge plate of pancakes the size of my face left to devour. Pancakes traditionally fill me up pretty quickly, and I've never been one to eat very many, let alone a plate that big. I was in trouble.

Have you ever seen the movie *The Great Outdoors*, with John Candy and Dan Aykroyd? There's a scene where both men's families eat together at a local spot in the middle of nowhere called Paul Bunyan's Cupboard. They have just sat down to order their meal when Dan Aykroyd's character Roman talks John Candy's character Chet into ordering something called "The Old 96er." The Old 96er is 96 ounces of prime aged beef steak, and if Chet or any other member of his party ordered the 96er and finished it, everybody would eat for free.

Chet started off strong but began struggling about halfway through, and visible meat sweats could be seen coming off his brow. He continued force-feeding himself meat until he could barely lift the fork to his mouth. With one last piece of meat left, he thought he was done, and a big smile warmed his delirious face.

Roman looked at the burly cook, who was standing overhead judging, and said, "Well, I think that just about does it."

The giant cook said, "He's not done yet."

Roman replied, "Well, he may take a little while with that last bite, but it'll go down."

"That ain't the last bite," the giant cook replied.

"Well, sure it is. There's nothing on that plate but gristle and fat." The cook just looked at him pointedly.

Chet squirmed in his seat, realizing he was not done and had to eat all the gristle and fat on his plate to accomplish the mission. That's exactly what I felt like in that moment. I was Chet Ripley looking down at my huge plate of pancakes. It might as well have been the fat and gristle from The Old 96er. There was zero chance I could shove that amount of food down my throat.

Time was ticking away.

I was scrambling and didn't know what to do. I thought about hiding the plate of food under the table or somehow putting the food in my cargo pockets, excusing myself to the bathroom, and flushing it down the toilet.

I looked around my table.

Most men were done eating, and I hadn't even started on my hotcakes. I looked at my teammate next to me and asked him if he wanted them.

He ended up splitting them with a teammate across from me.

I was relieved. My plate was clear, I was completely full, and my teammates bailed me out of what was sure to be some extra suffering. And not a moment too soon.

A coach walked into our room and told us it was time to move out. I wondered what was coming at us next. Since sunrise on Sunday, we had cleaned the complex at HQ and had been treated to a wonderful breakfast. I knew the heat was going to get turned up on us.

We walked out of the restaurant, made a left, and continued walking until we took another left to walk along a back alley behind the restaurant. That path would eventually lead us directly to HQ.

HAMBURGER HANDS

Once we were behind the restaurant, we were ordered to stop. The cadre approached us and told us that we would have to burpee broad jump all the way back to HQ. You could barely see HQ in the distance, and I figured it was roughly five to six blocks away. Was it a bad dream? Burpees suck, and broad jumps aren't much fun, either. But combining them both on a completely full stomach? It was going to be terrible.

The cadre signaled, and it was go time, so we formed up into two lines. The movement was slow and painful. As if broad jumps weren't bad enough, the push-up portion of the burpees on the street was starting to take its toll. Not on my chest like you might think, but rather on my hands. Hitting the deck repeatedly on blacktop and cement wasn't exactly doing wonders for my palms. They were getting cut and chafed and started bleeding.

Also, to make matters worse, my teammates were vomiting due to their bellies being full.

I was okay in that department since I didn't overeat. I scanned my peripheral, took stock of the misery we were all in, and went back to mental toughness basics. Control my breathing, get positive, set goals. My body was sore, hip flexors tight, hands bleeding, but I didn't care anymore. My mission was to make it to HQ, and that's all I focused on, one step at a time. I set goals to make it to the next street sign, curb, building, you name it—anything to keep my mind off the pain. Even though my hands resembled hamburger meat, my mind was still sharp and in the game.

After about 45 minutes, I could see HQ in plain sight, and it was only about a block away. This gave me extra energy. It was like running a race and seeing the finish line in sight only to kick it up a few notches and start sprinting the last quarter mile. Only it was not to be.

We were ordered to stop dead in our tracks. Did someone screw up?

I couldn't tell what was going on around me because I was so focused on the finish line. All I heard was the order to halt.

We were immediately instructed to form a line on the side of the alley parallel to the curb and get into plank position. Our feet were up on the curb, and our hands were on the street.

Planks, just what I wanted to do. My hands were already bleeding, and I was going to have to rest on them with my body weight. It sucked.

We held our positions. Minutes wore on. Doubt crept in our minds. Everyone's arms were shaking violently. All I could do was focus on my breathing. Breath control was something I constantly relied on to make it through very strenuous situations. I'd concentrate on breathing in for two seconds and then breathing out for four seconds. It was working. My body was trembling, but I was starting to control my mind.

Then, out of the corner of my left eye, I could see someone or something heading down the alley. The cadre whispered for us all to look strong and not show weakness.

The shadowy figure crept closer and closer until finally he was in plain sight. It was Mark Divine. He slowly walked past us one by one.

We did our best to hold our positions and look like we were tough. It was no different than when in school trying to look cool when you see someone you have a crush on or when your boss at work walks past you in the hall. You want to look your best.

He continued walking until he hit HQ, and I lost sight of him.

We were still holding our planks. I'm guessing it was for around 10 minutes.

Suddenly we were ordered to our feet. That was music to my ears. We were allowed to walk the short distance to HQ and hydrate. My hands were mangled, but I had made it, and I didn't vomit, which was a win.

After hydrating, we were told to clean up because we smelled like sweat, shit, and puke, and ordered to change into a new T-shirt, shorts, and shoes.

We hightailed into the gear room that my team had just cleaned. And of course, we had a time cap to that, too: ten minutes, to be exact.

I located my bag and yanked out the last pair of clean shorts, T-shirt, and socks I had brought. I was out of fresh gear, which meant I had to be getting close to the finish line, which would be sometime today. My feet were in good shape so no need for any special attention there. I was ready for whatever was to hit us next. My team formed up on the grinder, faced the ocean, and sorted into boat crews. This had become second nature. Everyone knew their place. Only one cadre greeted us and led us to the weight room situated just a few yards behind him. We were told to take our shoes and socks off before entering. Once inside the weight room, we were greeted with a surprise. It was Commander Divine. That was it, the pinnacle for me. I knew our weekend was drawing to a close, and there would be plenty of pain left, but having Commander Divine one-on-one with us in the room was a highlight.

He was and still is not only an inspiration but a mentor to me. I had read his books, and trained relentlessly using his SEALFIT programming. His methods had given me some sort of purpose and clarity on life. That's how powerful this stuff is, and I felt I owed him for it. Even though he was one of my mentors, we hadn't even had a 1:1 conversation yet. He didn't know me from anyone else in the crowd. Do you look up to anyone like that in your life? Someone you try to emulate but you haven't really ever met them in person? Well, I had, and I fell in love with the Unbeatable Mind and SEALFIT lifestyle, and if just 10% of it stuck with me, then I'd no doubt be a better man for it.

He greeted our class in a cool, calm demeanor and picked up right where he left off at Vail Lake, which was the last time he had spoken to us. He congratulated us on making it to that point in the training. Not many people get to experience a true Kokoro moment (Kokoro is a Japanese word that translates into the blending of heart and mind into action), but we had. He could tell we were all pumped with excitement. He brought the tempo down several notches, and we began doing some breath exercises as we sat cross-legged on the floor. We stretched and maneuvered through a 30-minute session of sun salutations, downward dogs, and other yoga poses. It felt amazing, and my body needed it for sure.

I was working up a sweat and feeling good. The last exercise we performed was a deadman's pose, which is where you basically play dead on the floor. I'm not sure how long we lay in that position because I fell asleep! Within minutes of lying down on the floor and closing my eyes, I was out. I remember dreaming of my wife and kids. We were all walking on the beach together several years in the future somewhere in Florida. It must have been part of some sort of future-me visualization. We were walking hand in hand, letting the seafoam hit our ankles, and our kids were laughing with pure joy. I glanced over at my beautiful wife with the sun beaming down on her blonde hair, gave her a smile, and then . . . .

BREAKOUT 2.0

"*Breakout!*" That word echoed in the yoga room where my team and I were physically in deadman's pose but mentally in La La Land. At first, I thought it was a bad dream. "*Breakout!*" I heard it again and immediately jumped to my feet. Then the sound of bull horns and screaming ensued. It was pure pandemonium.

We were told to bear crawl from our yoga mats to the grinder. We were immediately hit with cold water upon exiting. That woke me up. We were led to a pile of socks and shoes and told to find ours as quickly as possible all while additional cold water hit us on the face.

I heard one of my teammates shout my name, "Ritter." I looked in his direction, and he threw me one of my shoes. I had written my last name on the back of my shoes for a situation just like that one. Within minutes, I had both shoes but no socks. *Forget it. I don't want to wear wet socks anyway.* Our gear had been hosed down by the cadre. I put my shoes on, and as my feet maneuvered onto the cushioned soles, water sloshed and exited, finding any hole in the fabric to escape through.

We were reliving day one, hour one, all over again. This was Breakout version 2.0, only we'd already been up 48 hours. Dripping wet and still a little delirious from my nap, I stared at the cadre and awaited our next challenge.

What hit us next was a hardcore grinder PT session. This time, though, I knew what to expect and was listening attentively for the cues from the main instructor. Still, it was tough to keep up. We did push-ups and burpees until we couldn't lift our chests off the ground. Air squats by the hundreds and eight-count body builders until our legs trembled.

How much more are they going to make us do, I started asking myself. The all-too-familiar question crept back into my mind: Why am I here? I thought back to the "Why" statement I had written. I imagined my wife and kids standing by the cadre looking at me. Was I going to resemble a weak-minded little wimp with a defeatist attitude? *No. I'm going to be a strong-minded and powerful husband and dad. I got this. Easy day*, I told myself. I tapped into my mind gym and knew I wouldn't break. It wasn't a team event at the moment; it was survival, every man for himself, and me against them.

After a couple of hours of grinder PT 2.0, our session was over. We didn't lose a single soul. My entire class was intact, and my boat crew was looking strong. There wasn't much time for celebration. We were all instructed to pick up a log. Time for some real teamwork with another log PT session.

My boat crew shuffled over to the logs and grabbed the first one we could find. It didn't matter how much it weighed or what it looked like. We were ready for whatever.

For the next 30 minutes, we attentively listened to each command the cadre gave us and worked as a team to complete each movement. Up log, down log for reps. Military press from shoulder to shoulder for countless movements. Lunges with the log against our chest until our arms were numb. Sit-ups, chest presses. You name it, we did it.

We rocked the evolution, and you want to know why? Because we were moving as a team and putting out. We could have rocked those logs all day. Apparently, the rest of my class must have been rocking, too, because the cadre were noticing, and I could almost see a smile on some of their faces. On Sunday morning, after 48 hours of getting the crap knocked out of us, Kokoro class 38 was a real team. No more selfishness. We were a unified whole forged in the fire of adversity.

THE BIG FINISH

After log PT was over, we placed the logs back into the staging area. We were allowed to hydrate quickly and then informed that we had a timed run. This go-around, however, our entire team would have to finish under the time cap. We were instructed to run to Lookout Point, a spot about a mile away from HQ, where one could overlook the ocean and beach. We had ten minutes to make it there and back.

My class took off, and instead of every man for himself, we put the weaker runners up front and had them pace us. It was great. With our weakest runner up front, the run became a slow recovery jog. The sun was shining down on us, and we were all feeling great, knowing that the end was near.

We could feel a sense of pride and accomplishment. We made it to Lookout Point, took a few seconds to take in the scenery, and then made our way back to HQ.

I held my chest out, smiling from ear to ear. "Looking good, feeling good, ought to be in Hollywood" was playing in my head. Everything was going perfect until one of my teammates in my own boat crew came up lame about a quarter of a mile away from the finish line. His knee was locking up, and he could hardly move.

We gave him about 30 seconds to see if it would go away. It didn't. There was no way he could run back. He could barely walk.

I could feel our time ticking away, and we wouldn't make the time limit. Only one thing left to do. I picked him up and buddy carried him all the way back to HQ for the last quarter mile. In that moment, knowing our time was ticking away and our class would surely get beat down, adrenaline took over. I hoisted him up but couldn't really feel his body weight. He could have weighed 300 pounds for all I cared. Either way, we were all going to make it back in time.

As we rounded a corner, we had the finish line at HQ dead in our sights, and all of the cadre were lined up cheering us on. Some locals who happened to be around to witness it were also in the mix. They didn't know what was going on, and the look on their faces was priceless. I finished at the back of the pack, and as I crossed the finish line, I was excited as hell, tired, and ready for my buddy to hop off my back. "Congratulations," I remember being told by one of the cadres. "Great job," "congrats," "hooyah" were being tossed at us by all the cadre and spectators. I looked for my boat crew members, whom I had grown very close to during the weekend, and sought them out for celebratory hugs.

PSYCH!

Only there would be no hugs. In an instant, as if someone had magically thrown a switch and turned off the party, the cadre went from cheerleaders to tormentors. "You're not done. Get back in there for more PT!" The yelling had ratcheted back up, and it was pure chaos again. What a cruel joke. I felt like I had just finished a marathon, crossed the finish line, and received my medal only to be told I had another three miles left and to have my medal stripped away.

As we hightailed it back onto the grinder, I could see different stations set up for us. It would be no ordinary PT session. It was a "special" kind of party, and we were the guests of honor. The cement ground had water hoses, buckets, tires, stretchers, ice tubs, and all sorts of fun lying around just waiting for us. We were quickly split back into boat crews. Each crew would rotate stations until everyone got to experience the fun.

FIRST STATION

My group reported to the area that housed several water buckets and hoses. For the next 30 minutes, we were forced to lie face-up and take turns rolling on top of one another. Think of a fartlek run where the last runner is forced to sprint to the beginning of the pack. In this situation, however, there was no running. Everyone would lie down, and the person on the far left side would have to press themselves up on top of the next person and barrel roll down the line. If I had a dollar for every time someone landed on my satchel, I probably could have purchased a flight home with it. Oh yeah, one more thing. The cadre took turns throwing buckets of water on our faces and hosing us down.

After many barrel rolls, we were forced into a human centipede circle. We had to keep ourselves connected at all times, and our feet were supported by the shoulders and back of the person behind us. On the cadre's count, we would perform push-ups in unison. All it took was for one person to move out of order to throw our entire movement off course. And, you guessed it, all of this while being hosed down with cold water and buckets of it being thrown on us. Fun times indeed.

SECOND STATION

After more push-ups and planks than I care to count, we reported next to a stretcher. I hadn't seen them since our mountain phase up on Mt. Palomar. One person took each corner of the litter and hoisted the last guy up, and we walked around HQ. Sounds easy, right? Wrong.

In true SEALFIT fashion, the four support people were forced to wear blindfolds while the person on top of the litter gave directions on when to turn and move. Oh, and those socks we all had lost earlier before entering the yoga room? Those were our blindfolds. I got to wear someone's sweat-soaked, fungus-loaded, microbic tube sock around my face.

We all took turns supporting the litter and then riding on top shouting out orders. It was a cluster bomb. We were constantly running into things, but we didn't drop anyone. The one thing I feared most was running into was a cadre. I'm thankful that didn't happen. Mission accomplished in my book.

THIRD STATION

I ran over to the third station with the rest of my team after our blindfolded assault on the litter and ran into a familiar coach, Coach McLeod. Instead of buckets of water, ice, hoses, and other devices, he had chalk for us. Chalk?

We were instructed to get into plank position, the lean-and- rest version where our arms were extended straight out instead of being on our elbows and forearms. Then Coach Brad hit his watch. We held the plank for 60 seconds. I was already shaking like a leaf. Then another 60 seconds went by, then another, and another. It had been five minutes of violent shaking for me, but I hadn't dropped to my knees even once.

"Class, you've each held this plank for five minutes. The rest is up to you. Grab some chalks, and write out your 'Why' statement below on the pavement while keeping yourself in plank position. If you hit the ground, your five-minute buy-in starts over."

Easy day. I got this, I remember thinking. I eagerly took the chalk. With my left arm, I held myself up and wrote out my "Why" with my right hand. It looked like this:

"To be the best version of myself for my wife and kids. To be a better husband, father, and human being."

Short and sweet but very effective. Coach Brad walked over toward me and read it aloud. "Hooyah, Ritter. That's what I'm talking about."

I had been the first to finish, and it looked like others were struggling to remember or think of their "Why." It had always been front and center for me during the whole weekend and was a consistent reminder that kept me grounded when I wanted to quit. Coach Brad then ordered me to recover and head over to the tubs. I was on a slight high for having been the first one done and relieved to be out of plank position. Little did I know what I was in for next. My excitement would turn into terror as I was faced with my Achilles heel once again.

FOURTH STATION

Hmmm. What are these ice tubs for? There were two separate tubs, and in each one, there was ice-cold water filled to the top and, you guessed it, an actual layer of ice on top. There were five- pound bags of ice stacked up by the tubs for special effect. The cadre would periodically throw a new bag of ice in just to make sure the water temp was cold enough and to mess with our minds.

I was posted at one end of the first tub, and one of my teammates joined me at the other end.

When the cadre said "Go," we had to dive into the tub headfirst and move underwater to the other side of the tub. Once there, we had to hold our breath for 30 seconds under the water. This was very hard to do. I had trouble doing it in the pool and the lake let alone ice-cold water that takes one's breath away. The temperature of the water was so cold it shocks the human system, so the person starts to lose control of their breath.

My first attempt was unsuccessful. I came up too soon, and the cadre never gave me the signal to pop up.

They were right there in our face with a stopwatch. They started in on me, pretty relentless, too.

My teeth were chattering, and my body was quivering. All I could do was just sit there, freezing to death, taking the verbal abuse.

"We're going to keep you in here until you figure this out." I replied with a chattery "Hoo . . . yah."

"Do it again."

I took as deep a breath as I could manage and submerged my head under. Eyes closed, I concentrated on the sound of my heartbeat. I would not be denied again. Either I was staying under, or they would be bringing a limp, lifeless body out of that torture tub. Time was ticking away with each heartbeat, but so was my oxygen level. I wanted to pop my head back up out of the water but resisted the temptation and made myself hold on for five seconds longer. As I reached five seconds, I felt a tug on my shoulder, and I was hoping that was the all-clear signal to come up for air. Fortunately, it was. But it wasn't over.

Next, they gave me a plastic Coke bottle that had the bottom cut away. I was told to completely submerge underwater and breathe out of the plastic bottle until given the signal to pop up.

"Oh, and don't let me see you pop your head up again, Ritter, or you will pay dearly."

I sighed and swallowed some saliva, then sunk down until my head was under the water and my Coke bottle was the only thing sticking out of the water above the layer of ice. Weird thing was, it wasn't that bad. Sure, I had the initial shock of the cold water on my head, but I was starting to get used to it somewhat since my body was numb.

When I was underwater, I just closed my eyes, and the first thoughts that popped into my mind were of my family. I wondered what Leslie was doing. I'd be talking to her soon and couldn't wait to hear from my kids. I concentrated on my breath, making sure to take smooth controlled inhales and exhales and lowering my heart rate. After several minutes of being underwater, breathing out of a bottle, I felt a nice tug on my shoulder. On to the next ice tub.

This particular tub was on its own, placed away from everything else. *Odd*, I remember thinking, *what's so special about this one?* I'd find out very soon.

Once again, we had to climb into the ice-cold water headfirst, and I was at one end while my teammate was at the other. We just sat there, slowly freezing our balls off. Similar to our ocean torture session, I was pretty sure they'd crawled back into my stomach again.

Time continued to tick away, and I looked at my teammate while we both sat there trembling. The cadre were overly quiet, and that started to worry me a little. What could they be setting us up for? Five minutes passed, then ten.

Finally, one of the cadres starting talking and looked at his watch. "It's time."

Time? Time for what? I was ordered to rest my head on the back of the tub so my face was looking up at the sky and to close my eyes. *Okay, this just got real*, I remember thinking to myself. *What is going on? Are they going to put me in a choke hold now?*

All of a sudden, water was being poured on my face. It shocked me, plus I couldn't breathe, so I shook my head violently and popped forward. I opened my eyes. I could see my teammate having the same thing done to him. The cadre had a five-gallon bucket of water and was slowly pouring it all over his face. We were being waterboarded!

"Ritter, get back here."

The cadre started in on me again. This time, there was no shouting. We were just having a low-key conversation with only one exception: I was being waterboarded during it. I placed my head back into position. This time, I knew what to expect. As the water was being poured on my face, again I held my breath. But that only lasted so long, and after I exhaled all the carbon dioxide from my nose, I was out of breath and tried to suck oxygen down my mouth and throat. I violently shook and thrashed again, coming out of position.

One of the cadre said, "Ritter, you can't hold your breath this long. Find another way."

I was freaking out. What was I going to do? I glanced over at my teammate, and he was struggling just like I was. My breath was out of control, and I was in full-blown panic mode. I was forced to place my head back into position, and I glanced up at the sky. It was beautiful. The sky was blue, and the clouds were few and far between as the sun was beating down.

I closed my eyes and was back in hell and waited for the water to start rushing down my face. It started again. I wanted to freak out but held back. I just sat there and took it. Now I'm not sure how I figured this out, but chalk it up to divine intervention, the human spirit, or both. Something told me to relax and breathe through my mouth. I kept my mouth cracked open slightly, not enough to let water in but enough to keep an open airflow. Due to the restrictiveness of the airflow, I then took some quick, short breaths through my mouth to keep enough oxygen in my system, so I didn't pass out.

It worked.

I might have sounded like a pregnant woman at a Lamaze class, but it worked like a charm.

Having discovered this new technique, I became relaxed and just let the water roll over my face, making sure to feel every drop of water as it made streams across my skin.

Then the cadre started peppering me with questions. It had become an interrogation, or as some refer to it, the mad minute.

What's your name? Why are you here? How old are you? These were easy. Then I had to repeat whatever they said. First up was the first stanza of the poem "Invictus," then a few lines from the SEAL Creed, and finally something in Arabic. I had no clue what that phrase meant, but I was quickly reprimanded for it.

"Ritter, you just said 'Death to America.' Are you some kind of terrorist? Where's your home cell?"

The verbal abuse was on. All the while, mind you, water was being poured over my head. I energetically reminded the cadre that I wasn't a terrorist and that I love America. After they had their laughs at forcing me to degrade our own country, waterboarding class was over.

"Ritter, get out. You did well. Now, run over to that big tire over there."

"Hooyah!" and I was out of the ice-cold tub quicker than you can say *ISIS*.

Soaking wet after being waterboarded and a bit delirious from holding my breath under water in an ice tub, I walked rapidly across the grinder from one side to the other. I was told to head over to the big tire.

There were actually two in front of me, and I hadn't bothered asking which one. The first had six of my teammates spread out around it taking turns doing deadlifts with it.

The other was massive and about twice the size and weight of the former. There was no one with that tire.

After being in an ice bath for a while, the cold can numb various parts of your body. Problem was, it apparently had numbed my brain as well. For some stupid reason that still haunts me to this day, I chose to go over to the massive tire where no one else was. When I reached it, I just stood there looking around, dumbfounded and lost. I was only there a couple of seconds when that eerie feeling of "Oh, man I'm in the wrong place" set in. Problem was, I wasn't the only one who noticed my lack of attention to detail. A cadre was immediately on my ass.

"Ritter, what the **** are you doing?"

"I was told to go to the big tire, Coach."

"Do you think you're at the right one?" "No, Coach."

"Ritter, you're a bleeping idiot. Report to Coach L for extra sauce, and tell him you're an idiot."

"Hooyah!"

I knew I was in it deep. I'd made it all this way, through three days and two nights and over 48+ hours of PT, rucking, swimming, ocean torture, beatdowns, log work, etc. to get caught up like that? I reported to Coach L with a sad look on my face.

He looked at me with disgust and wondered why I was in his presence. "Why aren't you with the rest of your teammates?"

I quickly explained the situation and that "Taco told me to report to you for extra sauce, oh, and one more thing, that I'm an idiot."

"I see. Follow me, Ritter."

Coach L escorted me back to the massive tire where I had been all by myself.

"Have you ever seen the *Karate Kid*, Ritter?" Growing up in the '80s, it was one of my favorite movies. I mean, who didn't want to take Karate after seeing that movie?

"Hooyah, Coach," I replied.

"Then you are familiar with the crane kick, am I right?" "Hooyah," I said energetically.

"I want you to stand on top of the tire in crane kick position while saying, 'Coach L, I'm an idiot' until I say stop."

"Hooyah," and with that, I hopped up on the tire, which came up to my thighs, and awaited the go signal.

Coach L calibrated his watch and gave me the go signal.

I immediately stood with my right leg planted with a slight bend at the knee and my left knee raised up in the air to my midline. I raised both of my arms above my head with my hands tilted toward the ground ever so slightly. Mr. Miyagi would have been proud. I was in full crane position ready to do battle with the Cobra Kai. Only there was no target, no bully to fight, no real endgame. My opponent was myself, and as seconds passed, the balancing act took its toll. After 20 seconds, I dropped.

Coach L replied, "There's two ways to do something, the right way and again!" Now get back up there.

Again, I took to the crane position only to fall once more. "Aren't you forgetting to say something, Ritter?" Said, Coach L.

"I'm an *idiot*."

I began to repeat that phrase over and over and over again until I was told not to. I stood back up on the tire.

"Again," said Coach L, and for a third time, I took the crane position, and for a third time, I dropped.

"Balance isn't your strong suit, is it, Ritter?"

Coach L could see right through me. Although I might appear strong on the outside, my balance and flexibility were pretty flimsy. That's the beautiful thing about going through these types of crucibles. Everyone's weaknesses are revealed sooner or later, and everyone has weaknesses.

"So, you're a great runner? Great, then hop in the pool, and let's see what you've got in the water."

"So, you can do a lot of push-ups? Awesome, grab that ruck, and let's see you move weight over a long distance."

"You think you're a good leader? Great, then take your boat crew into the cold Pacific, and sit there until you're near hypothermic, and then let's see how well you lead."

You kind of get the picture. We all have weaknesses, and it's important to know what they are so we can work on them.

I was zero out of three attempts in holding my crane kick. Coach L told me that I would be on that tire until I could hold my position for 30 seconds straight, and we would be there all day if I had to. I started really doubting myself.

You think this sounds easy, right? Go ahead and try it. Right now, I want you to stand up and get into the crane position and hold it for 30 seconds without bringing your leg down. Hard enough for most, I'm betting. Now imagine doing it on top of a tire with uneven tread after you've been awake more than 50 hours getting the shit knocked out of you.

Coach L then told me he'd give me some help. He grabbed Taco, who was busy hosing down my other teammates. Taco came over with his hose.

"You need to concentrate, Ritter. Coach Taco will hose you down in the face to help focus. Ready? Begin."

Are you kidding me? I thought. *I'm having a hard time doing this dry, let alone with a water hose being force-fed onto my face.*

Coach Taco came over. "You're going to remember this one, Ritter." I think he even cracked a smile while saying it.

Within seconds, I was back up on the tire, holding the crane kick position and getting water shot in my face. It was my fourth attempt, and I only lasted 10 seconds until I came crashing down. I was pissed, took zero time to recover, and hopped back up. I made it to about 20 seconds on the fifth try but came crashing down again. My right knee had buckled since it had been carrying all of the weight. I was really beginning to think I was never going to make it. I mean, I tried five times with everything I had and couldn't do it.

"My kids could do this, Ritter," Coach L said sadistically.

My kids, of course! I had been trapped in my own head of self- doubt. I instantly visualized my own kids being there, watching me fall time and time again. I always told them to *NEVER* give up, and if you fall seven times, you get up eight. Time to prove it. I was soaking wet. Mind you, just because I had fallen off the tire doesn't mean that Coach Taco had turned the hose off.

My mindset instantly changed when I thought of my kids, Hallie and Brody. I hopped back up on that tire, with a slight smirk on my face, knowing I was going to win this time.

On my sixth try, I was finally able to hold the crane position for 30 seconds. Coach L shouted "Recover," and I eagerly dropped off the tire.

Coach Taco stopped soaking me with the hose and focused his attention on my other teammates. Coach L asked me what I had just learned. "That my balance is terrible," I replied.

He said bingo and told me that when I got back home and resumed training, I should focus on my weaknesses instead of my strengths. I instantly knew that meant swimming, balance, and flexibility for me.

Then I was told to join my other teammates who were putting in work on the other tire. I quickly ran over to join them, and for the rest of that evolution, we deadlifted a tractor tire up and down over and over again until the cadre told us to stop.

I'm an idiot.

PACK YOUR RUCKSACK

Double down on your weaknesses.

When I was in my mid-thirties, I noticed something about myself. Sure, I was "successful" by society's standards, but I constantly felt on edge and didn't feel like I was measuring up and being the kind of father and husband I could be. I'd spend multiple days on the road throughout the year and for work and for what? To say that I'm Marriott Platinum Elite? All that means is that you're never home.

And when I finally did come home from a work trip, I never really *came home*. Sure, I would walk in from the garage, take my shoes off, and enter my house, but I wasn't engaged with my family. I wasn't present. I couldn't find a way to shut work off.

What's worse, I'd often take it out on my kids if they spilled drinks or made messes. What a jerk! As if they were trying to have an accident. Not to mention how I must have been treating my wife, who was just glad I was home and relieved I could help out around the house. I was short with her, too, and didn't actively listen to her. Her conversations would go in through one ear and out the other. And if I came home to a house that wasn't clean, with dishes in the sink and loads of dirty clothes, I'd be in a bad mood and take it out on her. Why couldn't she keep up with the house while I was out busting my hump? Did she have any idea what it was like for me to be gone all the time? It's not like I was on vacation or something. Like I wanted to be away from home on a work trip, anyway.

I needed help. By sheer luck, I started listening to Mark Divine's *Unbeatable Mind* podcast one day while on the road for a work trip. He had on a guy by the name of Larry Hagner, who leads a tribe of men called The Dad Edge. It's a group of dads whose mission is to help men optimize their finances, marriage, connection with their kids, business, and health.

When I tuned in, Larry said something that has stuck with me to this day. He said, "What good is coming home with a pocket full of money to a house full of strangers?" Shots fired on that one. That hit me hard and shook me to the core. Then he spoke about coming home and shared some tips on how to create an environment where you leave your work mode behind and put your dad and husband hat on before setting foot in your house.

I followed his advice, and it worked. It changed my relationship almost overnight with my wife and kids. I realized that I was emotionally weak and needed help. I reached out to Larry, and he told me about his Dad Edge Alliance (DEA) group. It's a private group that men could join and then get placed into weekly mastermind calls to talk with other like-minded men about their struggles, and everyone on the call offers advice.

If I could improve my relationship with my wife and kids by listening to a guy I've never met, as he talked on a podcast for a few minutes, imagine what I could do in a tribe of like-minded individuals who meet weekly for an hour and discuss some of our most vulnerable and intimate thoughts. I decided to double down on my own weaknesses.

CHALLENGE

Tackle Your Five Mountains.

Why run from your weaknesses? Better yet, do you even know what they are? Take stock of your own situation right now, and write down the things you think you suck at. Now I want you to make a list of things that you aren't so good at. Categorize them into two groups: your professional/work life and your personal life. What you'll often find is your personal and professional weaknesses are not mutually exclusive. Most if not all of your professional weaknesses stem from your personal ones and vice versa.

In the book, *Unbeatable Mind*, author Mark Divine teaches the five mountains as a path to become the best version of yourself and become a world-centric authentic leader. By working on each mountain— whether it be the physical, mental, emotional, intuitional, or spiritual—you are growing daily on your path to self-mastery, which is a lifelong pursuit.

For this challenge, I want you to focus on your personal life. With luck, these weaknesses may even be the things you are scared of, which is probably why you've been avoiding them. No one wants to admit what they suck at, but it's how you grow as a fully integrated human being. Get real here. I just told you I was a total failure as a husband and dad and wasn't meeting my own standard regarding what or how I thought I should be operating in those roles.

Now rank your weaknesses, and prioritize which one you want to work on first. If you need help, check your ego at the door and find a coach, mentor, group, or someone else who can help you. *If you visit my website, schoolofgrit.org, you will find a free Five Mountain Assessment you can take to measure your baseline.* How can you begin on your path of self-mastery and becoming the best version of yourself if you don't know where you are right now? That's like trying to find an address on a map without knowing your current location. Get your bearings first. Give it a shot. What do you have to lose? If not now, when?

20

"YOU ARE SECURE!"

*"When I dig another out of trouble, the hole from which
I lift him is the place where I bury my own."*

—NORMAN VINCENT PEALE

"Form a height line. Grab logs," was our next command given over the megaphone.

We were all thinking the exact same thing: when would it be over? At this point, we'd all been up for over 50 straight hours. We waited patiently, standing at full attention. We could hear birds chirping and vehicles driving by on the side street adjacent to the grinder.

Then Commander Divine entered the scene and took charge. He wasted no time. There would be no speeches, callouts, or words of wisdom. Strictly business. His first words were, "Prepare to up log."

As a team, we squatted to the ground and placed our hands in position to pick it up.

"Up log."

We picked up the heavy log, and placed it on our left shoulder.

Commander Divine then asked us to close our eyes for the rest of the log PT session. "I want you to perform 10 perfect four- count overheads. If you fail, we'll hit the surf for three to four more hours of ocean PT."

The thought of spending another 3–4 hours getting wet and sandy left me salty, as I'm sure it did for the rest of my class, so we were all-in on nailing the movement.

Commander Divine began counting. "One."

We lifted our logs from our left shoulder resting position above our heads.

"Two."

We transferred the log from above our heads to our right shoulder.

"Three."

We lifted our logs from our right shoulder resting position to above our heads.

"Four."

We transferred the log from overhead to the left shoulder starting position. That was one total rep on our way to 10.

Now, I can't speak for the other boat crews since my eyes were closed the entire time, but my crew was stellar. We were moving in perfect harmony, and everyone was putting out. We'd become a well-oiled machine and could feel our way through the movements even with our eyes closed. On our 10th and final four- count overhead, we rested the log on our left shoulder, and a smile cracked on my face. I knew we had just successfully met Commander Divine's standard, but had the rest of my class followed suit?

With my eyes still closed, I heard Commander Divine tell us to hold our logs in the extended arm position (log above our heads) for 45 seconds. It would not be easy but would be totally doable if everyone on the team shared the load.

Within seconds, my arms started to shake, which caused me to start breathing deeply and heavily. I could hear some of the cadres walking up and down the boat crews and offering words of encouragement as we no doubt had looks of torment on our faces. I could hear people fighting and grunting all around me.

I heard one of the cadre say to suffer in silence, which meant we should keep our display of weakness quiet.

One of them walked to me and whispered in my ear, "Show no weakness, Ritter," which instantly sent me into full-on beast mode. No way was I dropping the log. I'd come too far to mess it all up. I concentrated on breathing through the pain, remembering some of the tactics I had learned during the weekend to build mental toughness. *Breathe. Think positive. This will all be over soon.*

Then I heard the six most wonderful words ever spoken. Commander Divine announced, "*Kokoro class 38 you are secure!*"

Did I hear that right, or am I imagining things? It took a couple of seconds for it to all sink in, for me to realize that with those magical words, my quest to find myself and set out on the greatest crucible in my life up to that point was finally over. I had done it. The event I had dedicated the previous six months of my life to training, living, breathing, and sleeping for had come to a close, and I didn't just survive, I thrived. Truth be told, if we would have had to go longer, I was ready for it, but I was definitely happy that it was over.

The scene on the grinder was pure bliss. Aside from marrying my beautiful wife and having our two kids, it was the happiest moment of my entire life. Never had I pushed myself so hard for so long physically, mentally, and emotionally, without sleep and with minimal food. There were handshakes and hugs as we embraced each other starting with our own boat crews and then opening up to the rest of our class and finally the cadres themselves. Grown men cried, and I'm talking about tears of pure joy. The cadres lined up to shake our hands, and one by one, we greeted every coach and looked them in the face as we offered our most sincere thank-you. It was a truly honorable moment, and I was lucky to be a part of it.

End Game.

Kokoro 38 class secured.

Kokoro 38 Cadre.

Coach Brad McLeod and me after securing Kokoro 38.

Before the after-party really started, Commander Divine congratulated us for our outstanding accomplishment. Very few have signed up for—and even fewer have graduated—his infamous camp. He delivered an after-action review and asked the group what we had learned about ourselves over the weekend.

Several guys chimed in with their own self-assessments. After every man took a turn discussing what he had learned over the weekend, Commander Divine then handed out some awards. Each of us was handed a certificate of completion hand-signed by Commander Divine himself. It read:

Kokoro 38

This certificate presented in honor of completion of SEALFIT
Kokoro Camp on July 24th–26th, 2015 to Brad Ritter.

Finally, to bring everything full circle, Commander Divine issued a final challenge in the form of a question. He asked us, "*What's next?*"

Pretty simple question, not-so-simple answer. His intent was for us to always be of a mindset where we are challenging ourselves and looking at the next event, business opportunity, or way to serve others. After all, if you aren't growing, you're slowly dying.

After we were officially dismissed and celebratory beers were handed out, there was only one person in the world I wanted to talk to, and that was Leslie. I dialed her up, and she answered on the second ring.

"Hello," Leslie answered. I could tell in her voice she was excited to hear from me. The last time she had heard from me was Thursday morning, which was about 3.5 days prior, and she hadn't heard a peep from me except for a "wish me luck" style of conversation right before I headed out for SEALFIT HQ early Friday morning.

"Hey, babe, I did it. I freaking did it." She could hear the jubilation in my voice.

"I just wanted you and the kids to know I made it and I'm okay." She was excited and relieved at the same time, although probably more of the latter. I know she was worried about me and probably didn't sleep well not knowing exactly where I was, what I was doing, and whether I was okay. She was just glad it was all over. Win or lose, she'd love me just the same.

I hated doing something like that to her, but sometimes in life, you have to go out on your own to forge your path. It's all part of your hero's journey. These are precious opportunities to get deep into your own head and master your self-dialogue. The path of self-mastery is an uncommon path and is also a lifelong pursuit. To achieve this mission, sometimes you have to be a little selfish and make it about you.

Aftermath.

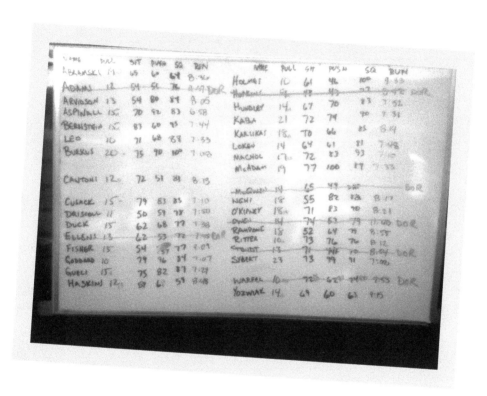

Our PST scorecard.

After party.

I left California the following day. It was bittersweet. On the one hand, I had just conquered something so difficult that many couldn't meet the minimum standard to even attend let alone finish. But that wasn't the only thing. I'd also met some of the most extraordinary people in the world: SEALs, teammates, teachers, mentors, etc., and forged a relationship with them that can never be duplicated. On the other hand, I was heading home a changed man who hadn't seen his wife and kids for some time. I couldn't wait to see them, and I wondered if they would recognize the changes in me. I felt reborn and this was Brad Ritter version 2.0 coming home.

The original t-shirt from class 001. Never given always earned.

I don't remember flying home because I slept almost the entire flight. But what I do remember was wearing the coveted black SEALFIT T-shirt I had just earned and proudly sporting it throughout the airport and onto the plane. Shortly after takeoff, I took out my notepad and started journaling my epic adventure. I mentally recalled the entire weekend and chicken scratched a timeline of events along with the evolutions that were happening at that specific time. I wanted to be able to remind myself of everything I had gone through, and those few pages of notes would provide just the very thing to jog my memory.

I never had any intention to turn those words into the book you're reading right now. I mean, we are literally talking about something I quickly jotted down into a notebook and had tucked away for safekeeping for almost a year before making the decision to write and publish a book about the experience. What you've just read is a condensed version of those 50 hours.

Kokoro Camp changed everything for me, and I do mean *everything*. It has altered the way I think. The experience changed the game of life for me. I'm not saying life for me is easy now. I deal with a lot of the same stuff you do. Being a husband, father, son, brother, cousin, uncle, friend, coworker, and entrepreneur isn't without its own sets of challenges. But after making it through an experience like this, life has gotten just a little bit easier. Those who have battled true adversity know exactly what I'm talking about. Because they know it can always be worse. And when adversity hits you in the face, you can always go back to that place of suffering to help you make it through.

Someone right now, right this very second, has been dealt a much crappier hand than you have, and they aren't complaining. They aren't quitting and throwing in the towel. They are getting after it each and every day, step by step, goal by goal. Each and every one of us puts a self-imposed ceiling on what we think we can or can't do. We are our own worst enemy, and we must master our inner dialogue in order to break those glass ceilings we put over ourselves.

Our mind will always follow the path of least resistance because it knows it's easier. We tend to stay clear of anything that requires extra thought, energy, emotion—basically all the "hard" stuff. I guess if I had to sum up my own message to you, it would be this:

Do hard stuff every day. Do things that suck, things that scare you. Do the common things uncommonly well.

That's how you learn and grow and create separation in life. That's how you make shifts in your mindset. By being in tough, scary, and uncomfortable situations, you get to examine your own inner dialogue and either listen and succumb to it or correct it.

The choice is yours and yours alone. No one will change the way you think for you. If you're doing it right, there will be times you'll want to quit along the way. That's the goal. That's where the growth happens. That's how you can train your mental toughness and emotional resiliency every day. That's your mind trying to trick you into going down the path of least resistance.

Don't allow it to happen. Teach yourself to shift and respond accordingly. Teach yourself to be unbeatable.

In those 50-plus hours that special weekend, I felt like I gained a couple of decades' worth of knowledge and experience. I was able to live out all the emotions of life, all the peaks and valleys. From dealing with injuries, to losing people you care for, to being broken down and hitting your all-time low and then finding the strength and power you have within yourself to persevere, and finally, pure joy and bliss. I finally found what I was looking for. I was looking for myself, my true self. I had finally met myself for the first time. I'd been stuck in a rut and felt too comfortable for far too long. I needed something or someone to come and break me loose.

You won't find it sitting at your desk punching away at your computer. You won't find it watching TV, or streaming YouTube, listening to music, or even reading a book. These things can help get you thinking and provide motivation, but there is only one way to change, and that is to put in the *daily* work and *do hard stuff.*

Don't let time run out on you. The time to act is now. Take massive action today!

PACK YOUR RUCKSACK

The P-word

Shortly after securing Kokoro Camp, Commander Divine was giving us an after-action review (debrief). He wanted to know what we had learned from our experience. Several men gave their responses, and then it was my turn.

There was so much going through my head and so many things I could have said, but I settled on one thing. I went back through the evolutions we had performed for over 50 hours, but one in particular was sticking out to me. It was the night ruck on Mt. Palomar on the very first evening. Not only did I hump my own gear all night, but I also carried my teammate's load, which made the evolution twice as difficult. I'm not complaining about that. I was one of the stronger ruckers of the group, and I was honored to do so.

What I didn't tell you was all the convincing and conversations I had to have with my teammate in order for him to offer up his gear. Right from the start, we could see he was going to struggle with walking up and down a mountain all night loaded down with gear after doing the Murph tribute Hero WOD. He was consistently falling behind and mentally just wasn't in the game. He'd go negative a lot, and we tried to push and pull him along so he could keep up with us. After a while of these shenanigans, I offered to take his gear so all he had to do was walk unassisted and without weight. He refused not once, not twice, but three times.

Only several hours later, after he was beaten down pretty hard by the terrain and added weight, did he finally ask if I would carry his backpack and weapon.

What I learned was a little something about pride, as I explained the situation to Commander Divine and the rest of the class. If generosity is giving more than you need, pride could be taking less than you need because you are too proud. It's a very dangerous emotion. In fact, it is one of the Seven Deadly Sins. But I got to see it play out right in front of me. My teammate was so arrogant that he let his own pride get in the way of asking for help. By the time he did, it was too late, and he was too far gone. That is evident because he quit right after the hike was over the next morning, after, of course, I had carried his gear most of the night. Commander Divine cracked a smile and agreed. He confirmed my suspicion and went on to say that pride is actually a negative emotion. It's okay to show pride in your work, for example, but too often, it comes at the expense of others. Lesson learned.

CHALLENGE

Ask For Help.

What are you struggling with right now? Maybe you haven't even started, but it's an idea in your head, and you're too afraid to ask for help. Or perhaps you're about halfway into a project and don't know which way to go. Don't wait too long. There is a point of no return.

My challenge to you here is to take action and ask people for help. I'm of the belief that most people want the same types of things that you want out of life. And the fact is, people actually like helping other people. Sounds absurd, right? The way the news and social media glorify all the negativity out there in the world makes it look bad (which is probably why I don't watch the news and am not very active on social media).

Asking for help does two things. It shows vulnerability and creates more trust in a relationship. It also makes the helper feel good since they are providing their own expertise. All you have to do is swallow your pride, check your ego at the door, and ask. If it truly takes a village, then why not use it?

"WHAT'S NEXT?"

**"Do today what others won't so you can do tomorrow
what others can't."**

—SMOKE JUMPERS CREED

So, back to the question that Commander Divine posed to my team upon completion of Kokoro 38: What's next? That question really stumped me, and it took a long time to figure out my own answer. I used to think my answer to that question was to keep challenging myself with other crucible-style events. I've completed some gnarly obstacle course races. I ran a 50K trail race solo, and even finished first in a 50-mile ruck with some friends to keep pushing myself. I do believe each and every one of us should tackle some sort of crucible once a year to keep our mind sharp and test our limits. After all, how do you know how far you can go unless you really push it? And what exactly is a crucible?

To me, a crucible event is one where you volunteer or perhaps even pay for an experience in which you'll meet part of yourself for the first time. It's the ultimate test, designed to challenge you on every level. It doesn't have to be a physical challenge, though. It could be learning another language, playing a new instrument, learning a new skill, getting an advanced degree, etc. There are an infinite number of ways to challenge yourself, grow, and learn about your own psyche.

Remember that if you aren't growing, you are slowly dying. But for me, while signing up for extreme physical events and completing them was fun, something was missing. Nothing I've tried lived up to the transformation at Kokoro Camp. This missing piece would soon reveal itself.

About a year after I completed Kokoro Camp, I was listening to Mark Divine's *Unbeatable Mind* podcast on my way home from work. On the podcast, he had a guest by the name of Larry Hagner, who runs a men's group called The Dad Edge Alliance. I made reference to this earlier in the "Double Down on your Weaknesses" section. The Dad Edge is a private group for dads who are looking to up their game in the fatherhood domain. I had mentioned that I liked what I was hearing so much that I contacted the owner and operator Larry Hagner. What I didn't tell you was that we met for dinner one evening in Indianapolis, and that dinner lasted about three hours. He was a big fan of Mark and was super interested in my story of why I chose to go to Kokoro Camp and the lessons I had learned along the way. I'm sure he could see the passion in my body language and vocal inflections as I spoke about the experience, how it changed my life, and how I use those lessons every day.

I asked him what his plans were with The Dad Edge. At the time, he had a successful podcast and large Facebook group dedicated to the show and was looking for a way to evolve. He told me how he wanted to create an *Alliance* (this is what is referred to now as DEA, which stands for Dad Edge Alliance), which would be a safe place for guys to go who really wanted to dig in deep to become the best versions of themselves through a brotherhood of like-minded men. These men would be vetted through an interview process, and each guy would be part of a team that would meet once a week to do life together remotely over video calls.

In that instant, as Larry shared with me his plans, I knew what I needed to do. The answer to Mark's question of "What's next" became crystal clear. On the spot, I volunteered to become Larry's first team leader. Serving others was something I had learned at Kokoro Camp, and I knew that I wanted to serve others in a big way, but I really didn't know how. It wasn't until Larry shared with me his plans that the opportunity revealed itself.

Since that dinner back in 2016, I've lead hundreds of men all over the world in weekly calls over video. It's truly remarkable what I've seen take place. Being remote and facilitating over video instead of together one-on-one in the same room provides a certain security blanket for people, and I find that guys, in particular, can be very quick to open up and show vulnerability. All it takes is for one courageous soul to get real about the issues they are dealing with in life, and others will follow suit. I've seen amazing transformations unfold:

- Guys with addictions being able to pull themselves out of the gutter

- Other guys who aren't showing up as a dad and husband now being the dad they had only dreamed of having when they were growing up

- Men who haven't been able to save for retirement and in credit card debt now living a life of no debt and financial freedom

- Men ditching the "dad bod" and getting in the best shape of their lives.

It's inspiring to say the least, and I get to be a part of the journey. I've had countless men on my own teams go on and become team leaders themselves, which is perhaps the most gratifying. But make no mistake here. I'm not trying to take the credit, and it's definitely not about me; it's about the team; it's about the tribe; it's about the men. I knew I was on the right path in finding my purpose and living it.

I wanted to take my purpose to the next level. As the saying goes, when the student is ready, the master will appear. As I referenced at the beginning of the book, you can grow your grit from the inside out and the outside in. I had spent countless hours growing from the outside in and it was time for me to balance this out by putting in the time and doing the work to grow grit from the inside out. And my mentor was a familiar face. Mark Divine offers an Unbeatable Mind coaching program that seeks to turn people into the best version of themselves by climbing the five mountains of physical, mental, emotional, intuitional, and spiritual development. The path of self-mastery is a lifelong journey, and if you get clear on your purpose, passions, and principles combined with a never- quit spirit, nothing can break you. You will be unbeatable. Anyone can achieve this. But in order to do so, you have to commit to the training and the discipline to do the work each and every day.

After a year-long in-depth study that was a crucible in its own right, I'm now a certified and licensed Unbeatable Mind coach. My purpose is to serve others through teaching, coaching, and facilitation.

I started my own coaching program, coincidentally called School of Grit. It's a lifestyle for those who despise mediocrity and want to take full ownership of their life and be part of a team. Not a traditional team you may have been conditioned into thinking like those commonly found in the business world but a real team that steps into courage, focuses on each other, and trains relentlessly.

If you spend any time at all with folks living in their golden years, it's the shots they didn't take that they remember and regret. Life is short. How will you leave a legacy for yourself and your family? How do you want to be remembered? Someone once told me the definition of hell is that on your last day on earth, the person you could have been will meet the person you became. How do you want that conversation to go?

If you'd like to learn more about me and my coaching services, please visit schoolofgrit.org

PACK YOUR RUCKSACK

The Arrival Fallacy

My friend Vincent Pugliese runs an excellent community called Total Life Freedom (totallifefreedom.com). It's a private group of generous, driven, self-employed freelancers and entrepreneurs who collaborate to achieve a life of time, money, and location freedom. He likes to say, "Success is never bought; it's rented, and the rent is due every day." Translation: you're never "there" and you never really "arrive." You have to keep grinding each and every day. Once you think you've made it to the top, that doesn't mean it's time to sit back and rest. The higher you climb, the farther you can fall, which is why it's even more important to focus and do the hard stuff.

We all know we should set goals in our life, whether they are for business or personal growth. But what happens when that goal you worked so long and hard to achieve is finally behind you?

In an article published by Wanda Thibodeaux on Inc.com[1], she writes that feeling blue after an achievement is actually pretty normal. We have neuroscience kicking us in the face while we're down. The brain releases dopamine, a hormone associated with both motivation and happiness, *in anticipation of* a reward. So, when you're planning and working hard for something, you're in a biological position to feel good. Each milestone gives you another dopamine hit, which makes you want to keep going toward your goal. But when you reach your goal, that release of dopamine drops. It's harder for you biochemically to have joy. This is what she refers to as the arrival fallacy.

If you are ridiculously sure you're going to reach the goal, you essentially can trick your brain into behaving as if you've already reached the end. The work already seems done, like a mere formality, so dopamine starts to drop. Then, when you actually get to the finish line, it doesn't feel as satisfying.

In the worst-case scenario, this can lead to you desperately hopping from goal to goal hoping something, anything, will make you happy. Achieving your goals rarely makes you as happy as you would expect. Think about it. How many people do you know have signed up for a race, completed it, and then just as quickly got out of shape? How many people have lost weight only to gain it all back? Say you finally retired after 30 years of working (or longer). That's awesome; now what? Leaving the military? Thank you for your service. Now, what's your new mission going to be? Arriving is a fallacy. Reaching our goals rarely makes us as happy as we think we'll be. And what if you spend all that time, blood, sweat, and tears to climb to the top only to see that the view sucks?

---

1 (https://www.inc.com/wanda-thibodeaux/why-you-might-feel-empty-after-reaching-a-huge-goal-and-how-to-move-on.html)

In order to achieve my dream of securing Kokoro Camp, I basically put my life on hold and dedicated every free moment to training for the event. Yes, I was joyful after completing arguably the toughest civilian training in the world. But shortly afterward, there was a void. I didn't have another event to train for. What was I going to do with my free time? I needed a new mission, a new goal, or perhaps even a new purpose.

FINAL CHALLENGE

Find Your Purpose.

This is my biggest challenge to you. It's the final piece to the puzzle but should be treated as the keystone and where you should start on your path of self-mastery and growing grit. It's that simple question that haunted me for years: What's your purpose? And it's the question that will remain long after you've achieved your goals and climbed those mountaintops.

There are many methods, strategies, and tactics you can use to help. But this isn't something someone can give you the answer to. You have to do the deep work and find it yourself. My advice is to seek out help and hire a coach or mentor who can guide you to the answer. But don't hire or ask just anyone. Make sure that person is living the kind of life you want for yourself and that they are eating their own dog food.

In the DEA, I had the pleasure of attending the first in-person summit back in 2018. The event was spectacular, and we had a guest speaker named Tuan Nguyen. Tuan is one of the most successful entrepreneurs I've ever met, but his heart and generosity are what truly won me over. I won't go into his personal story here, but if you're interested, you can find a great TEDx talk he delivered about volunteerism. As he spoke at our summit, I was drawn into his message and knew he was one of those people I wanted on my own personal board of directors.

You know the kind of people I'm talking about? The folks that you know, if you spend time with them, will 10x your life?

In his message, he explained how we can begin to identify our own unique gifts or superpowers. His **G.I. F. T.** analogy is what I want to share with you here. It helped me on my path to finding my own purpose in life. It goes a little something like this.

Given by your loved ones or a gift from God. What are you naturally talented in and in a sense born with?

Innate in your soul. What do you constantly think about? What drives you? What do you dream about? Think about your passions here.

Failures you've achieved. This is perhaps my favorite. What have you failed in? The only way we learn and grow is through failure. Nothing ventured, nothing gained. F.A.I.L. can also mean First Attempts In Learning.

Training I've received out of self-interest or education. What skills have you developed through studying and personal development?

I'm not saying that by going through the G.I. F. T. exercise, you'll find your purpose quickly. This can take years to reveal itself. But what I am saying is this is a great place to start. If you have trouble answering these questions, ask a loved one, family, or friends for help.

CONCLUSION

PACKING YOUR RUCKSACK

"You don't have to get ready if you stay ready."

—BRAD RITTER

It's not a matter of whether adversity will hit us but when. Why wait for it to come? I use the term rucksack or ruck to refer to the type of backpack most commonly used in the military. It's designed to carry a lot of weight for long periods of time and distance. Whether you are aware of it or not, we all wear rucks in life. The types of rucks I'm referring to aren't visible to most unless you take a closer look. Your personal ruck is all the weight of life that you carry around with you. It also houses all the tools and gear you will need for your journey. Packing your ruck is an art and not a science. Depending on the terrain, scenario, and mission you'll need different tools for different environments. Pack your own rucksack by properly equipping yourself for it. Seek out purposeful adversity. Invite it into your life, and do hard stuff. If something scares you but is good for you, what are you waiting for? You will find meaning through purposeful pain. I guarantee it. Take note of what worked and what didn't afterward so you can learn from your experience. And if the same event pops up again, you'll be better equipped to handle the situation.

Condition your mind, body, and soul to be ready for anything. You can grow your grit in the physical, mental, emotional, intuitional, and spiritual domains daily.

Over time, these incremental gains will have a compounding effect no different than a savings account. Imagine having a daily practice of growing grit, making those small deposits in yourself, and what you could look like in one day, a week, a month, a year, 30 years?

It's up to you. You have to be the one who decides that enough is enough, to take a stand, find yourself, and put in the work.

Once you're ready, your teacher will appear, and then you won't have to get ready if you stay ready. Be unbeatable!

PACK YOUR RUCKSACK.

Kokoro Camp 38 highlight reel.

APPENDIX

INVICTUS

"Invictus" is a short Victorian poem by the English poet William Ernest Henley (1849–1903). It was written in 1875 and published in 1888—originally with no title—in his first volume of poems, *Book of Verses*, in the section *Life and Death* (*Echoes*).

Out of the night which covers me, Black as the pit from
pole to pole, I thank whatever gods may be
For my unconquerable soul.
In the fell clutch of circumstance I have not winced nor
cried aloud. Under the bludgeoning of chance My head is
bloody, but unbowed.
Beyond this place of wrath and tears, looms but the Horror
of the shade, And yet the menace of the years Finds, and
shall find me, unafraid.
It matters not how strait the gate, How charged with
punishments the scroll,
I am the master of my fate
I am the captain of my soul.

SEAL ETHOS

In times of war or uncertainty, there is a special breed of warrior ready to answer our Nation's call. A common man with an uncommon desire to succeed. Forged by adversity, I stand alongside America's finest special operations forces to serve my country, the American people, and protect our way of life. I am that warrior.

My Trident is a symbol of honor and heritage. Bestowed upon me by the heroes that have gone before, it embodies the trust of those I have sworn to protect. By wearing the Trident I accept the responsibility of my chosen profession and way of life. It is a privilege that I must earn every day.

My loyalty to Country and Team is beyond reproach. I humbly serve as a guardian to my fellow Americans always ready to defend those who are unable to defend themselves. I do not advertise the nature of my work, nor seek recognition for my actions. I voluntarily accept the inherent hazards of my profession, placing the welfare and security of others before my own.

I serve with honor on and off the battlefield. The ability to control my emotions and my actions, regardless of circumstance, sets me apart from others. Uncompromising integrity is my standard. My character and honor are steadfast. My word is my bond.

We expect to lead and be led. In the absence of orders I will take charge, lead my teammates and accomplish the mission. I lead by example in all situations.

I will never quit. I persevere and thrive on adversity. My Nation expects me to be physically harder and mentally stronger than my enemies. If knocked down, I will get back up, every time. I will draw on every remaining ounce of strength to protect my teammates and to accomplish our mission. I am never out of the fight.

We demand discipline. We expect innovation. The lives of my teammates and the success of our mission depend on me—my technical skill, tactical proficiency, and attention to detail. My training is never complete.

We train for war and fight to win. I stand ready to bring the full spectrum of combat power to bear in order to achieve my mission and the goals established by my country. The execution of my duties will be swift and violent when required yet guided by the very principles that I serve to defend.

Brave SEALs have fought and died building the proud tradition and feared reputation that I am bound to uphold. In the worst of conditions, the legacy of my teammates steadies my resolve and silently guides my every deed. I will not fail.

RANGER CREED

Recognizing that I volunteered as a Ranger, fully knowing the hazards of my chosen profession, I will always endeavor to uphold the prestige, honor, and high esprit de corps of my Ranger Regiment.

Acknowledging the fact that a Ranger is a more elite soldier, who arrives at the cutting edge of battle by land, sea, or air, I accept the fact that as a Ranger, my country expects me to move further, faster, and fight harder than any other soldier.

Never shall I fail my comrades. I will always keep myself mentally alert, physically strong, and morally straight, and I will shoulder more than my share of the task, whatever it may be, one hundred percent and then some.

Gallantly will I show the world that I am a specially selected and well trained soldier. My courtesy to superior officers, neatness of dress, and care of equipment shall set the example for others to follow.

Energetically will I meet the enemies of my country. I shall defeat them on the field of battle for I am better trained and will fight with all my might. Surrender is not a Ranger word. I will never leave a fallen comrade to fall into the hands of the enemy and under no circumstances will I ever embarrass my country.

Readily will I display the intestinal fortitude required to fight on to the Ranger objective and complete the mission, though I be the lone survivor.

RANGERS LEAD THE WAY!

In my book, I write about the power of a team and how no one is truly self made. That Rambo, while a great movie, just isn't real. Well if there was a real Rambo, it might just be Congressional Medal of Honor recipient Master Sgt. Roy P. Benavidez. His story is unbelievable and I encourage you to google his name to learn of his selfless act of heroism. In his many presentations over the years, he often read this poem given to him by a nun to share with audiences.

Hello, remember me?
Some people call me Old Glory.

Others call me the Star-Spangled Banner. But whatever they call me, I'm your flag, The Flag of the United States of America. Something has been bothering me,

So, I thought I'd talk it over with you, Because it's about you and me.

Not long ago,

People were lining up

On both sides of the street to see a parade go by.

And naturally, I was leading that parade. Proudly waving in the breeze.

And when your daddy saw me coming, He would immediately remove his hat

And place it over his left shoulder.

So that his right hand would be over his heart. And you, you were standing there

Right next to your dad.

You didn't have a hat, and your little sister,

Not to be outdone, was standing right next to you. Both of you had your right hand over your heart. What has happened now?

I don't feel as proud as I used to. I'm still the same ol' flag.

I see children around playing, shouting. They don't seem to know or care

Who I am or what I stand for.

I saw an elderly man take his hat off, But when he saw others with theirs on,

He turned around and slowly walked away. Hey, I'm still the same ol' flag.

A few stars have been added since those parades long ago. A lot of blood has been shed.

Is it a sin to be patriotic anymore? Have you forgotten who I am?

What I stand for? And where I've been? Anzio, Guadalcanal, Korea and Vietnam. Take a good look one of these days
At the memorial honor wall. Of all the names of all those that never came back.
They gave their lives
For this great nation to be free under God. When you salute me, You salute each and every one of them. Well, it won't be long now and
I'll be coming down that street leading a parade. And proudly waving in the breeze.
So when you see me coming, Stand up straight and salute.
And I'll salute you by waving back. And then I know that you remember.

EVOLUTIONS

Breakout (3 hours)
PST #1
6-count burpees (135 reps)
Van ride (blindfolded with windows up and heater on full blast)
Breath-hold in lake
Low crawl 500 yards along the shore
Crab walk 500 yards
Team race up a hill (3 times)
3-mile run
A quick swim
5-minute perfect plank hold (3 rounds)
PST #2
Murph HERO WOD
26-mile ruck with weapon and water
Litter relay races (5 times)
6-mile light run
Pool competency
500 push-ups
6-mile light run
Log PT laps (each lap one mile)

Games—Hide-and-seek with a sniper, Burnouts on ropes and pull-up bars, KIM's memory games, and Rig takedown

Death by bear crawl with PVC pipe

Tug of war with a loaded-out U-Haul truck

8-count bodybuilders (100 reps)

2 hours of Log PT

Surf Torture

Walk for Life

Spring Cleaning

A big breakfast

1 hour of burpee broad jumps and plank

Warrior Yoga

Breakout 2.0 (2 hours)

Log PT

1-mile timed run as a team

False summit (Fake ending)

PT stations (human centipede, blind litter carry, plank, ice tubs, waterboarding, tire deadlift)

Log PT

Special 1:1 time with two coaches learning about the Crane Kick

RECOMMENDED READING LIST

8 Weeks to SEALFIT, Unbeatable Mind, Staring Down the Wolf and *The Way of The SEAL* by Mark Divine

The Mission, the Men, and Me by Pete Blaber

No Easy Day by Mark Owen

Fearless by Eric Blehm

American Sniper by Chris Kyle

Lone Survivor by Marcus Luttrell

Extreme Ownership by Jocko Willink and Leif Babin

Unbreakable by Thom Shea

Raising Men by Eric Davis

Can't Hurt Me by David Goggins

Men in Green Faces by Gene Wentz

The Battling Bastards of Bataan by John Doll

The Only Thing Worth Dying For by Eric Blehm

Start With Why by Simon Sinek

Band of Brothers by Stephen Ambrose

Gates of Fire by Steven Pressfield

Easy Makes Us Weak by Jim Brault *Tribes* by Seth Godin

Grit by Angela Duckworth

Power versus Force by David Hawkins, M.D., Ph.D

Breath by James Nestor

Becoming a Supple Leopard by Dr. Kelly Starrett

Living with a SEAL by Jesse Itzler

Tools of Titans by Tim Ferriss

The 4-Hour Workweek by Tim Ferriss

Discipline Equals Freedom by Jocko Willink

The Core Value Equation by Darius Mirshahzadeh

Mindset by Carol Dweck

The Art of War by Sun Tzu

The Daily Stoic by Ryan Holiday

Never Split the Difference by Chris Voss

Building a Story Brand by Donald Miller

Freelance to Freedom by Vincent Pugliese

This is Marketing by Seth Godin

Steal the Show by Michael Port

Debrief to Win by Robert "Cujo" Teschner

Your Income, Your Life by Jeff Bouwman

The Miracle Morning by Hal Elrod

Dad's Edge by Larry Hagner

Fundraising Freedom by Mary Valloni

Strengths Finder by Tom Rath

The 5 Love Languages by Gary Chapman

ACKNOWLEDGMENTS

I often get asked what the hardest part about writing a book is. Here's my 3-part answer.

#1 Writing a book is a scary, long, tedious, time-consuming process in which you have no idea if the work you are doing is going to amount to anything. Just like any other goal, break it down into manageable chunks of time and don't get discouraged. You will start off on fire, but somewhere along the way you will most likely become bored, discouraged, and lose interest. The worst thing you can do is start doubting yourself. Remember why you are doing this and above all else, Don't F'ng Quit!

#2 Publishing a "perfect" book won't happen. There will always be something you can tweak or rewrite. Your viewpoint on some of the things you thought and wrote about six months ago or longer can and will often change. Just roll with it. An 80% good enough book that is published is better than a 100% perfect book that never gets an ISBN and sees the light of day.

#3 Perhaps my biggest fear of all is forgetting to acknowledge someone who has helped me along the way. I've had lots of teachers, mentors, and all-around great people help me on my journey. My fear is forgetting to mention someone. Here's my attempt to acknowledge those special people in my life who helped to shape me into the person I am today. In the event you are reading this and you are one of those special people and don't find your name below, it's not done on purpose. In fact, call me out on it, and I'll happily buy you a drink of your choice the next time we are together.

In no particular order:

Leslie – to my wonderful wife and mother of our children. I don't know what you saw in me when I was a young lad working in the plumbing department at Menards, but thanks for agreeing to go out with me. The life we've built together is truly amazing, and each year I feel a stronger connection to you. It's said that opposites attract, and I believe that is what makes us work well together. I couldn't have gotten where I'm at today without your support. Life is easier with you in it. Thanks for having my back. Together we make an unbeatable team.

Hallie – You were the first born, and I'll always remember being the first person you ever saw as you came into this world. Your eyes focused on my face and at that moment, time stood still. In a world where most people try to fit in, just be you; everyone else is taken. You've got a big heart…let that steer your decisions in life. Learn to be comfortable while being uncomfortable and trust your gut. I've already seen great leadership qualities in you, and I can't wait to see the woman you grow up to be. P.S. Keep up your training; you are stronger than you know, and I'd hate to be on the receiving end of your roundhouse kicks.

Brody – When you were born, we had no idea what the gender was, and I was staring straight at your junk. The nurse let me "call the ball," and I shouted from the rooftops, "It's a boy." Mommy was so drugged up I don't even think she knew what was going on. That was it for me… having a healthy girl and boy made me the happiest father on earth at that moment in time. I love your determination, and you don't give up easily. Always remember to check your ego at the door and be a life-long learner. The more we learn, the more we find that we don't know. I pity the fool that breaks your sister's heart knowing that Bro- tank is on the loose. You were born with the Ritter curse, and those eyelashes of yours will serve you well throughout life. Stay humble and lead by example. Protect those who can't defend themselves. Be Sheepdog strong.

To Mom and Dad – thanks for always being there… from the baseball games to babysitting and everything in between. One of the many things I always cherished were our family vacations. I'm sure times were tough raising four kids on a single income, but somehow you always found a way to take us places, and for that I'm grateful. You've both taught me too many lessons to begin to even mention. Just know, through thick and thin, you both did it right as parents. Sure we had our ups and downs, but at the end of the day, you taught me that family is everything, which is something I continue to live my life by. I hope you both continue to enjoy the fruit of your labor, as it is well deserved. Life is short; do what you want when you want. If not now, when?

To Ryan, Jenna, and Geoff – I'll be really honest here. I had four years of pure bliss and then Mom and Dad started popping you all out left and right. Was I not good enough or did I do something wrong? All jokes aside, I couldn't ask for three better siblings. We've had our issues in the past, but at the end of the day, we all love each other and would be there for one another at a moment's notice. I only have one request for you three. Find what makes you happy and do it. If you feel drawn toward a certain thing, have the courage to pursue it and don't take shit from anyone. I look forward to many years of sibling rivalry.

To my grandparents – There's one constant theme that comes up with you four, and that is you all love your grandchildren. I have many memories of getting together for holidays and seeing you at ball games. Thanks for providing the best parents I could ask for. When my time on earth is gone, I look forward to reuniting with you in heaven one day.

To my aunts, uncles, and cousins – Some of my fondest memories were the many Thanksgivings and Christmas Eves we would all spend together. I always looked forward to seeing you all in our "controlled chaos" environment. I even had the opportunity to vacation with some of you up at Clark Lake, Michigan, or various places around the country.

Thank you for making those memories so special. My hope is that no matter what direction we go in or how far away we move, we all stay connected.

To my in-laws – being around my family and friends can be a crucible experience in and of itself that challenges you mentally and emotionally. Congrats on passing the test, and I appreciate you all.

To JB, Harv, Will, and Johnny – you guys truly are the jolliest bunch of assholes this side of the nuthouse.

JB, you're my best friend from high school. I always enjoy our philosophical discussions over Bud Light and bourbon. Harv, you're a great friend, and if I ever need a dinner recommendation, you are the first person I think of. Will, you're always loyal and a true cerebral assassin even if you did attend that school to the north. So excited for you to be a dad. Johnny, you're my go-to on all things PT and nutrition related. It's been fun to watch your career unfold. Proud of you, man. Keep grinding. Thank you all for letting this civilian hang around your brothers in arms.

Larry Hagner – I'll never forget hearing you on Mark's Unbeatable Mind podcast and then meeting you at Harry and Izzy's downtown Indy for dinner. That conversation lasted three hours, but what was talked about came to fruition in a big way. Thanks for allowing me to serve the guys in your tribe for over almost five years and taking a chance on me becoming your first team leader.

DEA Fight club – you guys have taught me so much. It was a pleasure leading you for so many years. There are so many to name, and I'm going to miss a bunch (find me and I'll buy you a beer if I don't mention you)…here we go; Jon Appino, Randy Harris, Brian Church, Shane Arbogast, Reggie Shah, Josh Long, Scott Reader, John Forsberg, Earl Murphy, Will Lowry, Ross Rousseau, Sean Hutchins, Javier Mesa, Tuan

Nguyen, Jeremy Roadruck, Malcolm Altheron, Mark Takacs, Chris Edgar, David Anderson, Chris Lesso, Devin Hightower, Greg Tredo, Steve Birch, Jordan McCrindle, Andrew Mundy, Phil Sperling, Dan Zehner, Andy Storch, Ben Killoy, Joel Giesting, Ben Esteban, Matt Jablonski, Phillip Lomboy, Aaron Goodwin, Alex Zaborenko, Scott Tewell, Nick Elkins, Michael Jeffrey, Warren Peterson, Judd Campbell, John Bauer, Dan Barnett, Robert Duffer, Chet Reed, Travis Parker, Jason Clinton, Dan Luigs, Adrian Chavez, Darren Bellew, Scott Kortright, James Hartzell Jr., Gary Guidi, Justin Gerards, Pat Rutherford, Brian Auten, Andrew Maple, Marc Hildebrand, Jeff Bonaldi, Tony Buchanan, Chet Reed, Michael Ferrante, Nick Sotelo, Pedro Echavarria, Craig Mills, Jason Grzywa and Omar Pinto. Fight Club forever!

School of Grit tribe – Team Alpha, Bravo, and A-team; You guys are the founder's and a big reason why I continue to pursue this dream day in and day out. Without you, there would be no tribe. Special shout outs to Earl Murphy, Scott Reader, John Forsberg, Will Lowry, Ross Rousseau, Mark Pearson and Chris Edgar.

Tuan Nguyen – to the Dude Buddha and all around badass. If wealth was measured by the size of your heart, then you my friend would be the wealthiest man in the world. I don't know exactly what you saw in me when we met several years ago, but I knew you were one of those people that I needed to surround myself with. Thanks for being a mentor in my life. Thank you for creating a world class advisory board of hooligans and yahoos. . . you know who you are!

Javier Mesa – my OG swim buddy. Through thick and thin we've been on some amazing adventures together. Thanks for trusting me to entice you into completing a SEALFit crucible and joining me on the path of becoming a certified UM Coach. We are just getting started!

Vincent Pugliese and the Freelance to Freedom tribe – Vinny my man, it has been a real treat watching your tribe grow. I always appreciate how you look to do things differently. I've learned a lot from you and your crew over the years. Keep grinding because the rent is due every day, my friend.

Mark Divine – I don't have the words; just know that you are a mentor in my life, and you've literally helped changed my mindset and provide a catalyst so I can live my purpose and become a world-centric leader. Hooyah!

To my Unbeatable Mind family. It all started with Team "Waya". You'll always be my first boat crew. Thanks to Cole Berschback, Javier Mesa, Hodi Hammond, Joe Oniwor, Judy Buchanan, Richard Charette, David Hamilton, and Joe MacDonald.

Team Mentor Program Alpha (MPA) – Richard Thompson, Luke Tan, Cole Berschback, Scott Francis, Matt Strachan, Craig Graves, Brett Magpiong, Mel Sliwka, Greg Robinson, Alex Pyrkotsch, Matt Halk, Steve Stewart, Bert Pacal, Karen Rowe, and Heather Parillo—iron sharpens iron. What an honor to be amongst such incredible humans. I still don't know how I was selected.

Bravehearts – you're the first UM boat crew I ever had the privilege of coaching and I hope we get to meet each other in person one day... Hooyah! Joe Martindale, Pri Yadav, Franco Cerutti, Vishal Kapoor, Brady Murray, Laura Eiman, Frank Kraetz and Birgit Krautscheid.

Coaches Jim Brault, Rob Ord, and Richard Thompson - thanks for believing in me. I look forward to training and growing with you all.

Coach Mel Sliwka – the first time I met you was at K38 after you handed me some gatorade after almost drowning during pool comp... and now we are teammates! Coach Boomer Alred – I look up to you bro, keep grinding.

SEALFIT cadre past and present with whom I either had the pleasure of working alongside or being "taught" by – Mark, Brad, Taco, Shane, Lance, Rick, Jeff, Faris, Derek, Will, Mel, Rob, Bill, Sid, Cramps, Trey, and Robert. What a great team. This is truly a world class event with world-class coaches.

SEALFIT tribe – to those folks getting after it every day, doing OPWODS and signing up for crucible experiences… Hooyah!

Amber Villhauer – you, Alexis, Caitlyn, Haley, and the rest of your team are the best marketing and launch strategists I've ever worked with. Thank you for your expertise and guiding me on my book launch journey. I'd recommend you to anyone reading this right now. Check out NGNG (No Guts, No Glory) to learn more!

Jennifer Harshman – I'll never forget hearing your voice on one of the Total Life Freedom calls. I was driving in the rain and you were talking about working with a book editor, and little did you know that I was in desperate need of one. Thank you for your hard work on this special project of mine.

Ashley Bunting – you and the team at Merack Publishing are second to none. You were able to listen to my concerns and deliver a product that blows me away. From the cover design, to layout, to production, getting this ready for prime time, and everything in between. You have been a joy to work with and I can't thank you enough. If anyone is looking for a top-notch publisher, please consider working with Merack and Ashley.

SEALGrinderPT (SGPT) – Brad McLeod, thank you for your awesome training tips, videos, and interviews. It was great meeting you in person at K38, and I look forward to training with you sometime soon.

Stew Smith – thanks for your training program and videos. I only wish I would have stumbled upon your swimming videos before I went to Kokoro Camp.

Angela Duckworth – If you hadn't written your book, Grit, and delivered an amazing TED talk, I don't know if I'd be where I am today. Your material made me question everything. Thank you!

Heroic Public Speaking (HPS) – Michael and Amy Port, you two run an amazing program, and I want to thank you for an amazing experience in Lambertville, New Jersey.

Simon Sinek – thanks for writing the book, *Start with Why*. It had a profound impact on me.

Hal Elrod – The Morning Miracle helped change my life. Thank you for sharing it with the world.

Seth Godin – I met you on a call that Vincent Pugliese had put together, and you shared some real gems with me. I love your writing and your blog. Keep up the great work!

Pete Blaber – The Mission, the Men, and Me is perhaps the best book on leadership I've ever read. Thanks for taking the time to write and publish it.

Jocko Willink – Discipline really does equal freedom! Keep putting great content out there, sir.

Larry and Ann Yatch – thank you for the training at SEALteamleaders!

Marcus Luttrell – No one likes telling a story, let alone writing a book and making a movie about getting their ass kicked, but I'm glad you did. I can't fathom what you went through over there and the long road to recovery, both physially and emotionally. Thanks for telling your story and also for the TNQ podcast.

David Goggins – you wrote my favorite book of 2018. What an incredible story of overcoming adversity. Thanks for sharing your stories!

Oakley – I love your gear! From the sunglasses to the boots, I'm a big fan. The light assault boots were amazing at Kokoro Camp.

Vermont Darn Tough – hands down the best socks you can buy! I'm still rocking my full cushion boot style six years later!

Ko's Martial Arts Academy – To Grandmaster Yun Sam Ko and his son Master Soon Ko. "A black belt is a white belt student who never quit." Thank you both for an outstanding school to practice and learn. I consider myself lucky to have found your Tae Kwon Do school and to be able to train with my family and friends. If you're looking for a Tae Kwon Do school, please consider Ko's. And if you're a parent, step off the sidelines and onto the mat. Train with your kids! It's easily one of the best decisions I've ever made as a parent.

Last but certainly not least. I want to personally thank those who helped me either directly or indirectly with writing Chapter 10, "It could always be worse." This part of the book was easily the most difficult. I wanted to portray Krista's life in the best light possible but how do you tell someone's story in a few paragraphs? I only hope I did it right. Thank you to my cousins Angie Cowan and Matt Ritter, my Aunt and Uncle Barb and Tony Ritter, and Jim Bugenhagen. I'd also like to thank those that had a hand in the celebration of life for Krista on Monday, April 8th 2019 at Chelsea Piers. I did not attend but I was lucky enough to read the speakers notes. Thank you to David Tewksbury, Suzanne McGoldrick, Debbie Gleicher, Angie Cowan, Jim Bugenhagen, and Roland Betts.

ABOUT THE AUTHOR

First and foremost, I'm a husband, father, brother, son, and friend. Family is #1 to me. I enjoy training hard, endurance events, the beach, fishing, shooting, and food. Professionally, I have over 20 years of combined experience ranging from the medical device, higher education, and specialty print industries. I started School of Grit after I graduated from SEALFit's infamous Kokoro Camp, which is renowned as the world's toughest civilian training. After graduation I wanted to find a way to serve others and help people take control of their lives and get unstuck. I accomplish this through a proven system that focuses on your physical, mental, emotional, intuitional, and warrior spirit. My job is to help you achieve a goal or produce a certain result. I will hold you accountable as well as celebrate your success. What I teach is a lifestyle. It won't be easy, but it will be worth it. It's for anyone who despises mediocrity and is willing to do the daily work. If you're ready to step into courage, focus on others, and train relentlessly, then you have found the right place.

RANDOM STUFF:

Certified and Licensed Unbeatable Mind Coach

SEALFit Basic Training Certification

Kokoro 38 Graduate

Head Coach for the Dad's Edge Alliance

To learn more and connect with Brad visit,
schoolofgrit.org